Myths
and
Legends
of the
World

Volume 3

John M. Wickersham
Editor in Chief

Macmillan Reference USA/An Imprint of The Gale Group
New York

Developed for Macmillan Reference USA by
  Visual Education Corporation, Princeton, NJ.

For Macmillan

Publisher: Elly Dickason

Editor in Chief: Hélène G. Potter

Cover Design: Irina Lubenskaya

For Visual Education

Project Director: Darryl Kestler

Writers: John Haley, Charles Roebuck, Rebecca Stefoff

Editors: Cindy George, Eleanor Hero, Linda Perrin, Charles Roebuck

Copyediting Supervisor: Helen A. Castro

Indexer: Sallie Steele

Production Supervisor: Marcel Chouteau

Photo Research: Susan Buschhorn, Sara Matthews

Interior Design: Maxson Crandall

Electronic Preparation: Fiona Torphy

Electronic Production: Rob Ehlers, Lisa Evans-Skopas, Laura Millan, Isabelle Ulsh

Macmillan Reference USA
1633 Broadway
New York, NY 10019

Printed in the United States of America
1 2 3 4 5 6 7 8 9 10

Library of Congress Cataloging-in-Publication Data

Myths and legends of the world / John M. Wickersham, editor in chief.
        p. cm.
      Includes bibliographical references and index.
      Contents: v. 1. Abel-Coriolanus — v. 2. Corn-Io — v. 3. Iphigenia-Quetzalcoatl — v. 4. Ra-Zoroastrian mythology.
      ISBN 0-02-865439-0 (set : alk. paper)
      1. Mythology—Juvenile literature. 2. Legends.   [1. Mythology—Encyclopedias. 2. Folklore—Encyclopedias.]   I. Wickersham, John M. (John Moore), 1943–
BL311 .M97   2000
398.2—dc21   00-030528

Iphigenia

In Greek mythology, Iphigenia appears in legends about the Trojan War†. She was killed by her father, Agamemnon, leader of the Greek forces, in exchange for favorable wind from the gods. Euripides† and Aeschylus also include the story of Iphigenia in their dramas.

In the myth, Greek ships on their way to attack Troy† were stuck in the port of Aulis because of unfavorable winds. There are a number of different explanations for the difficulty. Most suggest that Agamemnon was being punished for somehow offending the goddess Artemis†. Agamemnon was told that the gods would send winds for his ships if he would sacrifice Iphigenia to Artemis. Knowing that his wife, Clytemnestra, would never agree to the sacrifice, Agamemnon dispatched a message asking her to send Iphigenia to him so she could be married to the Greek hero Achilles†.

At this point in the myth, the story varies. According to some versions, Agamemnon actually did sacrifice Iphigenia. Clytemnestra never forgave him and arranged to kill him when he returned from the war. In other versions, Artemis spared Iphigenia by replacing her on the sacrificial altar with a female deer. Artemis then sent Iphigenia to the land of Tauris, where the girl acted as priestess of Artemis's temple there. A later myth says that Iphigenia's brother Orestes traveled to Tauris to search for a statue of Artemis. He was captured and about to be sacrificed, when Iphigenia recognized him. They both escaped with the help of the goddess Athena† and the god Poseidon†. *See also* ACHILLES; AGAMEMNON; CLYTEMNESTRA; ORESTES.

Ishtar

deity god or goddess
benevolent desiring good for others

In the ancient Near East, Ishtar was an important and widely worshiped mother goddess for many Semitic† peoples. The Sumerians† called her Inanna, and other groups of the Near East referred to her as Astarte.

A complex **deity**, Ishtar combined the characteristics—both good and evil—of many different goddesses. As a **benevolent** mother figure, she was considered the mother of gods and humans, as well as the creator of all earthly blessings. In this role, she grieved over human sorrows and served as a protector of marriage and motherhood. People also worshiped Ishtar as the goddess of sexual love and fertility. The evil side of Ishtar's nature emerged primarily in connection with war and storms. As a warrior goddess, she could make even the gods tremble in fear. As a storm goddess, she could bring rain and thunder.

Some myths say that Ishtar was the daughter of the moon god Sin and sister of the sun god Shamash. Others mention the sky god Anu, the moon god Nanna, the water god Ea, or the god Enlil, lord of the earth and the air, as her father. Most myths link her to the planet Venus.

Ishtar appears in many myths, but two are especially important. The first, part of the Babylonian *Epic of Gilgamesh,* tells how Ishtar offered to marry the hero-king Gilgamesh because she was

Ishtar was worshiped as both a good and evil goddess by the people of the ancient Near East. They honored her as the protector of marriage and motherhood as well as a warrior and storm goddess.

impressed by his courage and exploits. According to the **epic,** Gilgamesh refused her offer and insulted Ishtar, reminding the goddess of all the previous lovers she had harmed. Enraged, Ishtar sent the fierce Bull of Heaven to kill Gilgamesh, but he and his friend Enkidu killed the beast instead.

The other well-known myth of Ishtar concerns her descent to the **underworld** and sacrifice of her husband Tammuz (also known as Dumuzi). In this story, Ishtar decided to visit the underworld, which was ruled by her sister Ereshkigal, perhaps to seize power there. Before departing, she instructed her follower Ninshubur to seek the help of the gods if she did not return.

To reach the underworld, Ishtar had to pass through seven gates and remove a symbol of her power—such as an article of clothing or a piece of jewelry—at each one. At the last gate, the goddess, naked and deprived of all her powers, met her sister Ereshkigal, who announced that Ishtar must die. She died immediately, and her corpse was hung on a stake.

Meanwhile, the god Enki learned from Ninshubur that Ishtar was missing and sent two messengers who restored her to life. However, in order to leave the underworld, Ishtar had to substitute another body for her own. The goddess offered her young husband, Tammuz, to take her place. This tale of death and rebirth was associated with fertility and linked to the seasons and agricultural cycles, much like the story of Persephone in Greek mythology.

Temples to Ishtar were built throughout the ancient Near East. Among the most famous were those at the cities of Erech, Babylon, Ur, and Nineveh. Her **cult** was very popular and may have included **rituals** associated with sexual love. *See also* ANU; ENLIL; GILGAMESH; INANNA; SEMITIC MYTHOLOGY; SHAMASH; UNDERWORLD.

epic long poem about legendary or historical heroes, written in a grand style
underworld land of the dead

cult group bound together by devotion to a particular person, belief, or god
ritual ceremony that follows a set pattern

Isis

deity god or goddess
resurrection coming to life again; rising from the dead
cult group bound together by devotion to a particular person, belief, or god

The great mother goddess of ancient Egypt, Isis was the sister and wife of the god Osiris†. Together these two **deities** played a major role in many stories in Egyptian mythology, particularly in myths about rebirth and **resurrection.** The **cult** of Isis became very popular in Egypt and eventually spread to other parts of the Mediterranean world, including ancient Greece and Rome.

According to Egyptian mythology, Isis was the daughter of the earth god Geb and the sky goddess Nut. Her sister and brothers were Nephthys, Set, and Osiris. These six deities—Geb, Nut, Isis, Osiris, Set, and Nephthys—belonged to an important group of nine Egyptian gods called the Great Ennead of Heliopolis.

†*See **Names and Places** at the end of this volume for further information.*

underworld land of the dead

The cult of Isis, the mother goddess of ancient Egypt, spread to many parts of the Mediterranean world, including Greece and Rome.

One famous myth about Isis tells how she discovered the secret name of the sun god Ra and increased her power. According to the story, Isis found Ra asleep one day, snoring loudly and saliva dripping from his mouth. She collected the saliva and mixed it with earth to form a poisonous serpent. Then she placed the serpent on a path that Ra took every day.

When Ra awoke and started on his way, the serpent bit him, causing terrible pain. He called to the other gods for help, but all were helpless except Isis, who promised to cure him if he revealed his secret name. At first Ra refused, but eventually the pain became unbearable. He told Isis the name, and she gained new powers. This story was associated with a major aspect of Isis's character, her skill in magical arts.

One of the most important myths associated with Isis was the story of Osiris's death and resurrection. According to this tale, the god Set became jealous of his brother Osiris, who ruled as king of Egypt. One day Set tricked Osiris and sealed him inside a box. Set then placed the box adrift on the Nile River, which carried it to the distant land of Byblos.

Isis searched for and found the box and then brought it back to Egypt, where she concealed it. However, Set discovered the hiding place and cut Osiris's body into many pieces and scattered them throughout Egypt. After recovering the pieces, Isis used her magical powers to restore life to Osiris, who then went to live in the **underworld.**

Sometime before this happened, Osiris and Isis had had a son named Horus. Isis kept the child hidden from Set so that he could grow up and avenge his father's death. She protected Horus against all dangers, even restoring him to life once after he was

bitten by a scorpion. When Horus became a young man, he fought his uncle Set. But Isis took pity on Set and allowed him to escape. Angry at his mother, Horus cut off her head. Thoth, the god of magic and wisdom, changed the severed head into a cow's head and reattached it to Isis's body. Some ancient statues and paintings of the goddess show her with a cow's head, and she is often linked to the goddess Hathor. Eventually, Isis went to live with Osiris in the underworld.

The ancient Egyptians regarded Isis as a perfect mother, and she was worshiped as a protector goddess because of the way she sheltered Horus from danger. In the roles of mother and magician, she also cured the sick and restored the dead to life. As the mother of Horus, who took his father's place on the throne of Egypt, Isis also was thought to play a key role in the succession of Egyptian kings. *See also* AFTERLIFE; EGYPTIAN MYTHOLOGY; HORUS; OSIRIS; RA (RE); SET; UNDERWORLD.

Isolde

See *Tristan and Isolde.*

Itzamná

deity god or goddess
culture hero mythical figure who gives people the tools of civilization, such as language and fire
ritual ceremony that follows a set pattern

Itzamná was one of the most important **deities** of Mayan mythology. The ruler of the heavens and of day and night, he was often shown in Mayan art as a pleasant, toothless old man with a large nose. He was also identified as the son of the creator god Hunab Ku.

In various myths, Itzamná appears as a **culture hero** who gave the Maya the foundations of civilization. According to legend, he taught them to grow corn, to write, to use calendars, and to practice medicine. He also introduced a system for dividing up the land, and he established **rituals** for religious worship.

Itzamná is sometimes linked with the sun god Kinich Ahau and the moon goddess Ixchel. The goddess may have been Itzamná's wife or a female form of his deity. Like Itzamná, she gave people many useful skills, such as weaving. However, Ixchel had a destructive nature and could cause floods and other violent events, while Itzamná was always kind and protective toward humans. *See also* MAYAN MYTHOLOGY.

Ivan the Terrible

tsar Russian ruler
aristocracy privileged upper classes of society; nobles or the nobility

Ivan Vasilyevich, better known as Ivan the Terrible, was the first **tsar** of Russia. Crowned in 1547, he ruled Russia until his death in 1584. During his long reign, Ivan created a large empire, made various reforms of government and society, and consolidated power under a strong centralized state. However, legends grew up about Ivan's extreme cruelty and the reign of terror his large force of personal bodyguards waged against the Russian **aristocracy.**

Ivan's reputation had a great impact on Russian poetry, music, art, and legend. The character of Ivan appears in a number of legends, and his life and deeds have inspired poems, operas, and films. Russian composer Nikolai Rimsky-Korsakov wrote an opera called *Ivan the Terrible.* Russian director Sergei Eisenstein made a famous film, *Ivan the Terrible,* with music by Sergei Prokofiev.

Izanagi and Izanami

deity god or goddess
underworld land of the dead
primeval from the earliest times

In Japanese mythology the two **deities** Izanagi (The Male Who Invites) and Izanami (The Female Who Invites) are the creators of Japan and its gods. In one important myth, they descend to Yomi-tsu Kuni, the **underworld** and land of darkness. Stories about Izanagi and Izanami are told in two works from the A.D. 700s, the *Kojiki* (Records of Ancient Matters) and the *Nihongi* (Chronicles of Japan).

According to legend, after their birth Izanagi and Izanami stood on the floating bridge of heaven and stirred the **primeval** ocean with a jeweled spear. When they lifted the spear, the drops that fell back into the water formed the first solid land, an island called Onogoro. Izanagi and Izanami descended to the island and became husband and wife. Their first child was deformed, and the other gods said it was because Izanami spoke before her husband at their marriage ceremony.

The couple performed another wedding ceremony, this time correctly. Izanami soon gave birth to eight lovely children, who became the islands of Japan. Izanagi and Izanami then created many gods and goddesses to represent the mountains, valleys, waterfalls, streams, winds, and other natural features of Japan. However, during the birth of Kagutsuchi, the fire god, Izanami was badly burned. As she lay dying, she continued to create gods and goddesses, and still other deities emerged from the tears of the grief-stricken Izanagi.

When Izanami died, she went to Yomi-tsu Kuni. Izanagi decided to go there and bring his beloved back from the land of darkness and death. Izanami greeted Izanagi from the shadows as he approached the entrance to Yomi. She warned him not to look at her and said that she would try to arrange for her release from the gods of Yomi. Full of desire for his wife, Izanagi lit a torch and looked into Yomi. Horrified to see that Izanami was a rotting corpse, Izanagi fled.

Angry that Izanagi had not respected her wishes, Izanami sent hideous female spirits, eight thunder gods, and an army of fierce warriors to chase him. Izanagi managed to escape and blocked the pass between Yomi and the land of the living with a huge boulder. Izanami met him there, and they broke off their marriage.

Izanagi felt unclean because of his contact with the dead, and he took a bath to purify himself. A number of gods and goddesses, both good and evil, emerged from his discarded clothing as Izanagi bathed. The sun goddess Amaterasu appeared from his left eye, the moon god Tsuki-yomi appeared from his right eye, and Susano-ô came from his nose. Proud of these three noble children, Izanagi divided his kingdom among them. ***See also*** AMATERASU; JAPANESE MYTHOLOGY; SUSANO-Ô; UNDERWORLD.

Janus

Janus was the Roman god of beginnings, gates, and doorways. He was associated with the start of day and the first month of the year, called January after him. The Romans mentioned Janus first when including a list of gods in their prayers, and they named the Janiculum, one of the seven hills of Rome, in his honor.

Like a doorway that can be entered from two directions, Janus was usually pictured with two faces, one looking forward and one looking back. The temple to Janus in the Roman Forum had two sets of doors facing east and west. These doors were open during a war and closed in periods of peace.

Janus appears in one myth as the defender of an important Roman gateway. When the city was under attack by a tribe known as the Sabines, Janus flooded the gate with a hot spring to prevent the invaders from entering the city. In another story, Janus used his two faces while pursuing a lover. The goddess Cardea was known for leading her admirers to a cave and then running away. When Janus accompanied her to the cave, he saw with the face in the back of his head that she was turning to leave and caught hold of her before she could escape.

Japanese Mythology

The mythology of Japan has a long history dating back more than 2,000 years. It became part of two major religious traditions: Shinto, an **indigenous** religion, and Buddhism, which developed in India and came to Japan from China and Korea.

Japanese mythology includes a vast number of gods, goddesses, and spirits. Most of the stories concern the creation of the world, the foundation of the islands of Japan, and the activities of **deities,** humans, animals, spirits, and magical creatures. Some myths describe characters and events associated with particular places in Japan. Others are set in legendary locations, such as the heavens or the **underworld.**

Sources for Japanese Myths

For many centuries myths were transmitted orally in Japan. In A.D. 712, a written version of the mythology, the *Kojiki* (Records of Ancient Matters), was compiled for the Japanese **imperial** court. The tales in the *Kojiki* tell of the creation of the world, the origin of the gods, and the ancestry of the Japanese emperors, who claimed descent from the sun goddess Amaterasu.

Another early source of Japanese mythology is the *Nihongi,* or *Nihonshoki* (Chronicles of Japan). Completed in 720, this work also includes various myths and legends, and it helps establish the **genealogy** of the imperial family. The *Nihongi* was greatly influenced by

Hachiman, one of the most popular gods of Japanese mythology, was the patron of warriors.

Japanese Deities	
Deity	**Role**
Amaterasu	goddess of the sun and fertility who brings light to the world
Hachiman	god of warriors, known for his military skill
Inari	god associated with rice and merchants
Izanagi	creator god
Izanami	creator goddess
Kagutsuchi	god of fire
Susano-ô	violent god associated with storms and the sea, Amaterasu's brother
Tsuki-yomi	moon god, Amaterasu's brother

Chinese and Korean history and mythology. Both the *Kojiki* and the *Nihongi* contain elements of Taoism, a Chinese religious movement that was introduced to Japan by the 600s.

Major Deities and Characters

In Japanese mythology, everything in nature has a *kami*—a deity or spirit. As a result, the Japanese **pantheon** is enormous, with some sources claiming that there are millions of different spirits and deities. Throughout Japan, local myths and legends tell about the *kami* of a particular place, such as a rock, a pair of trees, or a mountain. However, several major deities appear in significant roles in a number of stories from different regions.

The two most important creator deities are Izanagi and his sister Izanami. According to the myths, they made the islands of Japan as well as many of the gods and goddesses. Izanagi and Izanami also appear in a story about a descent to Yomi-tsu Kuni, a land of darkness and death associated with the underworld.

Perhaps the best-known Japanese deity is the sun goddess Amaterasu. Said to be the ancestor of the imperial family, she brings light into the world and is responsible for fertility. Her shrine at Ise is the most important shrine in Japan.

Amaterasu has two brothers: the moon god Tsuki-yomi and Susano-ô, a powerful and violent god often associated with storms. Of the two, Susano-ô plays a more important role in mythology, appearing in a number of major legends, including several with Amaterasu.

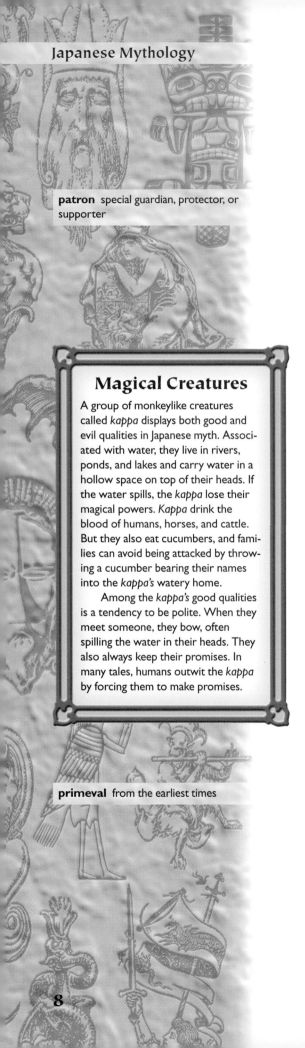

patron special guardian, protector, or supporter

Magical Creatures

A group of monkeylike creatures called *kappa* displays both good and evil qualities in Japanese myth. Associated with water, they live in rivers, ponds, and lakes and carry water in a hollow space on top of their heads. If the water spills, the *kappa* lose their magical powers. *Kappa* drink the blood of humans, horses, and cattle. But they also eat cucumbers, and families can avoid being attacked by throwing a cucumber bearing their names into the *kappa's* watery home.

Among the *kappa's* good qualities is a tendency to be polite. When they meet someone, they bow, often spilling the water in their heads. They also always keep their promises. In many tales, humans outwit the *kappa* by forcing them to make promises.

primeval from the earliest times

Ôkuninushi, a descendant of Susano-ô (possibly his son), is a central character in the Izumo Cycle, a series of myths set in the Izumo region of western Japan. Like the heroes in the legends of other cultures, Ôkuninushi has many adventures and undergoes various ordeals.

One of the most popular deities of Japanese mythology is Hachiman, a **patron** of warriors. The character of Hachiman is based on the emperor Ôjin, who lived in the A.D. 300s and was renowned for his military skills. According to tradition, after Ôjin died he became the god Hachiman. In the 700s, Hachiman became part of the Shinto pantheon.

The god Inari appears in few myths, but he is important because of his association with the growing of rice, the major food crop in Japan. Thought to bring prosperity, Inari is the patron of merchants and sword makers.

Among the many spirits and creatures in Japanese mythology are the *tengu,* minor deities that are part human and part bird. According to tradition, they live in trees in mountainous areas. The *tengu* enjoy playing tricks on humans but resent being tricked themselves. They are more mischievous than wicked.

The Oni, a more threatening group of spirits, may have originated in China and traveled to Japan with Buddhism. These horned demons, often of enormous size, can take human or animal shape. Sometimes invisible, the Oni have the ability to steal the souls of humans. They can be very cruel and are associated with various evil forces such as famine and disease.

Japanese mythology also includes other Buddhist deities. In addition to stories about the life of Buddha, many tales concern Amida, the ruler of a paradise called the Pure Land. Kannon, the protector of children and women in childbirth, and Jizô, who rescues souls from hell, are also important Buddhist figures.

Major Myths and Themes

The most important stories in Japanese mythology deal with creation and the goddess Amaterasu. Deeply rooted in nature, they vividly describe the formation of the landscape and the origin of forces such as fire, wind, and light.

Creation Myth. According to the *Kojiki,* in the beginning there was only a **primeval** ooze, out of which heaven and earth were formed. Life emerged from this mud. In heaven three deities—followed by two others—appeared. These five became the Separate Heavenly Deities. They were followed by the Seven Generations of the Age of the Gods, two single deities and five male and female couples. The two single deities came out of a reedlike substance floating in the ooze.

When the youngest pair of deities—Izanagi and Izanami—were born, the other gods ordered them to make solid land out of the material drifting in the sea. Standing on the floating bridge of heaven, Izanagi and Izanami stirred the primeval ocean with a

One story from Japanese mythology features a young hero named Yoshitsune and the king of the *tengu,* a group of half-human and half-bird deities. In this illustration, Yoshitsune grabs the king's nose.

jeweled spear. When they pulled up the spear to see if any material had gathered on it, drops of salty water dripped down into the sea and formed an island called Onogoro. Izanagi and Izanami left heaven and went to live on the island. They married and produced eight children, who became the islands of Japan.

Izanagi and Izanami then created gods and goddesses of the trees, mountains, valleys, streams, winds, and other natural features of Japan. While giving birth to the fire god Kagutsuchi, Izanami was badly burned. As she lay dying, she produced more gods and goddesses. Other deities emerged from the tears of her grief-stricken husband.

When Izanami died, she went to Yomi-tsu Kuni, the land of darkness and death. Izanagi followed her there and tried to bring her back. But Izanami's body had already begun to decay, and she hid in the shadows and told Izanagi that she could not leave. Izanagi could not resist looking at his beloved wife one last time. When he lit a torch and saw her rotting corpse, he fled in terror. Angry that Izanagi had seen her, Izanami sent hideous spirits to chase him. Izanagi managed to escape, and he sealed off the passage to Yomi-tsu Kuni with a huge boulder. Izanami remained there and ruled over the dead.

Feeling unclean from his contact with the dead, Izanagi decided to bathe in a stream to purify himself. As he undressed, gods and goddesses emerged from his discarded clothing. Others came forth while he washed. Susano-ô came from his nose, Tsuki-yomi emerged from his right eye, and Amaterasu appeared from his left eye. Izanagi divided the world among these three gods. He gave Susano-ô control of the oceans, assigned Tsuki-yomi the realm of the night, and made Amaterasu the ruler of the sun and the heavens.

Myths of Amaterasu. One famous myth tells how Susano-ô, Amaterasu's brother, was unhappy with his share of the world and caused much destruction. Banished to Yomi-tsu Kuni, he asked to go to heaven to see his sister the sun goddess one last time. Amaterasu became concerned that Susano-ô might be planning to take over her lands. The two agreed to a contest to prove their power. If Susano-ô won, he could stay in heaven forever, but if he lost, he would have to leave.

Amaterasu asked for her brother's sword, which she broke into three pieces and chewed in her mouth. When Amaterasu spit out the pieces, they turned into three goddesses. Susano-ô then took a string of five star-shaped beads that Amaterasu had given him. He put the beads in his mouth, chewed them, and spat out five gods.

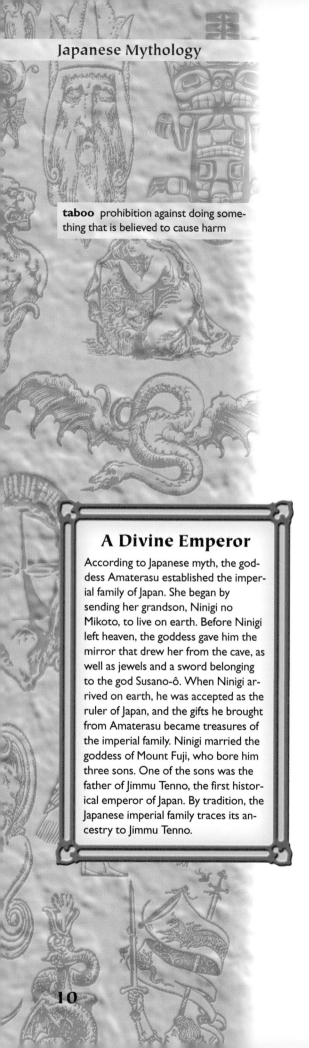

taboo prohibition against doing something that is believed to cause harm

A Divine Emperor

According to Japanese myth, the goddess Amaterasu established the imperial family of Japan. She began by sending her grandson, Ninigi no Mikoto, to live on earth. Before Ninigi left heaven, the goddess gave him the mirror that drew her from the cave, as well as jewels and a sword belonging to the god Susano-ô. When Ninigi arrived on earth, he was accepted as the ruler of Japan, and the gifts he brought from Amaterasu became treasures of the imperial family. Ninigi married the goddess of Mount Fuji, who bore him three sons. One of the sons was the father of Jimmu Tenno, the first historical emperor of Japan. By tradition, the Japanese imperial family traces its ancestry to Jimmu Tenno.

Susano-ô claimed victory because he had produced five gods and Amaterasu had produced only three goddesses. However, Amaterasu pointed out that he had created these gods from her possessions, which proved that her power was actually greater than his. Susano-ô refused to acknowledge defeat, and Amaterasu allowed him to remain in heaven.

While in heaven, Susano-ô began doing things that offended his sister and violated important **taboos.** He destroyed rice fields, made loud noises, and dirtied the floors of her palace. Finally, Susano-ô killed one of the horses of heaven, skinned it, and hurled it into the hall where Amaterasu was weaving cloth. This so angered Amaterasu that she hid in a cave and refused to come out.

When the sun goddess concealed herself, the world was plunged into darkness, plants stopped growing, and all activities came to a halt. Desperate for Amaterasu's return, 800 gods gathered to discuss ways of getting her to leave the cave. A wise god named Omori-kane proposed a solution.

The gods hung a mirror on the branches of a tree outside the cave. Then they had a young goddess named Ama-no-uzume dance to music while they laughed loudly. Amaterasu heard the noise and wondered what was happening. Opening the door to the cave a little, she asked why the gods were so happy. They told her that they were celebrating because they had found a goddess superior to her.

Curious at who this goddess might be, Amaterasu opened the door wider to look and saw her own image in the mirror. When she paused to gaze at her reflection, a god hiding nearby pulled her completely out of the cave. Another god then blocked the entrance with a magic rope. After Amaterasu emerged from the cave, her light shone once again, and life returned to normal. To punish Susano-ô for his actions, the gods banished him from heaven.

The Izumo Cycle. The Izumo Cycle of myths features the god Ôkuninushi, a descendant of Susano-ô. One of the most famous stories is about Ôkuninushi and the White Rabbit.

According to this tale, Ôkuninushi had 80 brothers, each of whom wanted to marry the same beautiful princess. On a journey to see the princess, the brothers came upon a rabbit with no fur in great pain at the side of the road. They told the animal that it could get its fur back by bathing in saltwater, but this only made the pain worse. A little while later, Ôkuninushi arrived and saw the suffering rabbit. When he asked what had happened, the rabbit told him how it had lost its fur.

One day while traveling between two islands, the rabbit persuaded some crocodiles to form a bridge so it could cross the water. In return the rabbit promised to count the crocodiles to see whether they were more numerous than the creatures of the sea. As the rabbit neared the far shore, the crocodiles realized that the promise was only a trick to get the rabbit across the water. Furious, the last crocodile seized the rabbit and tore off its skin.

*† See **Names and Places** at the end of this volume for further information.*

After hearing this story, Ôkuninushi told the rabbit to bathe in clear water and then roll in some grass pollen on the ground. The rabbit followed this plan, and new white fur soon grew on its body. The rabbit, who was actually a god, rewarded Ôkuninushi by promising that he would marry the beautiful princess. Ôkuninushi's success angered his brothers, and a number of other myths in the Izumo Cycle tell about the struggles between them.

Legacy of Japanese Mythology

Mythology plays an important role in the lives of the Japanese people today. Myths and legends are the basis of much Japanese art, drama, and literature, and people still learn and tell stories about the gods and goddesses. Traditional *kagura* dances are performed to honor the deities at Shinto shrines. Legend traces the origin of this ancient art form to the dance that drew the goddess Amaterasu from her cave. *See also* AMATERASU; BUDDHISM AND MYTHOLOGY; DEVILS AND DEMONS; GIANTS; INARI; IZANAGI AND IZANAMI; KOJIKI; NIHONGI; SUSANO-Ô; TRICKSTERS; UNDERWORLD.

Jason

centaur half-human, half-animal creature with the body of a horse and the head, chest, and arms of a human

oracle priest or priestess or other creature through whom a god is believed to speak; also the location (such as a shrine) where such words are spoken

In Greek mythology, Jason was the leader of a band of adventurers who set out on a long journey to find the Golden Fleece†. Although he succeeded in this quest, he never achieved his true goal—to become king of the land of Iolcus. Jason's story is one of violence and tragedy as well as adventure, partly because of his relationship with the enchantress and witch Medea.

Background to the Quest. Like many Greek heroes, Jason was of royal blood. His father was King Aeson of Iolcus in northwestern Greece. The king's half brother Pelias wanted the throne himself and overthrew Aeson while Jason was still a boy. Jason's mother feared for his safety. She sent him away to be guarded by Chiron, a wise **centaur** who took charge of the boy's education. Chiron taught Jason hunting and warfare, music and medicine. Some accounts say that the centaur also gave Jason his name, which means "healer," in recognition of the boy's skill in the medical arts.

At about the age of 20, Jason headed back to Iolcus, determined to gain the throne that rightfully belonged to him. On the way, he helped an old woman across a flooded stream and lost one of his sandals. Unknown to him, the old woman was the goddess Hera† in disguise. She vowed to destroy Pelias, who had failed to worship her properly, and to help Jason.

An **oracle** had warned Pelias to beware of a man wearing one sandal. When Jason arrived in Iolcus, the king confronted him. Jason identified himself and declared that he had come for his throne. Prevented by the laws of hospitality from attacking Jason openly, Pelias resorted to trickery. He said that if Jason could bring him the fabled Golden Fleece, he would make him his heir. Pelias believed that obtaining the heavily guarded fleece from the distant land of Colchis was a nearly impossible task.

Jason, a Greek hero, led the Argonauts on the quest for the Golden Fleece. Here, Jason finds the ram's hide hanging on a tree.

demigod one who is part human and part god

The Quest. Jason assembled a band of brave adventurers— including the sons of kings and gods and some other former students of Chiron—to accompany him in his quest. They sailed in a magic ship called the *Argo* and were known as the Argonauts. Among them were the famous musician Orpheus† and the **demigod** hero Hercules†.

The Argonauts' eventful journey to Colchis, their seizure of the Golden Fleece, and their long voyage home became the subject of many tales and works of art. They might never have succeeded without the help of Medea, the daughter of King Aeëtes of Colchis, who fell in love with Jason. Some versions of the story say that Hera persuaded Aphrodite, the goddess of love, to inspire Medea's passion. Both a clever woman and a witch with knowledge of magic, Medea would be a useful helpmate to Jason.

When Jason arrived in Colchis, Aeëtes set harsh conditions for handing over the Golden Fleece, including the accomplishment of several seemingly impossible tasks. Jason had to yoke two fire-breathing bulls to a plow, sow a field with dragons' teeth, and then fight the armed warriors that grew from those teeth. In all these trials, Medea used her magic powers to protect and guide

*† See **Names and Places** at the end of this volume for further information.*

Jason. Then after Jason promised to marry her, she helped him steal the fleece from the serpent that guarded it.

With the fleece on board, the *Argo* sailed away from Colchis, pursued by Medea's brother Apsyrtus. Apsyrtus caught up with the ship and spoke with Jason, promising to let him keep the Golden Fleece if he would give up Medea. However, Medea objected to this plan. When she and Jason next met Apsyrtus, Jason killed him.

Return to Iolcus. After a long journey home with many adventures along the way, Jason and the Argonauts finally arrived back in Iolcus. Jason delivered the Golden Fleece to Pelias. Meanwhile, Medea decided to get rid of Pelias (accounts differ on whether Jason knew of her plan). She persuaded the king's daughters that she could make their father young again, but first they would have to cut him up and put him in a pot. This procedure led only to a messy death, and the horrified people of Iolcus drove Jason and Medea away. The couple settled in Corinth, where they lived for ten years and had several children.

Their peaceful interlude ended when Creon, the king of Corinth, offered Jason his daughter in marriage. Jason accepted and divorced Medea. Enraged at this shabby treatment, Medea sent the new bride a poisoned wedding gown, which killed her when she put it on and killed Creon as he tried to save her. Some versions of this myth say that, to punish Jason still further, Medea went on to kill the children she had borne him, while other accounts say that the angry Corinthians killed them. Either way, the children perished and Medea fled to Athens.

According to some accounts, Medea killed Jason at Corinth as part of her bloodbath. Much more common, though, is the story that Jason lived out his last days at Corinth, alone and broken by tragedy. One day as he sat near the *Argo,* which was rotting away, a piece of wood broke off from the ship and fell on him, killing the one-time hero of the Golden Fleece. *See also* ARGONAUTS; GOLDEN FLEECE; GREEK MYTHOLOGY; MEDEA.

Jerome, St.

St. Jerome, an early Christian scholar who lived around A.D. 400, is considered one of the early Latin Fathers and Doctors of the Roman Catholic Church. He became well known for his translation of the Bible from Greek and Hebrew into Latin. Called the Vulgate, his work remained in use until 1979.

According to legend, a lion limped into St. Jerome's monastery in Bethlehem one day. The other monks ran away in fear, but Jerome calmly looked at the lion's paw and removed a large thorn. Thereafter the lion became his companion. The other monks felt that the lion should work for his food as they did, so Jerome told the lion to guard the monastery's donkey. However, one day the lion neglected his duty, and thieves stole the donkey. Noticing that the donkey was missing, the monks accused the lion of eating it and forced the lion to do the donkey's work. Although innocent, the lion obeyed the order without complaint. Some time later, the lion saw the donkey in a caravan passing by the monastery and brought it back to the monks to prove his innocence.

Paintings of St. Jerome usually show him accompanied by a lion. His feast day is September 30.

Jezebel

prophet one who claims to have received divine messages or insights

prophecy foretelling of what is to come; also something that is predicted

In the Book of Kings I and II of the Bible, Jezebel was the wife of Ahab, king of Israel. She favored the worship of the god Baal† and ordered the deaths of many Hebrew **prophets.** Because of her actions, the prophet Elijah cursed her, saying that dogs would eat her body by the walls of the capital city.

After Ahab died, Jezebel's son Jehoram and a warrior named Jehu both claimed the throne. Jehu killed Jehoram and became king. He went to Jezebel's palace, where she was waiting for him dressed in beautiful clothes. When Jezebel taunted Jehu from her window, however, he ordered her servants to throw her out the window. Although he later declared that she should receive a proper burial, her body had been eaten by dogs in the street, fulfilling Elijah's **prophecy.** Evil women have since come to be called Jezebels. *See also* BAAL.

Job

Job is the name of a book in the Hebrew Bible and the name of the book's main character. Many scholars consider the Book of Job to be one of the finest works of literature ever written. It focuses on the question of why the innocent suffer.

Job, a wealthy man, blessed with a loving wife and family, is known for his goodness and devotion to the will of Yahweh, the Hebrew god. The Bible indicates that Job's prosperity and general good fortune are a reward for his goodness and belief in Yahweh. However, in a meeting between Yahweh and his heavenly advisers, Satan questions Job's faith, claiming that he is faithful because of the many blessings he enjoys. If Job were to suffer misfortune, suggests Satan, he would curse Yahweh as readily as he now praises him. Satan challenges Yahweh to test Job's faith, and Yahweh accepts the challenge.

Yahweh inflicts a number of terrible misfortunes on Job. He kills Job's children and causes him to lose all his wealth, but Job's belief in the goodness of Yahweh remains unshaken. This show of faith does not convince Satan, however, who says that physical pain and suffering would cause Job to abandon his belief. So Yahweh causes Job to be afflicted with painful boils all over his body, and still his faith remains firm.

Job's faith is tested by both Yahweh (God) and Satan. This stained glass window shows Satan torturing Job.

†*See Names and Places at the end of this volume for further information.*

At this point three friends visit Job, supposedly to comfort him by explaining why Yahweh is causing him to suffer. They suggest that Job must be guilty of some sin, because Yahweh only punishes the wicked. Knowing that he is a righteous man, Job refuses to accept their arguments. Finally Job pleads with Yahweh to end his suffering and asks him to explain why he is tormenting a good man. Yahweh appears to Job in all his glory, overwhelming him with his magnificence. He proceeds to question Job about the mysteries of the universe. When Job cannot answer, Yahweh asks him how he could possibly hope to understand the will of the almighty if he cannot explain the workings of nature. Job accepts this answer and renews his faith in Yahweh, who rewards him by restoring his health and prosperity.

In the end, Yahweh offers no answer to the question of why the innocent must suffer. Instead, the Book of Job delivers the message that one must believe in the goodness of Yahweh, even in the face of seemingly unjust punishment.

Jocasta

oracle priest or priestess or other creature through whom a god is believed to speak; also the location (such as a shrine) where such words are spoken
prophecy foretelling of what is to come; also something that is predicted

In Greek mythology, Jocasta was the wife of King Laius of Thebes†. An **oracle** warned that their child would kill his father and sleep with his mother. To prevent this prediction from coming true, Laius left their first baby on a mountain to die. However, a shepherd found the child and took him to King Polybus of Corinth, who raised the boy and named him Oedipus.

Many years later, the oracle repeated the **prophecy** to Oedipus. Hoping to avoid his fate, Oedipus fled Corinth and his adoptive parents. While traveling, he killed a stranger who insulted him. The stranger was actually his real father, Laius. Oedipus continued his journey until he reached Thebes, where he outwitted a monstrous sphinx that had been terrorizing the city. As queen of Thebes, Jocasta agreed to marry Oedipus. She gave birth to two sons, Eteocles and Polynices, and two daughters, Antigone and Ismene. When Jocasta later discovered that Oedipus was her son and that the horrible prophecy had come true, she committed suicide. *See also* ANTIGONE; GREEK MYTHOLOGY; OEDIPUS; SPHINX.

John Henry

John Henry, a mighty laborer who outperformed a mechanical drill, is a character who first appeared in African American songs and ballads. He can be seen as a symbol of black strength and of African Americans' refusal to be crushed. In more general terms, John Henry also represents the human will and spirit, which a machine may defeat but can never duplicate.

The character of John Henry sometimes receives the kind of exaggerated treatment given to other larger-than-life figures such as Paul Bunyan. For example, John Henry is said to have weighed 44 pounds at birth and to have gone looking for work after his first meal.

His story is linked to the spread of railroads across the United States as the Industrial Age got into full swing in the years after the American Civil War (1861–1865). John Henry became a "steel-drivin'

man," someone who swung a heavy hammer at a steel drill, driving it into rock to make railway tunnels through hills and mountains. The Chesapeake and Ohio Railroad drove the Big Bend Tunnel through West Virginia's Allegheny Mountains in the early 1870s, and legend places John Henry there.

All versions of the story agree that John Henry was the strongest and best hammerer of all, a man who wanted to be buried with his hammer in his hand. Then the railway company found a steam-powered drill that it claimed could work faster and better than even John Henry. The "steel-drivin' man" entered a contest with the drill, working until he was exhausted and ready to fall. In the words of one song:

> The man that invented the steam drill
> Thought he was mighty fine.
> John Henry drove his fifteen feet,
> And the steam drill only made nine.

John Henry beat the steam drill in that contest, but the victory was a costly one. He "died with his hammer in his hand," say some accounts, while others claim that he died that night in his bed, worn and broken from the strain of the contest. ***See also* BUNYAN, PAUL.**

Johnny Appleseed

Johnny Appleseed was the name given to John Chapman, an eccentric wanderer who planted apple trees on the American frontier. Like Davy Crockett and Daniel Boone, Chapman was a real person from the early history of the United States whose deeds were romanticized and embroidered by later writers until the man became a folk legend.

Chapman was born in Massachusetts in 1774, shortly before the outbreak of the American Revolution. As a young man, he settled in Pittsburgh, which then looked out on the frontier of American settlement in the Ohio River valley. He became an orchardist, someone who cultivates trees to sell their fruit or the seedlings of new trees.

In the early 1800s, Chapman began traveling west into the Ohio Territory with bags of apple seeds and loads of seedlings to sell to the pioneers settling there. When he came upon pioneers who could not afford to buy from him, he gave his seeds and seedlings away or exchanged them for a meal or a piece of cast-off clothing. Although he owned a sizable portion of land himself, Chapman preferred the life of a wanderer and became famous for his simple tastes. He often walked barefoot, no matter what the weather, and he was content to wear any old clothes he could find. In later life, he favored a shirt made out of a coffee sack with armholes cut in it.

Chapman came to be known on the frontier as Johnny Appleseed. His gentle and generous behavior won the affection and respect of everyone he met. Even the Native Americans of the region, who were involved in conflicts with white settlers over land ownership, treated Johnny Appleseed kindly.

By the time Chapman died in 1845 near Fort Wayne, Indiana, he had planted apple orchards across a large part of the Midwest. Vachel Lindsay's poem *In Praise of Johnny Appleseed* and Charles Allen Smart's play *The Return of Johnny Appleseed* are among the literary works that have helped promote his legend.

Jonah

prophet one who claims to have received divine messages or insights

The book of Jonah in the Bible tells the story of a **prophet** who was commanded by the Hebrew god Yahweh to go to the city of Nineveh and preach so that the people there might be saved. Jonah, however, did not feel they deserved salvation and boarded a ship going in the other direction. When a huge storm came up, he admitted it was caused by his disobedience to Yahweh. The crew threw Jonah into the sea, where a great fish swallowed him. The fish spat him onto land three days later, and Jonah went to Nineveh.

After hearing Jonah preach, the king of Nineveh ordered his subjects to repent, causing Yahweh to spare them. Because Jonah was angry that Yahweh had saved so many wicked people, he left the city, hoping it would be destroyed. Yahweh decided to teach Jonah a lesson. First he caused a plant to grow to shade Jonah from the sun during the day; later he sent a worm to eat it. When Jonah expressed regret at losing the plant, Yahweh scolded him for taking pity on a plant that he did not make grow, while feeling no sorrow for thousands of people in Nineveh. Jonah is usually portrayed in art with the great fish or resting in the shade of the plant.

Juggernaut

incarnation appearance of a god, spirit, or soul in earthly form

Juggernaut (Jagannatha), a form of the Hindu god Vishnu's **incarnation** Krishna, is worshiped at the religious city of Puri in India. A temple to Juggernaut there dates from the A.D. 1100s. According to one legend, a priest chose the site for the temple when he saw a crow dive into the nearby Bay of Bengal. Inside the temple is a horrifying wooden image of Juggernaut with a black face and a gaping mouth as red as blood.

Several festivals are held at the temple each year, the most important being the Chariot Festival in midsummer. On this occasion, the image of Juggernaut is placed on a 60-foot-high cart and pulled through the town by hundreds of people. Occasionally worshipers have thrown themselves beneath the wheels of the cart to be crushed as a sacrifice to Jagannatha. This practice gave rise to the English word *juggernaut,* meaning a person or power that crushes anything in its path. *See also* HINDUISM AND MYTHOLOGY; KRISHNA.

Julian Hospitaller, St.

St. Julian Hospitaller is the **patron** saint of innkeepers, travelers, and boatmen. According to **medieval** legend, Julian was a nobleman who was told by a stag that he would kill his parents. To avoid this fate, Julian fled to another land where he married a wealthy widow. In the meantime his parents went searching for him, and one day they came across his castle while he was away.

patron special guardian, protector, or supporter
medieval relating to the Middle Ages in Europe, a period from about A.D. 500 to 1500

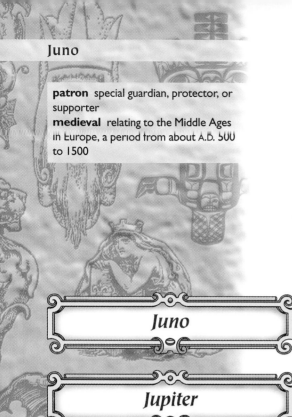

They told his wife who they were, and she allowed them to sleep in her bed. When Julian came home and found two people in his room, he killed them both

After discovering what he had done, Julian and his wife left the castle and opened an inn for travelers and a hospital for the poor. One night Julian risked his life to ferry a dying leper across the river near the inn. The leper turned out to be an angel sent by God to tell Julian he had been forgiven because of his good deeds. In paintings, St. Julian is often shown on horseback with a stag at his side. Many hospitals and inns are named after him.

Juno

See *Hera.*

Jupiter

See *Zeus.*

Kachinas

Spirits known as kachinas are central to the religion and mythology of the Pueblo Indians of the American Southwest, in particular the Hopi who live in Arizona. These groups believe that kachinas are divine spirits present in features of the natural world such as clouds, winds, thunder, and rain. They are also ancestral spirits that help connect humans with the spirit world.

Each Pueblo tribe and village has its own distinct kachinas. There may be more than 500 in total, and all are equally important. The Pueblos revere the kachinas and look to them for help, especially in bringing rain to water corn and other crops.

The kachinas dwell in sacred mountains and other sacred places. However, they spend half of each year living near Pueblo villages. During this time, the men of kachina **cults** perform traditional **rituals** linked with the presence of the spirits. They wear costumes and elaborate masks and perform songs and dances associated with specific kachinas. The Pueblos say that during these rituals each dancer is temporarily transformed into the spirit being represented.

Kachinas are also portrayed in elaborately carved wooden dolls adorned with the costumes and masks that identify them. The Hopi and other Pueblo peoples

The Hopi and other Pueblo peoples use kachina dolls to teach their children about divine and ancestral spirits. These wooden figures are often elaborately carved and adorned; this one has horns and feathers.

cult group bound together by devotion to a particular person, belief, or god
ritual ceremony that follows a set pattern

use these dolls to teach their children about the hundreds of different kachinas. *See also* CORN; KOKOPELLI; NATIVE AMERICAN MYTHOLOGY.

Kali

See *Devi.*

Katonda

Katonda, the creator god worshiped by the Buganda people of East Africa, is considered the father of the gods as well as the king and judge of the universe. He has many different titles, including Kagingo (master of life), Gguluddene (the gigantic one), Namuginga (the shaper), and Ssewannaku (the eternal one).

According to the Buganda, Katonda rules over a vast number of spirits that help him run the universe. He ranks the spirits of the dead on the basis of their worthiness, making them advisers, warriors, and even slaves. Spirits that are ranked may return as animals to earth, where they are respected by humans. Unranked spirits are not allowed on earth, and the living perform **rituals** to keep them away. Katonda's main spirit helpers are Kibuka, the god of war, and Walumbe, the spirit of death. After organizing the spirit world and ranking the spirits, Katonda leaves his deputies to run the universe. He only becomes involved to act as a judge in very difficult matters involving the spirits. *See also* AFRICAN MYTHOLOGY; KIBUKA.

ritual ceremony that follows a set pattern

Kibuka

Kibuka is the war god of the Buganda tribe of East Africa. According to legend, the king of the Buganda asked Kibuka's brother, the great god Mukasa, for assistance in a war. Mukasa sent Kibuka to help but told him to be sure the enemy did not know where he was stationed. He also warned his brother to avoid contact with the opponent's women.

On one occasion, Kibuka stayed hidden in a cloud, where he killed the enemy by shooting arrows, winning the battle for the Buganda. Afterward, Kibuka became interested in a woman taken as a prisoner and took her back to his hut. When she discovered who he was, she escaped and told her people about his hiding place in the cloud. During the next battle, the enemy's archers shot arrows into the cloud where Kibuka was hiding and killed him. *See also* AFRICAN MYTHOLOGY.

Kojiki

Together with the *Nihongi,* the *Kojiki* (Records of Ancient Matters) is the earliest and most important chronicle of early Japan. Compiled in A.D. 712 by Ô no Yasumaro, the *Kojiki* records events from the mythological age of the gods up to the death of Empress Suiko in A.D. 641. The three-volume work is a valuable resource for understanding Japan's mythology, traditions, art, and religious beliefs. In addition, it is one of the classics of Japanese literature.

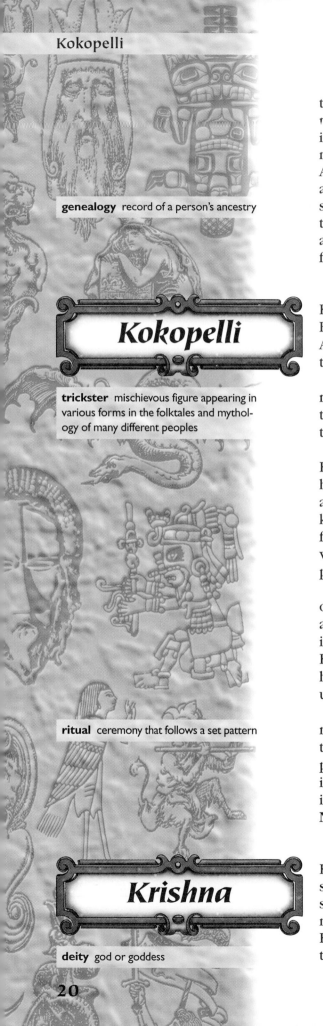

genealogy record of a person's ancestry

Kokopelli

trickster mischievous figure appearing in various forms in the folktales and mythology of many different peoples

ritual ceremony that follows a set pattern

Krishna

deity god or goddess

The *Kojiki* had two main purposes: to reinforce the idea that the emperor was descended from the gods and to determine the ranks of the leading Japanese families in society. During the 600s, increased contact with China had introduced the Japanese to many aspects of Chinese society, including its royal court system. After Japan imported the Chinese court system, the *Kojiki* created a history of the court similar to that of the Chinese. The work presents the **genealogy** of the most prominent families in Japan and traces the family history of the Japanese emperor back to the creation of heaven and earth. The *Kojiki* also includes myths on the founding of Japan. *See also* JAPANESE MYTHOLOGY; NIHONGI.

Kokopelli is a kachina, or spirit, found in the mythology of the Hopi, Zuni, and other Pueblo Indians of the American Southwest. A complex character, he plays various roles, including those of fertility spirit, **trickster,** and hunter.

Images of Kokopelli are among the oldest that survive in ancient rock art in the Southwest. He is also a popular figure on painted pottery. Usually depicted as a humpbacked figure playing a flute, he often carries a large bag on his back and has antennae like an insect.

The Hopi have several fertility kachinas connected with Kokopelli. In some Hopi tales, Kokopelli's bag contains gifts that he uses to attract women. In others, he carries a baby on his back and leaves it with a young woman. The Hopi also have a female kachina called Kokopell' Mana. During ceremonial dances, a performer dressed as Kokopell' Mana challenges Hopi men to race with her. If she catches her opponent, she knocks him down and pretends to mate with him.

Kokopelli is identified with various insects. Kuwaan Kokopelli, or the Robber Fly Kachina, is named after a humpbacked fly that is always mating. Like Kokopell' Mana, this kachina represents fertility. In a tale about how Kokopelli guided the Hopi to a new land, Kokopelli is either a locust or a grasshopper. When an eagle dares him to pass an arrow through his body, he cleverly slips the arrow under one of his wings.

Kokopelli's flute is similar to the flutes used in Native American religious **rituals.** As a hunter, Kokopelli may play the flute to attract the mountain sheep he is hunting. The Zuni call him a rain priest and connect him and his music with the gift of rain. According to the Hopi, Kokopelli warmed the land and the winds by playing his flute as he led them to their homeland. *See also* KACHINAS; NATIVE AMERICAN MYTHOLOGY.

Krishna, one of the most popular Hindu gods, is revered as a supreme **deity** and the eighth **incarnation** of the god Vishnu. Worshiped as a restorer of order to the world, he appears in a number of myths and legends. The most important source of stories about Krishna is the *Mahabharata,* the great Hindu **epic** written between 400 B.C. and A.D. 200, and the *Bhagavatam,* written later.

Hindus worship Krishna, one of the most popular Hindu gods, as a supreme god and restorer of order to the world. Here, Krishna lifts a mountain.

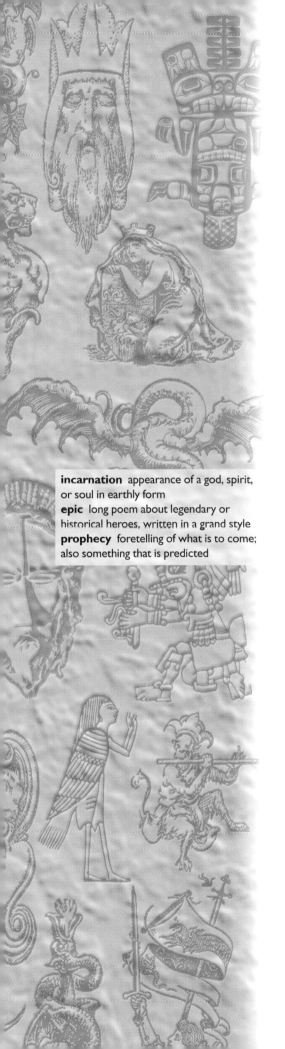

incarnation appearance of a god, spirit, or soul in earthly form

epic long poem about legendary or historical heroes, written in a grand style

prophecy foretelling of what is to come; also something that is predicted

Birth and Childhood. According to myth, Krishna was the son of Vasudeva and Devaki. His uncle, the wicked King Kamsa of Mathura, heard a **prophecy** that he would be killed by the eighth child of his sister Devaki. As a result, Kamsa vowed to kill the child. However, when Devaki gave birth to Krishna, her eighth child, the god Vishnu helped switch him with the newborn child of a cowherd and his wife. This couple raised Krishna as their own son.

From birth, Krishna exhibited great powers. Once when his father was carrying him, the baby Krishna dipped his foot in the waters of a raging river. The waves parted, allowing Vasudeva to cross.

After the evil Kamsa discovered that Krishna was alive, he sent demons to destroy the child. Krishna managed to overcome them all. He put an end to the ogress Putana by sucking the life out of her and caused a cart to crush the monstrous flying demon named Saktasura. He also destroyed Trinavarta, a whirlwind demon, by smashing it against a rock.

As Krishna grew up, he often amused himself by playing pranks on people. He also enjoyed teasing the daughters of the cowherds and had many romantic adventures.

Struggles Against Evil. When Krishna reached manhood, Kamsa lured him and his brother Balarama to Mathura to a wrestling contest. As the brothers entered the city, Kamsa released a wild elephant to trample them. Krishna killed the beast. Next Kamsa sent his champion wrestlers to fight the brothers, but Krishna and Balarama defeated them all. Finally, Kamsa ordered his demons to kill Krishna's real parents, Vasudeva and Devaki. Before this could take place, however, Krishna killed Kamsa, thus fulfilling the prophecy made years before.

21

After killing Kamsa, Krishna led his **clan,** the Yadavas, to the fortress city of Dvaraka. He settled there and married a beautiful princess named Rukmini. He later took other wives as well.

The climax of Krishna's long struggle against the forces of evil came with the great war between two families: the noble Pandavas and their evil cousins the Kauravas. Krishna served as the charioteer of Arjuna, one of the Pandava leaders. Although he took no part in the fighting, Krishna gave advice to Arjuna, and the Pandavas eventually defeated the Kauravas and rid the world of much evil. The conversations between Krishna and Arjuna are found in a section of the *Mahabharata* called the Bhagavad Gita.

After the war, Krishna returned to Dvaraka. One day while he sat in the forest, a hunter mistook him for a deer and shot an arrow at him. The arrow pierced Krishna's heel, his only vulnerable spot. After Krishna died, his spirit ascended to Goloka, a heavenly paradise, and his sacred city of Dvaraka sank beneath the ocean. *See also* BHAGAVAD GITA; DEVILS AND DEMONS; HINDUISM AND MYTHOLOGY; INDRA; MAHABHARATA, THE; SHIVA; VISHNU.

Lady of the Lake

The Lady of the Lake, an enchantress also known as Viviane or Nimuë, appears in many of the tales of King Arthur. According to legend, she lived in a castle beneath a lake surrounding the mystical island of Avalon. She raised Lancelot and gave Arthur the magical sword Excalibur, which he treasured. When Arthur was near death, she saved him by taking him to Avalon.

Arthur's magician Merlin fell in love with the Lady of the Lake, but she did not return his affection. However, she did persuade him to teach her some of his magic. While the two were traveling together, the Lady of the Lake used the spells she learned from Merlin to imprison him in a tower with invisible walls (in some versions of the story she traps him in a tree or cave instead).

The Lady of the Lake was also associated with Pelleas, one of the knights of the Round Table. When Pelleas was rejected by Ettard—the woman he loved—the Lady of the Lake took care of him. She and Pelleas fell in love and were married. *See also* ARTHUR, KING; AVALON; EXCALIBUR; LANCELOT; MERLIN.

Lancelot

In the **medieval** legends about King Arthur of Britain and his knights, Lancelot is the greatest knight of all. In time, however, Lancelot's love for Guinevere, the king's wife, leads him to betray his king and sets in motion the fatal events that end Arthur's rule.

Lancelot is generally considered to be a French contribution to the Arthurian legends†. He first appears in the **romances** of the French writer Chrétien de Troyes in the 1100s. However, some students of mythology see Lancelot as a later version of Celtic† heroes or even of older images of gods associated with lightning and fertility.

Like many heroes of myth and legend, Lancelot enjoyed a royal birth and an unusual upbringing. He was the son of King Ban of

† *See **Names and Places** at the end of this volume for further information.*

Lancelot, the greatest knight in King Arthur's court, appears in many stories based on medieval legend. In this illustration from the 1400s, Perceval and Lancelot on horseback attack Galahad.

chivalry rules and customs of medieval knighthood

adultery sexual relationship between a married person and someone other than his or her spouse

Benoic in western France, but he was raised by a mysterious figure known as the Lady of the Lake, who appears in various roles in the Arthurian tales. For this reason, he is sometimes called Lancelot of the Lake.

The Lady of the Lake prepared the youth to excel in all the knightly virtues and pastimes and then presented him to King Arthur's court. There Lancelot became the foremost knight, the model of **chivalry** and the good friend of the king. Unfortunately, however, Lancelot also fell in love with Queen Guinevere.

Some of Lancelot's knightly feats had to do with Guinevere. On one occasion, he rescued her after she had been kidnapped by a rival prince, but he had to humble his pride and ride in a lowly cart to do so. The same prince later accused Guinevere of **adultery,** and Lancelot fought as her champion. His love for Guinevere was such that he resisted the charms of a maiden called Elaine of Astolat, who died of love for him. Another Elaine, this one the daughter of King Pelleas, proved more enterprising. She tricked Lancelot into sleeping with her, pretending that she was Guinevere. Elaine bore Lancelot's son, Galahad, who grew into a pure

23

morality ideas about what is right and wrong in human conduct

and sinless knight. As Christian **morality** played an increasing role in the Arthurian legends over time, Galahad came to replace his flawed father as the supreme knight of Arthur's Round Table.

The uproar over Lancelot's affair with Guinevere tore King Arthur's court apart—as those who opposed Arthur had hoped that it would. Some of the knights followed Lancelot to France and set up another court, while others remained with Arthur. The two sides went to war until a rebellion led by Arthur's nephew Mordred broke out in Arthur's realm and the king had to return to Britain to suppress it. Arthur was mortally wounded fighting against the rebel army and was carried away to the island of Avalon. When Lancelot returned to Britain, Arthur's court was no more. Guinevere, in the meantime, had become a nun. Lancelot followed her example and devoted himself to religious service as a monk until he died. ***See also*** ARTHUR, KING; ARTHURIAN LEGENDS; GALAHAD; GUINEVERE; HOLY GRAIL; LADY OF THE LAKE.

Laocoön

seer one who can predict the future
prophecy foretelling of what is to come; also something that is predicted
epic long poem about legendary or historical heroes, written in a grand style

In Greek and Roman mythology, Laocoön was a **seer** and priest of the god Apollo† in the ancient city of Troy†. He played a notable role in the last days of the Trojan War† and met a violent death with his twin sons, Antiphas and Thymbraeus.

Toward the end of the Trojan War, the Greeks placed a large wooden horse before the gates of Troy. Laocoön hurled a spear at it and warned the Trojans not to bring the horse into the city. He said, "I fear the Greeks even when they offer gifts." Soon afterward, the Trojans ordered Laocoön to sacrifice a bull to the god Poseidon†. While he was making the sacrifice near the sea, two great serpents emerged from the water and crushed Laocoön and his sons to death. The Trojans interpreted this event as a sign of the gods' disapproval of Laocoön's **prophecy,** and they brought the horse into the city, an action that led to their downfall. Hiding inside the horse were Greek soldiers, who opened the gates of Troy at night, allowing the Greek army to enter and destroy the city.

Some stories say that the death of Laocoön and his sons was punishment from Athena† or Poseidon for warning the Trojans against the wooden horse. This is the reason given in the *Aeneid,* an **epic** by the Roman poet Virgil. According to other legends, however, Apollo sent the serpents to kill Laocoön as punishment for an earlier wrong—breaking his vow to the god that he would never marry or have children. ***See also*** ANIMALS IN MYTHOLOGY; GREEK MYTHOLOGY; ROMAN MYTHOLOGY; SEERS; SERPENTS AND SNAKES; TROJAN WAR.

Laocoön was the Trojan priest who predicted the fall of Troy. This ancient Roman sculpture shows Laocoön in his struggle with the serpents that Apollo sent to punish and kill him.

†*See* ***Names and Places*** *at the end of this volume for further information.*

Lares and Penates

deity god or goddess

In Roman mythology, Lares and Penates were groups of **deities** who protected the family and the Roman state. Although different, the Lares and Penates were often worshiped together at household shrines.

Considered spirits of the dead, Lares guarded homes, crossroads, and the city. Every Roman family had its own guardian, known as the *Lar familiaris,* to protect the household and ensure that the family line did not die out. Each morning Romans prayed and made offerings to an image of the *Lar familiaris* kept in a family shrine. Deities known as *Lares compitales,* who guarded crossroads and neighborhoods, were honored four times a year in a festival called the Compitalia. Another group of deities, the *Lares praestites,* served as the guardians of the city of Rome.

The Penates, originally honored as gods of the pantry, eventually became guardians of the entire household. They were associated with Vesta, the goddess of the hearth. The main function of the Penates was to ensure the family's welfare and prosperity. The public Penates, or *Penates publici,* served as guardians of the state and the object of Roman patriotism. According to legend, they were once the household gods of Aeneas†, the mythical ancestor of the Roman people. **See also AENEAS; ROMAN MYTHOLOGY; VESTA.**

Lear, King

Shakespeare's play *King Lear* has been produced on stage and film numerous times since its first performance in 1605. Here is a scene from a 1993 production of the Royal Shakespeare Company.

medieval relating to the Middle Ages in Europe, a period from about A.D. 500 to 1500

King Lear, a legendary ruler of ancient Britain, is a tragic figure who loses his authority through his own foolishness. The aging king decides to divide his kingdom among his three daughters and asks each of them to declare their love for him. King Lear's two oldest daughters, Regan and Goneril, flatter him with grand, but insincere, expressions of devotion. By contrast, Lear's youngest daughter, Cordelia, conveys only her natural, true love for her father.

Angered by what he perceives as Cordelia's insufficient love, Lear splits the kingdom between Regan and Goneril. Their treachery, however, soon becomes clear as they strip their father of all his authority and possessions. Lear then realizes the sincerity of Cordelia's love. Fearing that she will reject him because of the way that he treated her earlier, he goes to her and finds that she welcomes him with generosity and compassion.

One of the primary sources of King Lear's legend is the *History of the Kings of Britain* by the **medieval** English writer Geoffrey of Monmouth. In this version, Lear regains authority over his lands after joining Cordelia and her husband, although he dies a few years later. The legendary king is best known through William Shakespeare's play *King Lear.* In this version, Lear goes mad after he is humiliated by his two older daughters. When Cordelia learns of her father's condition, she raises an army to fight her sisters' forces. Cordelia's army is defeated, and she is imprisoned and hanged. King Lear dies soon thereafter of a broken heart over the death of his daughter. **See also CELTIC MYTHOLOGY.**

deity god or goddess

ritual ceremony that follows a set pattern

cult group bound together by devotion to a particular person, belief, or god

Lebe

In the mythology of the Dogon people of West Africa, the god Amma, the supreme **deity,** created eight ancestors and eight families and organized human existence on earth. Lebe was the eighth ancestor and the first one to die. At the time, death had not yet come to humans.

Lebe, an old man, was instructed to die (or at least appear to die) and to allow himself to be buried. After Lebe did this, the seventh ancestor took the form of a snake, swallowed Lebe, and then vomited his bones. These were transformed into colored stones that fell to earth and formed the shape of a body. The pattern and arrangement of the stones helped determine the nature of social relationships, particularly marriages. After Lebe was swallowed, all that was pure and good in the ancestors went into the stones, while everything impure was cast away. The stones also symbolized the life force of the ancestors, and Lebe's death allowed this life force to be passed on to all human beings. Each year the Dogon people perform a special **ritual** in honor of Lebe's sacrifice. *See also* AFRICAN MYTHOLOGY.

Leprechauns

A leprechaun is a tiny elf or fairy from Irish folklore who is supposed to know the whereabouts of hidden treasure—usually a pot of gold. A leprechaun is typically pictured as an old man wearing a bright red vest, an old-fashioned cocked hat, a leather apron, and heavy leather shoes with silver buckles.

According to most legends, a person who catches a leprechaun and threatens him may be able to convince him to reveal the location of the treasure. However, finding a leprechaun is not easy. The best way is to sneak up while he is mending his shoes, the only time he sits still for very long. After catching a leprechaun, a person must stay alert because leprechauns are very clever and can easily outsmart humans.

Leprechauns are great mischief makers who often play pranks on people, such as riding their sheep or dogs during the night or causing small accidents around the house. Occasionally they "adopt" a family and faithfully follow the members during their travels. However, if not treated well, a leprechaun will abandon the family after causing trouble. Some stories claim that leprechauns are the offspring of evil spirits and bad fairies. However, one legend says that the leprechaun is actually the Irish god Lug. After the Irish people forgot the old gods, Lug became a fairy cobbler named Lugh Chromain, which means "little stooping Lug." *See also* CELTIC MYTHOLOGY; DWARFS AND ELVES; LUG.

Lethe

In Greek and Roman mythology, Lethe was one of five rivers in the underworld, or the kingdom of the dead. Drinking from Lethe (whose name means "forgetfulness") caused the souls of the dead to forget all knowledge of their previous lives.

Some Greek religious **cults** taught their members not to drink from Lethe after they died. They believed that it was important to remember the mistakes of one's past lives so that, when reborn,

oracle priest or priestess or other creature through whom a god is believed to speak; also the location (such as a shrine) where such words are spoken

Leviathan

primeval from the earliest times

chaos great disorder or confusion

Leza

deity god or goddess

one would be wiser in the next life. To avoid Lethe's waters, they told their followers to drink from a spring named Mnemosyne (meaning "memory") that was near the Lethe.

Springs called Lethe and Mnemosyne were located at a cave near the Greek town of Lebadeia. The cave, which contained an **oracle,** was believed to be an entrance to the underworld. *See also* AFTERLIFE; HADES; STYX; UNDERWORLD.

The sea serpent Leviathan is mentioned several times in the Old Testament of the Bible. Legends about this immense and powerful creature were based on earlier stories about Tiamat, a dragon defeated by the god Marduk in a Babylonian creation myth. Later a similar tale appeared among the ancient Canaanites, who claimed that the god Baal slaughtered a seven-headed **primeval** serpent named Lotan.

In the Bible, Leviathan roamed the sea, breathing fire and spewing smoke from his nostrils. The book of Psalms describes how the Hebrew god Yahweh struggled with the many-headed Leviathan and killed it during a battle with the waters of **chaos.** Yahweh then created the universe, day and night, and the four seasons. Scriptural references to the end of time say that the flesh of Leviathan will be part of a feast served on the Day of Judgment. *See also* BAAL; CREATION STORIES; DRAGONS; MARDUK; SEMITIC MYTHOLOGY; SERPENTS AND SNAKES; TIAMAT.

Various Bantu-speaking peoples of central and southern Africa believe in a supreme **deity** called Leza. A sky god and creator spirit, Leza is the subject of several myths. According to a story told by the Basubiya people, Leza taught humans different arts as well as the proper way to worship him. When he finished, Leza returned to his home in the sky on a spiderweb. The people tried to follow him, but the spiderweb broke and they fell to earth.

In a legend told by the Ila people, a woman who had lost all the members of her family decided to find Leza to ask him why he made her experience such sorrow. She built a ladder to the sky, but it crashed to earth. While searching for a road to the sky, she told the sad story to people she met. They explained that all people were meant to suffer and that she was not alone in her sorrow. The woman never found Leza, and she, too, eventually died.

In yet another story, told by the Kaonde people, Leza once gave three gourds to a honeybird and instructed it to take them to humans. He told the bird that two of the gourds contained seeds and that humans could open these. The third gourd, however, should remain closed until Leza came to earth. While carrying the gourds, the bird became curious and opened all of them. Two held seeds, but the third contained death, sickness, and dangerous animals. Leza could not capture these unpleasant things, so humans were forced to build shelters to protect themselves. *See also* AFRICAN MYTHOLOGY.

Lilith

incantation chant, often part of a magical formula or spell

amulet small object thought to have supernatural or magical powers
medieval relating to the Middle Ages in Europe, a period from about A.D. 500 to 1500

In Jewish mythology, Lilith was a female demon who killed newborn children in the night. She was associated with an ancient Babylonian demon called Lilitu, whose name often appeared in magical spells and **incantations.**

According to Jewish legend, Lilith was the original wife of Adam, the first man created by God. She often quarreled with Adam and eventually left him. God sent three angels—Senoy, Sansenoy, and Semangelof—to find Lilith and bring her back. They found her at the Red Sea, where she was giving birth daily to numerous demons. When Lilith refused to return to Adam, God punished her by causing 100 of her children to die each day. He then created Eve to be Adam's companion.

Furious at her punishment, Lilith began to kill the newborn babies of others. Parents could protect their children from her attacks by placing near the child an **amulet** bearing the names of the three angels sent to find her. Up to **medieval** times, Jewish people often kept amulets to ward off Lilith and her demon children, the *lilim*. ***See also*** ADAM AND EVE; ANGELS; DEVILS AND DEMONS; SEMITIC MYTHOLOGY.

Lion

See ***Animals in Mythology.***

Loch Ness Monster

medieval relating to the Middle Ages in Europe, a period from about A.D. 500 to 1500

The Loch Ness Monster, known affectionately as Nessie, is a legendary marine animal associated with Loch Ness, the largest and deepest lake in Scotland. Legends about the monster have been told for centuries.

The first reported sighting was made in the A.D. 500s by St. Columba, an Irish missionary who had come to Scotland to spread Christianity. According to legend, Columba stopped the monster from attacking a man by making the sign of the cross and ordering the beast to leave.

The Loch Ness Monster is not just a beast from **medieval** mythology, however. A number of people have reported sighting it in modern times, describing the creature as about 30 feet in length with a long neck and flippers in the middle of its body. Such descriptions are similar to that of an extinct dinosaur called the plesiosaur.

Various attempts to find evidence that would either prove or disprove the existence of such an animal in Loch Ness have not been successful. As a result, the legend of the Loch Ness Monster continues. ***See also*** ANIMALS IN MYTHOLOGY; DRAGONS; MODERN MYTHOLOGY; MONSTERS; SERPENTS AND SNAKES.

Loki

In Norse† mythology, Loki was a **trickster** who caused endless trouble for the gods but who also used his cunning to help them. He lived in Asgard, the home of the gods, and he served as a companion to the great gods Thor† and Odin†. Loki enjoyed mischief

The trickster Loki arranged the death of Odin's son Balder. One day, while the gods were tossing objects at Balder in fun, the evil Loki tricked the blind god Höd into touching Balder with mistletoe. The touch of that plant, the one thing that could harm Balder, killed him.

trickster mischievous figure appearing in various forms in the folktales and mythology of many different peoples
supernatural related to forces beyond the normal world; magical or miraculous

and disguise and could change his form to imitate any animal. At first the gods found him amusing, but eventually they became tired of his tricks and grew to dislike him.

Nevertheless, Loki helped the gods on many occasions. One time a giant disguised as a builder came to Asgard, and offered to build a wall within a year and a half in exchange for Freyja, Odin's wife. Thinking the task was impossible, the gods agreed to the deal. However, the giant had a powerful stallion that could perform great feats of labor. When it looked as if the giant would succeed, Loki disguised himself as a mare and lured the stallion away, preventing the wall from being completed. The mare later gave birth to an eight-legged horse called Sleipnir, which Loki gave as a gift to Odin.

Loki had a number of wives and children. With his second wife, the giantess Angrboda, he had three fearsome offspring: a **supernatural** being named Hel, a serpent named Jormungand, and a wolf named Fenrir. As these creatures grew larger and more terrifying, the gods decided to get rid of them. They cast Hel into the dismal realm called Niflheim, where she became the goddess of the dead. They threw Jormungand into the sea, and they bound Fenrir with magical chains and fastened him to a huge rock.

As time went on, Loki grew increasingly evil. Angry with the gods because they now disliked him, he arranged the death of Odin's son Balder. Loki discovered that Balder could be harmed only by mistletoe. One day while the gods were tossing objects at Balder in fun, Loki gave a piece of mistletoe to the blind god Höd and told him to throw it at Balder. The mistletoe struck Balder and killed him.

The gods held a banquet in honor of Balder to which, naturally, Loki was not invited. But he showed up anyway, insulted the gods, and then fled again when they became angry. To escape detection, Loki disguised himself as a fish, but the gods knew his tricks by this time and caught him in a net.

To punish Loki, the gods captured two of his sons, Narfi and Vali. They turned Vali into a wolf and let him tear his brother Narfi to pieces. They then took Narfi's intestines and used them to tie Loki to rocks in a cave. A giantess named Skadi hung a great snake over Loki's head, and when its venom dripped onto Loki's face, it caused terrible pain. Loki would twist in agony, causing the whole world to shake. It is said that Loki will remain in that cave until Ragnarok, the end of the world, arrives. ***See also*** BALDER; FENRIR; FREYJA; GIANTS; HEL; NORSE MYTHOLOGY; ODIN; RAGNAROK; THOR; TYR.

Lucretia

According to legend, Lucretia was the beautiful wife of the early Roman army commander Lucius Tarquinius Collatinus. During a military expedition, Lucius and the other Roman leaders talked about how moral and good their wives were. They decided to return to Rome to see if the women were actually as faithful as each man claimed. They found only Lucretia at home; the other wives were misbehaving while their husbands were away.

One of the men in the group, Sextus Tarquinius, was the son of the Roman king. Fascinated by Lucretia's beauty and goodness, he went to see her again and raped her at knifepoint. Lucretia made her husband and father swear to avenge the deed and then killed herself. According to Roman legend, people were so outraged by the incident that they overthrew the monarchy and founded the Roman Republic. The story of Lucretia appears in works by the Italian artists Botticelli and Titian and in Shakespeare's poem *The Rape of Lucrece*. **See also ROMAN MYTHOLOGY.**

Lug

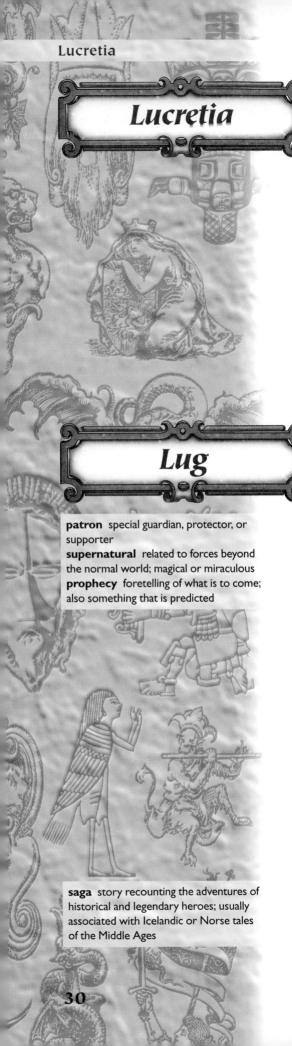

patron special guardian, protector, or supporter

supernatural related to forces beyond the normal world; magical or miraculous

prophecy foretelling of what is to come; also something that is predicted

saga story recounting the adventures of historical and legendary heroes; usually associated with Icelandic or Norse tales of the Middle Ages

An important and popular deity in Celtic† mythology, Lug (or Lugh) was a god of the sun and light known for his handsome appearance and skills in arts and crafts. A **patron** of heroes, Lug appears in many Irish and Welsh legends.

Lug was the son of Cian and the grandson of Balor, the king of the evil Formorians, a race of violent, **supernatural** beings who lived in darkness. Warned by a **prophecy** that he would be killed by his grandson, Balor locked his daughter Ethlinn in a crystal tower. In spite of his efforts, she gave birth to a son. Balor ordered the infant drowned, but a Celtic priestess rescued the child and raised him. According to some legends, Lug was raised by the smith god Goibhniu, his father's brother.

When Lug reached manhood, he went to the court of Nuada, the ruler of the Tuatha Dé Danaan, to offer his services as a warrior and master crafts worker. The Tuatha Dé Danaan, another race of supernatural beings, were the sworn enemies of the Formorians. Lug soon became involved in the ongoing war between the two groups. Besides getting magic weapons from the craft gods Goibhniu, Luchta, and Creidhne, Lug also helped organize the military campaigns of the Tuatha Dé Danaan.

During one battle King Nuada fell under the spell of Balor's evil eye, which had the power to destroy those who looked at it. Lug pierced the eye with a magic stone and killed Balor, thus fulfilling the prophecy and defeating the Formorians as well.

Lug became king of the Tuatha Dé Danaan, married the mortal woman Dechtire, and had a son named Cuchulain, who became a great hero. In a **saga** called the Cattle Raid of Cuailgne, Lug fought alongside Cuchulain in battle and soothed and healed him when he was wounded.

Eventually defeated by invaders, the Tuatha Dé Danaan retreated underground and were gradually transformed into the

†See **Names and Places** at the end of this volume for further information.

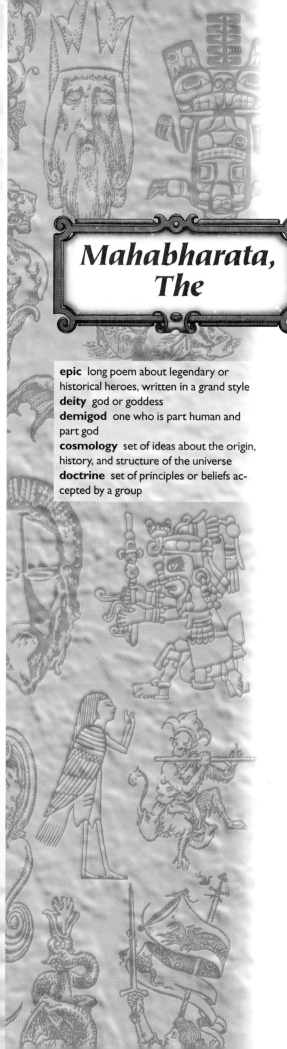

fairies of Celtic folklore. Meanwhile, Lug became a fairy crafts worker known as Lugh Chromain, a name that later turned into leprechaun—the tiny sprite or goblin of Irish folklore. *See also* CELTIC MYTHOLOGY; CUCHULAIN; DWARFS AND ELVES; LEPRECHAUNS.

Mahabharata, The

epic long poem about legendary or historical heroes, written in a grand style

deity god or goddess

demigod one who is part human and part god

cosmology set of ideas about the origin, history, and structure of the universe

doctrine set of principles or beliefs accepted by a group

One of the major **epics** of India and the longest poem in the world, the *Mahabharata* is a sacred Hindu text. It consists of many legends and tales revolving around the conflicts between two branches of a mythical family. The stories—which involve **deities, demigods,** and heroes—contain elements of **cosmology,** philosophy, and religious **doctrine.** A section of the epic called the Bhagavad Gita is the most important religious text of Hinduism.

Origin, Setting, and Background. Although tradition holds that an ancient sage, or wise man, called Vyasa wrote the *Mahabharata,* it was almost certainly composed by a number of different poets and then collected into a single work sometime between 400 B.C. and A.D. 200. The epic reached its present form about 200 years later. It contains nearly 100,000 verses and is divided into 18 sections called *parvans.*

The *Mahabharata* is set in the kingdom of Kurukshetra on the northern plains of India along the Ganges River. The opening *parvans* explain the ancestry of the major characters and provide background for the central conflict of the work. That conflict begins when the rightful heir to the throne of Kurukshetra, a blind prince named Dhritarashtra, is passed over in favor of his younger brother Pandu. Instead of taking the throne, however, Pandu goes to the Himalaya mountains to live as a hermit, leaving Dhritarashtra on the throne after all.

Rivals for Power. Before Pandu left Kurukshetra, his two wives gave birth to five sons, who became known as the Pandavas. They lived at the royal court with their cousins, the 100 sons of Dhritarashtra known as the Kauravas.

When the Pandavas came of age, the eldest, Yudhishthira, demanded the throne from his uncle, claiming that he was the rightful heir. A feud broke out between the two branches of the family, and the Kauravas eventually forced the Pandavas into exile in the forest.

While in exile, the Pandavas entered a tournament to win the hand of a beautiful princess named Draupadi. The Kauravas also entered the contest, but the Pandava brother Arjuna won the princess, who became the common wife of all five Pandavas.

After the tournament, King Dhritarashtra called the Pandavas back to his court and divided the kingdom among them and his own sons. Unhappy with this settlement, the Kauravas challenged the Pandavas to a game of dice and won back the entire kingdom by cheating. Once again, the Pandavas were forced into exile.

The *Mahabharata* is a sacred Hindu text and the longest poem in the world. Its story revolves around conflicts between two branches of a mythical family. This painting illustrates a scene from the poem.

War and Aftermath. After many years of wandering, the Pandavas returned to reclaim the kingdom, but the Kauravas refused to give up control and both sides prepared for war. The god Krishna, a relative of both the Pandavas and Kauravas, supported the Pandavas. Although he took no part in the fighting, he served as charioteer for the Pandava brother Arjuna and gave him advice. Their conversations make up the section of the *Mahabharata* known as the Bhagavad Gita.

The Pandavas and Kauravas met in a series of battles on the plains of Kurukshetra. In the end, the Pandavas emerged victorious after killing all their cousins. The Pandavas gained the kingdom, and the oldest brother, Yudhisthira, took the throne.

The Pandavas ruled peacefully, although their uncle Dhritarashtra mourned the loss of his sons and frequently quarreled with his nephews. Dhritarashtra eventually went to live in the forest and died there. Some time later, Yudhisthira gave up the throne and went with his brothers and their wife, Draupadi, to live on Mount Meru, the heaven of the god Indra.

Other Tales and Impact. The conflict between the Pandavas and Kauravas makes up only a portion of the *Mahabharata*. The work includes many other tales about deities and heroes and covers an enormous range of topics. The stories present complex philosophical ideas that form the basis of the Hindu faith—codes of conduct, social duties, and religious principles.

The *Mahabharata* became immensely popular in India and throughout Southeast Asia. The work inspired many ancient works of art, such as Indian miniature paintings and the elaborate sculptures of the ancient temples of Angkor Wat and Angkor Thom in Cambodia. Today the *Mahabharata* remains the most important Hindu epic and continues to serve as the foundation for religious faith and mythology. ***See also*** BHAGAVAD GITA; HINDUISM AND MYTHOLOGY; INDRA; KRISHNA.

Manco Capac

In the mythology of the Incas, Manco Capac was the founder of their nation and a **culture hero** who set the Incas on the road to glory. There are several versions of his story.

The best-known source, *The Royal Commentaries of the Inca* by Inca Garcilaso de la Vega, relates that the sun god was distressed that the people of earth did not live in a civilized way. As he crossed the sky each day, he saw that they wore only leaves and

animal skins for clothing, lived in caves, and gathered wild plants and berries for food. So the sun god decided to send his son Manco Capac and daughter Mama Ocllo to teach the people how to improve their way of life. He gave his children a golden rod and told them to push it into the ground wherever they stopped to rest. When they reached a spot where the rod sank completely into the ground with a single push, they should build a sacred city of the sun, to be named Cuzco.

Setting out from Lake Titicaca, Manco Capac and Mama Ocllo wandered across the land and finally came to a valley where the golden rod sank easily into the soil. There they gathered all the people from near and far and taught them how to build homes, weave cloth, make tools, and grow crops. They also taught the people how to use weapons so that they could defend themselves and defeat others.

Another version of the myth says that Manco Capac was one of six siblings who emerged from a cave near Cuzco. The siblings gained control over the people of the earth, and Manco Capac became the first ruler of the Incas. Still another tale says that Manco Capac deceived people into believing that he was the son of the sun god. He did this by standing on a mountain wearing silver plaques that shone in the sun and made him look like a god. *See also* INCA MYTHOLOGY.

Manticore

The manticore (also known as martichora) was a mythical animal with a human head and face, a lion's body, and a scorpion's tail. According to legend, this fast, powerful, and fierce beast attacked and devoured people.

First described by the Greek physician Ctesias in the late 400s or early 300s B.C., the manticore was said to have originated in India. It was mostly red, had pale blue or gray eyes, and had three rows of sharp teeth stretching from ear to ear. The manticore's voice sounded like a combination of a trumpet and a reed pipe. Its tail was equipped with stinging quills that the creature could shoot like arrows.

In **medieval** Christianity, the manticore was a symbol of the devil. It appeared in a number of bestiaries, books containing pictures or descriptions of mythical beasts. The manticore was also featured in medieval **heraldry** on items such as coats of arms, banners, and family trees. *See also* ANIMALS IN MYTHOLOGY; MONSTERS.

Manu

In Hindu mythology, the gods created Manu, the first man, who gave life to all humans. According to legend, he was the earth's first king and the ancestor of all the kings of India. The most famous tale involving Manu tells of a great flood that destroyed everything on earth.

One day Manu was washing his hands in a bowl of water when he saw a tiny fish there. The fish pleaded with Manu to be placed in a larger vessel of water to survive. In return, the fish promised to save Manu from a great flood that was to come and carry away all living beings. Manu put the fish in a bigger bowl, but the fish grew so rapidly that he had to transfer it to an even larger tank. The fish continued to grow until Manu eventually threw it into the sea. At that point, the fish told him that he should build a great ship to save himself from the coming flood. He also instructed Manu to take into the ship two of each animal on the earth as well as seeds from every kind of plant.

When the flood came, Manu used a rope to tie his boat to a large horn growing out of the fish. Pulling the ship through the rough waters, the fish came to the Himalaya mountains. There it told Manu to tie the ship to one of the mountains and wait until the waters receded. After the flood, Manu became lonely because only he and the animals aboard the ship had survived. He offered a sacrifice and was rewarded with a wife, with whom he began to repopulate the earth.

In several Hindu texts the fish appears as the god Brahma or Vishnu. The story of Manu and the flood also has parallels with the biblical stories of Noah's Ark and Adam and Eve. ***See also*** ADAM AND EVE; FLOODS; HINDUISM AND MYTHOLOGY; NOAH.

Marduk

chaos great disorder or confusion
epic long poem about legendary or historical heroes, written in a grand style
primeval from the earliest times
deity god or goddess

The Babylonians believed that Marduk, the chief god, created the world, the first calendar, and humans. In recognition of Marduk's power, the other gods built him a temple in Babylon.

The chief god of the Babylonians†, Marduk created an ordered world out of the original state of **chaos.** His exploits are described in the Babylonian creation **epic** known as the *Enuma Elish.*

Before the birth of Marduk, there were two **primeval** gods: Apsu, god of the sweet waters; and his wife, Tiamat, goddess of the salt waters. This pair produced children, who in turn gave birth to Marduk and other **deities.** In time, a great conflict arose between the young gods and the primeval gods. Tiamat created an army of demons to attack and destroy the young gods. After giving her son Kingu the tablets of destiny, which allowed him to command the gods in her service, Tiamat placed him in charge of the army. The young gods chose Marduk as their champion to do battle with Tiamat. He accepted on the condition that he be named the leader of all the gods.

Armed with a net, a bow, a mace, and the four winds, Marduk went out to face Tiamat. She appeared in the form of a dragon. Marduk caught Tiamat in his net, but she opened her mouth to swallow him. At that point, Marduk drove fierce winds into her mouth, causing her body to blow up like a balloon. He then shot an arrow at Tiamat's heart and killed her. After splitting her body into two pieces, he set one piece in the sky to create the heavens and the other at his feet to form the earth.

Marduk took the tablets of destiny from Kingu and placed them on his own chest to proclaim his power over the gods. Then he created time by establishing the first calendar. Finally, he killed Kingu and used his blood to create humans as servants of the gods. In recognition of his power, the other gods built a great temple to Marduk in the city of Babylon. ***See also*** CREATION STORIES; ENUMA ELISH; TIAMAT.

†*See **Names and Places** at the end of this volume for further information.*

Mars

Mars was a major Roman **deity,** second only to Jupiter† in the Roman **pantheon.** He began as a protector of agriculture but later became the god of war, honored throughout the realm of the conquering Romans. The Romans admired Greek culture and absorbed Greek deities into their own. They came to identify their own war god, Mars, with the Greek war god, Ares, but Mars was a more dignified and popular figure.

According to legend, Juno, the queen of the gods, gave birth to Mars after being touched by a magic plant. He was originally associated with vegetation and fertility. As the Romans became increasingly warlike, Mars gradually developed into a god of war, but he never lost his connection with agriculture and the plant world entirely. The Romans honored him with festivals in his month, March, which occurs at a time of the year when new growth begins in the fields and military campaigns resume after a winter break.

Mars's high place of honor in the Roman pantheon comes in part from his role as an ancestor of Rome. According to the story of the founding of Rome, Mars was the father of Romulus and Remus, twin boys born to a human priestess and raised by a wolf. Romulus later founded the city of Rome, and the Romans believed that Romulus's divine father would come to their aid in times of crisis or disaster. The wolf and the woodpecker, animals involved in the saving of the twins, were sacred to Mars. Picus, a Roman god who took the form of a woodpecker, was Mars's companion.

One story about Mars relates that the god's sacred shield had fallen from the sky in the time of the early Roman king Numa Pompilius. Believing that the shield was vital to the well-being of Rome, Numa had 11 identical shields made and hung all 12 of them in a shrine to confuse any thief who might try to steal Mars's shield. Numa also established an order of priests called the Salii to guard the shields. For many years, Roman priests continued to wear the old-fashioned armor and to perform **ritual** war dances during the March festivals of Mars.

Soldiers throughout the empire offered sacrifices to Mars before and after battles. They also honored the goddess Bellona, who appeared as Mars's sister, wife, and daughter in various myths. The Campus Martius, a large field outside Rome where soldiers exercised, was sacred to Mars. *See also* Ares; Roman Mythology; Romulus and Remus.

Masewi and Oyoyewi

Masewi and Oyoyewi are twin brothers who play a prominent role in the creation myths of the Acoma people of the American Southwest. In these stories, their mother, Iatiku, gave birth to people, and they emerged into the light from underground at a place called Shipap. Masewi and Oyoyewi, Iatiku's warrior sons, became the leaders of the people. As **culture heroes,** they performed many great deeds, such as summoning rain and instructing others how to make offerings to beneficial spirits called kachinas. Like twins in other Native American traditions—such as the Zuni Ahayuuta brothers and the Navajo warrior

twins—Masewi and Oyoyewi sometimes indulged in irresponsible and mischievous behavior between their acts of heroism.

One Acoma story tells how Masewi and Oyoyewi were responsible for bringing rain. Each night they danced outside their mother's house to ensure that the water in her medicine bowl did not dry up. However, Iatiku grew tired of the dancing, so the twins went away to prove that they controlled the rains. After they left, the water in the bowl dried up, and Iatiku asked everyone for help in bringing rain. Desperate, she pleaded with her children to return. They finally did, but only after many years of drought had led to starvation among their people. The return of the twins brought rain, and the people realized the power of Masewi and Oyoyewi. *See also* CREATION STORIES; KACHINAS; NATIVE AMERICAN MYTHOLOGY; TWINS.

Maui

trickster mischievous figure appearing in various forms in the folktales and mythology of many different peoples
culture hero mythical figure who gives people the tools of civilization, such as language and fire
immortality ability to live forever

In Polynesian mythology, Maui was a powerful **trickster** god best known for creating the Pacific islands. A son of the god Tangaroa and a woman, he performed many deeds to improve the lives of humans, such as making the sky higher and the day longer. Endowed with magical powers, this small but exceedingly strong god and **culture hero** tried but did not succeed in achieving **immortality.**

Maui created the islands while out on a fishing trip with his brothers. First he fashioned a magic fishing hook from his grandmother's jawbone. Then, as his brothers looked on, Maui cast the hook into the water and began to pull up from the ocean floor the islands on which the Polynesians now live.

On another occasion Maui was out walking and came upon a girl who complained that the sky was so low it kept falling on her and preventing her from doing her chores. Eager to impress the girl, Maui pushed hard and succeeded in raising the sky.

In order to give people more hours of daylight to tend their gardens, cook their food, and make cloth, Maui made the days longer. With the help of his brothers, he caught the sun in a net and beat it with his grandmother's magic jawbone. The sun was so bruised and bloodied by this battering that from that time on it could only limp slowly across the sky.

Maui tried to become immortal by tricking Hina, the goddess of death, as she lay sleeping. He crawled into her body and tried to pass through it, but the goddess was awakened by the call of a bird and promptly crushed Maui to death. *See also* POLYNESIAN MYTHOLOGY; TRICKSTERS.

Mayan Mythology

The Mayan civilization flourished in **Mesoamerica** from around 300 B.C. until the Spanish conquest of the early A.D. 1500s. The mythology of the Maya had many elements in common with those of other civilizations of the region. But the Maya developed their own variation of the Mesoamerican **pantheon** of gods and goddesses, the stories about them, and the image of the universe and the place of humans in it.

Mesoamerica cultural region consisting of southern Mexico and northern regions of Central America
pantheon all the gods of a particular culture

deity god or goddess

divination act or practice of foretelling the future
ritual ceremony that follows a set pattern

In Mayan mythology, the gods and heroes had many different names and appearances, stories occurred in varying forms, and scenes and figures changed and shifted with confusing rapidity. Beneath this seeming confusion, though, lay a sense that the universe was an orderly, structured place and that proper behavior toward the gods played an important role in maintaining its harmony and balance.

Background and Sources. The earliest known images of Mesoamerican gods were created by the Olmec civilization of Mexico. Emerging sometime after 1400 B.C., the Olmecs lived along the southern coast of the Gulf of Mexico for roughly a thousand years. They built pyramids that were sacred places where the human realm touched the realm of the gods. They also carved enormous stone heads as images of their leaders and created a long-distance trade network across Mesoamerica to obtain valued items such as jade.

The Olmec pantheon probably included **deities** of rain, corn, and fire, as well as a feathered serpent god. These figures reappeared in the myths of later Mesoamerican peoples. Olmec art included images of jaguars and of creatures that were part jaguar, part human. People of the region believed that magicians could turn themselves into jaguars.

The Zapotecs, Toltecs, and Aztecs were among the Mesoamericans who inherited and built upon Olmec traditions. So did the Maya, who were concentrated in the lowlands of Mexico's Yucatán Peninsula and in a highland region that extends from the present-day states of Tabasco and Chiapas into Guatemala. The Maya enjoyed their greatest wealth, power, and success from around A.D. 300 to 900. Historians call this their Classic period. During this time, the Maya built vast stone cities and ceremonial centers such as Tikal and Palenque. After the Classic period, Toltecs from central Mexico arrived in the Yucatán and eventually merged with the Maya. Their influence shaped late Mayan civilization at Chichén Itzá and Mayapán.

The Maya shared in a common Mesoamerican culture. The peoples of the region believed in the same gods and myths, built temples in the form of pyramids, practiced **divination,** and had an interest in astronomy. They also had a ball game in which teams competed to pass a ball of solid rubber through a stone ring or hoop. Only certain men and gods could play this game. Sometimes it was simple sport, sometimes a sacred **ritual.** Scholars do not know the full meaning of the Mesoamerican

The Maya played a ball game in which teams competed to pass a rubber ball through a stone ring or hoop. Although the meaning of the game is not clear, the players may have represented the struggle between light and dark, and the ball may have symbolized the movement of stars through the heavens.

Mayan Deities

Deity	Role
Ah Puch (Yum Cimil)	god of death and destruction, brought disease and was associated with war
Chac	rain god
Cizin (Kisin)	god of death, linked with earthquakes
Hun-Hunahpú (Ah Mun)	god of maize and vegetation
Hunahpú and Xbalanqúe	twin sons of Hun-Hunahpú, tricked the lords of the underworld
Itzamná	chief god, ruler of heaven, of night and day, and of the other deities
Ixchel	goddess of fertility, pregnancy, and childbirth
Kinich Ahau	sun god, sometimes considered an aspect of Itzamná
Kukulcan (Quetzalcoatl)	Feathered Serpent, god of learning and crafts

ball game, but it may have represented the movement of the heavenly bodies or a symbolic kind of warfare that ended in human sacrifice.

The Maya also shared the elaborate calendar system used across much of Mesoamerica. One part, called Haab by the Maya, was a 365-day calendar based on the sun's annual cycle. The other, called Tzolkin, was a 260-day sacred calendar. The two calendars meshed in a cycle known as the Calendar Round, which repeated every 52 years. The Maya used the calendar both for measuring worldly time and for sacred purposes, such as divination. Each day in the Calendar Round came under the influence of a unique combination of deities. According to the Maya, the combination that occurred on a person's date of birth would influence that person's fate.

Like other Mesoamerican cultures, the Maya used a writing system based on symbols called glyphs that represented individual syllables. They recorded their mythology and history in volumes known as codices. Although the Spanish destroyed most Mayan documents, a few codices have survived. Other written sources of Mayan mythology include the *Popol Vuh*, the sacred book of the Quiché Maya of Guatemala; and the *Chilam Balam* (Secrets of the Soothsayers), writings by Yucatecan Maya that date from the 1600s and 1700s and contain much traditional lore. Accounts by Spanish explorers and missionaries—such as Diego de Landa's description of Mayan life and religion in the Yucatán with the first key to the written language (ca. 1566)—provide useful information. Inscriptions found at **archaeological** sites are also helpful.

archaeological referring to the study of past human cultures, usually by excavating ruins

underworld land of the dead

maize corn

primeval from the earliest times

rite ceremony or formal procedure

Major Deities and Characters. The chief god of the Maya was Itzamná—ruler of the heaven, of day and night, and of the other deities. Itzamná was a culture hero, a figure credited with giving people basic tools of civilization, such as language and fire. Said to have been the first priest and the inventor of writing, Itzamná was also linked to healing. His wife, Ixchel, was goddess of fertility, pregnancy, and childbirth. Women made pilgrimages to her shrines.

Ah Puch, often shown with decomposing flesh and a head like a skull, was the god of death and destruction. He brought disease, was associated with war, and ruled the lowest level of the Mayan **underworld.** The modern Maya call him Yum Cimil (lord of death). Cizin or Kisin (stinking one) is another death god. He is linked in particular with earthquakes, which often strike Mesoamerica with devastating force. The ancient Maya depicted him as a dancing skeleton with dangling eyeballs. His opponent was the god of **maize** and vegetation, called Ah Mun and or Hun-Hunahpú, often shown with an ear of maize growing from his head.

The sun god was Kinich Ahau, sometimes said to be one aspect of Itzamná. He was associated with jaguars. The rain god, a major figure in all Mesoamerican mythologies, was called Chac by the Maya. He was often portrayed as a fisherman or as a figure with the features of a fish or reptile. Like Itzamná and other Mayan deities, Chac could appear in four forms, each associated with a particular color and compass direction. (This fourfold aspect is a common feature of Mesoamerican mythology.) Quetzalcoatl, the Feathered Serpent, called Kukulcan by the Maya, was also a figure of great importance throughout Mesoamerica.

Major Themes and Myths. The Maya believed that creation was related to divination and magic, and they often referred to their heroes and creator gods as diviners. The men and women who practiced divination regarded it as a form of creation similar to the divine miracle that produced the world and humankind.

Like the Aztecs and other Mesoamericans, the Maya believed that the present world is only the most recent in a series of creations. The earlier ones perished or were destroyed one after the other, just as this world will one day come to an end too.

According to the *Popol Vuh*, creation began with the god Huracan, who blew as a great wind over the **primeval** ocean, causing the earth to rise from the depths. Then Xpiacoc and Xmucane, "old man and old woman," performed magical **rites** that helped Huracan and other creator deities form plants, animals, and eventually the human race. The gods fashioned the first man out of clay, and he melted into the water. The next race of people, made of wood, were dull, spiritless, and easily destroyed by fire. For their third attempt, the gods mixed yellow and white maize flour together and made the First Fathers, the ancestors of men, from the dough.

The First Fathers were worshipful, handsome, and wise—too wise, the gods decided. Fearing that their creations would become

The Pyramid of Kukulcan (Quetzalcoatl) in the ancient Mayan city of Chichén Itzá was constructed around 1050. The Maya probably used the pyramid as a calendar. The pyramid's four sides face north, west, south, and east, and each side has 91 steps. Together with the top step, that adds up to 365 steps—the number of days in a year.

too powerful, the gods blew fog into the First Fathers' eyes, taking away some of their knowledge. The gods then made the First Mothers. Finally they created the sun to bring light to the world.

One section of the *Popol Vuh* tells the myth of the Hero Twins, sons of the maize god Hun-Hunahpú. The lords of death, seeing the maize god and his twin brother play the ball game constantly, grew annoyed and summoned the two to Xibalba. The brothers fell into a series of tricks and traps, which allowed the lords of death to sacrifice them and to hang Hun-Hunahpú's head from a tree. But the maize god's twin sons, Hunahpú and Xbalanqúe, grew up to be even more skilled ballplayers.

When in turn the lords of death summoned the twin sons to the underworld, Hunahpú and Xbalanqúe had tricks of their own. They played the ball game every day, and each night they passed some test. Eventually, they decided to set a trap for the lords. In the final part of their trick, the twins cut themselves in pieces and then restored themselves to wholeness. The underworld gods wanted to try the same trick. However, after the twins cut up the

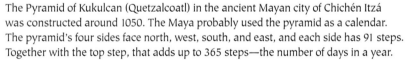

†*See **Names and Places** at the end of this volume for further information.*

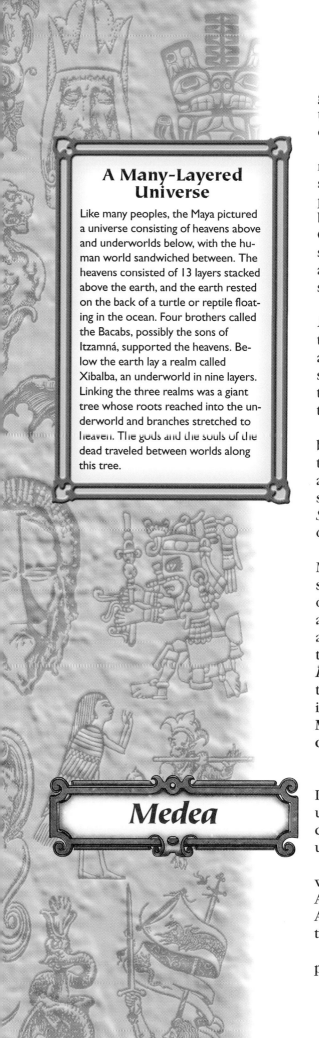

A Many-Layered Universe

Like many peoples, the Maya pictured a universe consisting of heavens above and underworlds below, with the human world sandwiched between. The heavens consisted of 13 layers stacked above the earth, and the earth rested on the back of a turtle or reptile floating in the ocean. Four brothers called the Bacabs, possibly the sons of Itzamná, supported the heavens. Below the earth lay a realm called Xibalba, an underworld in nine layers. Linking the three realms was a giant tree whose roots reached into the underworld and branches stretched to heaven. The gods and the souls of the dead traveled between worlds along this tree.

gods, they simply left them in pieces. The twins then restored their father and their uncle to life before passing into the sky to become the sun and moon.

The mythology of the ancient Maya included the belief that humans had been put on earth to nourish the gods. Human sacrifices served this purpose. So did the ritual called bloodletting, in which priests or nobles pierced parts of their bodies and offered the blood to the gods or to ancestors in exchange for guidance. Clouds of smoke from burning blood offerings were thought to summon the Vision Serpents, images of snakes with Mayan gods and ancestors coming from their mouths. Such visions probably symbolized the renewal and rebirth made possible by sacrifice.

Legacy. Striking images of the deities and myths of Mayan civilization can be found today in archaeological sites. Southern Mexico and northern Central America are dotted with the remains of great stone cities and temples that are still yielding a wealth of information about the history and culture of the ancient Maya. Some of these sites have become tourist attractions and educational centers.

Other remnants are literary. Mayan texts—those recorded by both Native American and Spanish chroniclers in the years after the Spanish conquest, as well as new translations of inscriptions and codices—are available to interested readers. Some have inspired modern writers. Stories in Charles Finger's *Tales from the Silver Lands* and Miguel Angel Asturias's *Men of Maize* are based on the *Popol Vuh.*

There is a living Mayan legacy as well. The descendants of the Maya number about 5 million today. Proud of their heritage, they still tell old myths at festivals and funerals, although perhaps less often than they used to. Some of them remember the old gods, asking Chac for rain, thanking Hun-Hunahpú for a good harvest, and fearing that Ah Puch is prowling about, hungry for victims. In the Yucatán, a television series called *Let Us Return to Our Maya Roots* promoted traditional language and customs. The mythology that once expressed the visions and beliefs of much of Mesoamerica remains part of a culture that is still alive. ***See also*** AZTEC MYTHOLOGY; HUNAHPÚ AND XBALANQÚE; ITZAMNÁ; MEXICAN MYTHOLOGY; POPOL VUH; QUETZALCOATL; TWINS.

Medea

In Greek mythology, Medea was an enchantress and witch who used her magic powers to help Jason† and the Argonauts in their quest for the Golden Fleece†. Later, after Jason betrayed her, she used her witchcraft to take revenge.

The daughter of Aeëtes, king of Colchis, Medea first saw Jason when he arrived at the king's palace to request the Golden Fleece. According to some accounts, Hera, queen of the gods, persuaded Aphrodite, the goddess of love, to make Medea fall in love with the young hero.

Aeëtes had no intention of handing over the Golden Fleece but pretended that he would do so if Jason successfully performed a

series of tasks. He was to yoke fire-breathing bulls to a plow, sow a field with dragons' teeth, and then fight the armed warriors who grew from those teeth. In return for his promise to marry her, Medea gave Jason a magic ointment to protect him from the bulls' fiery breath and told him how to confuse the warriors so that they would fight among themselves. Following Medea's instructions, Jason completed the tasks he had been set.

Aeëtes promised to hand over the Golden Fleece, but Medea knew that he would not keep his word. She led Jason and the musician Orpheus† into the sacred grove where the fleece was kept, guarded by a vicious serpent. Orpheus sang the serpent to sleep, enabling Jason to escape with the fleece. Medea then joined Jason and the Argonauts as they set sail in the *Argo,* pursued by her brother Apsyrtus. When Apsyrtus caught up with them, he promised to let Jason keep the Golden Fleece if he would give up Medea. Jason refused and killed Apsyrtus.

Eventually the Argonauts arrived back at Iolcus, which was ruled by Jason's uncle Pelias. Pelias had gained the throne by killing Jason's father, King Aeson. Medea brought Aeson back to life by boiling his remains in a pot with magical herbs. In this way, she tricked Pelias's daughters into thinking that they could restore their father to youth by cutting him up and boiling him in a pot. Pelias died a gruesome death, and the furious inhabitants of Iolcus drove out Medea and Jason.

The couple married and settled in Corinth, where they raised several children. Their happy days ended when Creon, the king of Corinth, offered Jason his daughter Glauce in marriage. Anxious to please the king, Jason abandoned Medea and prepared to marry Glauce. Medea took her revenge by sending Glauce a poisoned wedding gown that burned her alive. By some accounts, before fleeing to Athens, she also killed the children she had borne to Jason.

Aegeus, the king of Athens, agreed to protect Medea if she married him and bore him children. They produced a son, Medus (or Medeius), who stood to inherit the throne. However, Aegeus was unaware that he already had a son, Theseus, from a previous marriage. When Theseus came to Athens to claim the throne, Medea recognized him, persuaded Aegeus that Theseus planned to kill him, and prepared a cup of poisoned wine for the young man. Just as Theseus was about to drink the wine, Aegeus recognized the sword that Theseus carried, realized that Theseus was his son, and knocked the cup from the young man's hand. By some accounts, Medea then fled to a region in Asia that came to be known as Media in her honor and whose inhabitants became known as Medes. *See also* ARGONAUTS; GOLDEN FLEECE; JASON; THESEUS.

Medusa

Medusa, one of three sisters in Greek mythology known as the Gorgons, had a destructive effect upon humans. In many myths, she appeared as a horribly ugly woman with hair made of snakes, although occasionally she was described as being beautiful. In

†See **Names and Places** at the end of this volume for further information.

both forms, Medusa's appearance was deadly: any person who gazed directly at her would turn to stone.

Although the two other Gorgons were **immortal,** Medusa was not. One of the best-known legends about her tells of how the Greek hero Perseus killed her. Perseus and his mother, Danaë, lived on the island of Seriphos, which was ruled by King Polydectes. The king wanted to marry Danaë, but Perseus opposed the marriage. Polydectes then chose another bride and demanded that all the islanders give him horses as a wedding gift. Perseus, who had no horses, offered to give Polydectes anything else. Because no man had ever survived an encounter with the Gorgons, Polydectes challenged Perseus to bring him the head of Medusa.

With the help of the goddess Athena† and a group of **nymphs,** Perseus obtained special equipment for his task: a sharpened sickle, a cap that made the wearer invisible, and a pair of winged sandals. He also polished his bronze shield so that he could see Medusa's reflection in it and not gaze directly at her. Wearing the magic cap and following Medusa's reflection in his shield, Perseus crept up on the Gorgons. He cut off Medusa's head in one swipe and put it in a bag. The drops of blood that fell from the head turned into Medusa's two sons—Chrysaor and Pegasus—by the god Poseidon†.

With the help of the magic sandals, Perseus flew off before the other Gorgons could catch him. When he reached Seriphus, he held up Medusa's head and turned Polydectes to stone. Perseus later gave the head to Athena, who mounted it on her shield. *See also* DANAË; GORGONS; GREEK MYTHOLOGY; NYMPHS; PEGASUS; PERSEUS.

Melanesian Mythology

Melanesia, an area in the southwest Pacific Ocean, consists of thousands of islands and a remarkable variety of cultures. These individual cultures possess different mythologies and **deities.** The main island groups of the region are New Guinea, New Caledonia, Vanuatu (formerly New Hebrides), New Britain, the Solomon Islands, the Admiralty Islands, the Trobriand Islands, and the Fiji Islands.

Foundations of Religion and Myth

No single religion or mythology unifies Melanesia. Each island or community has its own distinct beliefs and its own collection of legends and mythological beings. Nevertheless, the mythologies of Melanesia do share certain basic elements and themes. For example, the names of the characters and the details of their stories differ from island to island, but the activities in which they are involved often have much in common.

Supernatural Spirits and Forces. **Supernatural** beings, including ancestral spirits and spirits of nonhuman origin, play an important role in the lives of Melanesians. The islanders believe that ancestral spirits continue to influence the way people act in everyday life. Ancestor worship is a significant part of their religion.

immortal able to live forever

nymph minor goddess of nature, usually represented as young and beautiful

deity god or goddess

supernatural related to forces beyond the normal world; magical or miraculous

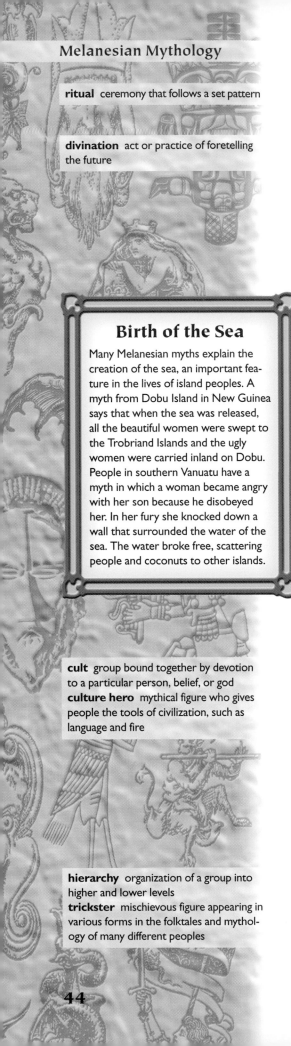

ritual ceremony that follows a set pattern

divination act or practice of foretelling the future

Birth of the Sea

Many Melanesian myths explain the creation of the sea, an important feature in the lives of island peoples. A myth from Dobu Island in New Guinea says that when the sea was released, all the beautiful women were swept to the Trobriand Islands and the ugly women were carried inland on Dobu. People in southern Vanuatu have a myth in which a woman became angry with her son because he disobeyed her. In her fury she knocked down a wall that surrounded the water of the sea. The water broke free, scattering people and coconuts to other islands.

cult group bound together by devotion to a particular person, belief, or god
culture hero mythical figure who gives people the tools of civilization, such as language and fire

hierarchy organization of a group into higher and lower levels
trickster mischievous figure appearing in various forms in the folktales and mythology of many different peoples

Summoned through prayer and **ritual,** supernatural beings and forces can be controlled to a large extent by the use of magic, which is central to Melanesian religion. The presence and activities of ancestral spirits are revealed in dreams and by **divination.** Evidence of their effect on human society can be seen in the health, well-being, and prosperity of the people.

Music plays a key role in Melanesian religious rituals. Throughout the islands the sounds of instruments such as drums and reed flutes are thought to be the voices of spirits and other supernatural beings. Today the use of instruments is usually restricted to men, but some myths tell how they originally belonged to women until men stole them or obtained them through trickery.

Closely related to the belief in spirits is the concept of mana, a supernatural power independent of any spirits or beings, yet linked to them. A characteristic of persons and objects as well as of spirits, mana can be either helpful or harmful. Anything uncommon or out of the ordinary—such as a weapon that has killed many animals or a great hero who defeats many foes—is said to possess mana.

Cargo Cults. A distinctive feature of many Melanesian cultures is the cargo **cult,** a religious movement created in response to European influence during colonial times. Cargo cults helped Melanesians explain the role of Europeans in the universe. When Europeans first arrived, the Melanesians were impressed by the huge amounts of material goods, or "cargo," they brought with them. The islanders believed that the Europeans must have acquired such wealth through strong magic, and they gradually developed cargo cults in an effort to gain knowledge of this magic for themselves. Religious in nature, cargo cults also had a political side, and they stressed resistance to foreign domination of their societies.

Members of the cargo cults believed that one day an ancestral spirit, tribal god, or **culture hero** would bring cargo to the people, leading to an age of prosperity, justice, and independence from foreign powers. To prepare for this day, the cults built structures representing docks for boats, runways for planes, and shelters for storing the cargo when it arrived. Such activities disrupted traditional economic practices and caused drastic changes in some parts of Melanesian society. Colonial authorities feared such changes and tried to put an end to the cults, but with little success.

Major Gods and Characters

Melanesian mythology has neither a supreme deity nor a distinct **hierarchy** of gods and goddesses. Instead, each cultural group possesses its own supernatural spirits, culture heroes, **tricksters,** and other beings that appear in local myths and stories.

Creator Gods and Heroes. Most cultural groups have creation myths that explain or describe the origin of the world.

This bark painting from New Guinea shows Ruban, a figure of knowledge.

Melanesians, however, believe that the world has always existed, so they have few stories about creation. Yet various figures do play roles in changing parts of the world and in the formation of islands and features of the landscape.

On the Banks Islands of Vanuatu, the first being in the world was Qat, a creator god and hero who fashioned islands and covered them with trees, animals, and plants. Qat also made humans by carving dolls from wood and then dancing and singing them into life. Then he created day and night so that people could work and then sleep.

In the islands of Vanuatu and New Britain, a creator god made twin brothers, To-Kabinana and To-Karvuvu, by sprinkling the ground with his own blood. To-Kabinana became a creator hero who produced many good things, while To-Karvuvu was responsible for the evil and troubles in the world. In Papua New Guinea, the sky god Kambel made people and the moon. He also created the clouds, which pushed up the sky and separated it from the earth.

Tricksters and Other Spirits. According to the Kiwai people of New Guinea, the trickster Sido could change his skin like a snake. He was killed by a powerful magician and then wandered the world seducing women and children. After losing his human wife, Sido transformed himself into a gigantic pig. Finally, he split himself open so that the pig's backbone and sides formed the house of death, the place where people go when they die.

Another mythological figure of New Guinea is Dudugera, known as the "leg child" because he sprang from a cut in his mother's leg. The people of his village mocked and bullied Dudugera, who one day told his mother to hide under a rock because he was going to become the sun. Dudugera soared into the sky and shot fire spears, which burned vegetation and killed many living things. To stop Dudugera from destroying everything, his mother threw mud or lime juice at his face, and it turned into clouds that hid the sun.

Marawa, the spider, is a friend of Qat. When Qat created humans Marawa tried to do the same, but his wooden figures turned into rotting corpses. That is how death came into the world. Tagaro, a trickster of Vanuatu, destroyed his evil brother Meragubutto by persuading him to enter a burning house to gain more magic and thus increase his power.

The mythologies of Melanesia include many spirits associated with nature and animals. The Adaro are sun spirits, part fish and part human, who use rainbows as bridges and come to earth

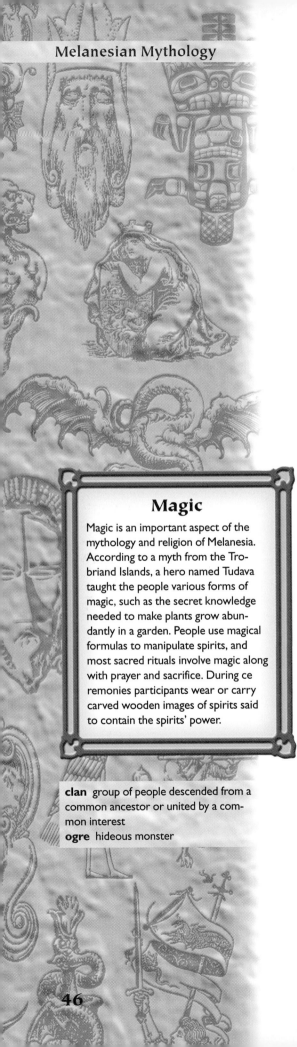

Magic

Magic is an important aspect of the mythology and religion of Melanesia. According to a myth from the Trobriand Islands, a hero named Tudava taught the people various forms of magic, such as the secret knowledge needed to make plants grow abundantly in a garden. People use magical formulas to manipulate spirits, and most sacred rituals involve magic along with prayer and sacrifice. During ce remonies participants wear or carry carved wooden images of spirits said to contain the spirits' power.

clan group of people descended from a common ancestor or united by a common interest

ogre hideous monster

during sun showers. The Bariaus are shy spirits that live in old tree trunks. The Kiwai of Papua New Guinea say that they are descended from Nuga, a half-human, half-crocodile creature created long ago from a piece of wood.

Major Themes and Myths

Throughout Melanesia some common mythological themes and characters appear. Many myths deal with two fundamental issues: where people came from and what happens after death. Certain characters—such as snakes, monsters, and twins—can be found in legends from numerous islands.

Myths of Origin. Melanesians have several basic stories about how the first humans appeared. In some places these beings descended from the sky. The Ayom people of Papua New Guinea, for example, say that Tumbrenjak climbed down to earth on a rope to hunt and fish. When he tried to return to the sky, he found the rope cut. His wife threw down fruits and vegetables, including cucumbers that became women. The offspring of Tumbrenjak and these women became the ancestors of different cultural groups.

In other places, the first beings came from the sea or emerged from underground. Among the Trobriand islanders, the ancestors of each **clan** emerged from a particular spot in a grove of trees, or from a piece of coral or a rock. The Keraki of Papua New Guinea believe that the first humans emerged from a tree, while others say that they came from clay or sand, blood, or pieces of wood.

Snakes, Monsters, and Twins. Snakes appear in the myths of many Melanesian peoples as a symbol of fertility and power. In some myths they are said to control rain; in others, animals and humans emerge from their slaughtered bodies. Some snake-beings wander from place to place giving gifts to humans and teaching them how to grow crops or perform magic. The Arapesh of New Guinea believe that spirits called *marsalai* live in rocks and pools and sometimes take the form of snakes or lizards. The *marsalai* shaped different parts of the landscape and then became guardians of their territory.

Many Melanesian peoples believe in monstrous **ogres** that eat people. An ogre killer becomes a hero by slaying these monsters. Ogre killers often perform other great feats as well. According to a myth from Vanuatu, a terrible ogre killed everyone except a woman who hid under a tree. The woman gave birth to twin sons who destroyed the ogre and cut it into pieces, an act that enabled the people who had been eaten by the ogre to come to life again. The people reestablished their society and began to follow new rules of behavior.

Twin brothers appear as central characters in many other Melanesian myths. These pairs often include one wise and one foolish brother, such as To-Kabinana and To-Karvuvu. Myths about twins may also represent the presence of both helpful and harmful forces in nature, such as nourishing rains and violent storms.

Afterlife. People throughout Melanesia generally believe in an afterlife. Among the Kiwai of Papua New Guinea, the land of the dead is known as Adiri; in Vanuatu one of its names is Banoi. The god of the dead also has various names; in parts of New Guinea he is called Tumudurere.

In Vanuatu people say that humans have two souls—one goes to an afterlife while the other takes the form of an animal, plant, or object. The route taken by souls to the land of the dead is often well defined. The people of the Fiji Islands believe that this path is dangerous and only the greatest warriors can complete the journey. In other places, the success of the journey depends on whether the proper funeral rites have been carried out.

Souls that go to the afterlife often visit the land of the living as ghosts by taking on human or animal form. Ghosts sometimes help the living, but they can also frighten them and interfere with certain activities. Some places have special types of ghosts, such as beheaded men with wounds that glow in the dark or the ghosts of unborn children.

Legacy of Melanesian Mythology. In some areas of Melanesia, mythology remains a powerful force in society, particularly where traditional religious systems and cult practices have been left relatively undisturbed. In other areas, traditional beliefs have been modified, usually as a result of modernization or the introduction of Christianity. Yet even where change has occurred, mythology continues to play an important role. It has helped Melanesians make sense of the changes in their society and in their relationship to the broader world by providing ways of understanding and interpreting events. *See also* AFTERLIFE; ANIMALS IN MYTHOLOGY; CREATION STORIES; MICRONESIAN MYTHOLOGY; POLYNESIAN MYTHOLOGY; TWINS.

Melanesia does not have a single religion or mythology. Instead, each island or cultural group has its own spirits, heroes, and characters that appear in local myths and legends. This photo shows a Vanuatu sculpture of a religious figure.

Menehune

In Polynesian mythology, the Menehune were a group of little people—about 2 feet tall—who lived in caves in the forests. The Hawaiians used to warn travelers to watch out for the Menehune because they shot tiny arrows at people who bothered them. Left alone, the Menehune were harmless. Hard working, they had to complete any task they undertook in one night. Similar creatures were said to have built temples on the island of Java and to have planted entire forests on Tonga, all in one night.

In time, the Menehune appeared in New Zealand, where the Maori called them the Patu-pai-arehe. According to tradition, these creatures had fair hair and light skin. Like their Hawaiian counterparts, the Patu-pai-arehe lived in the forests and were generally harmless. It was said that they carried off the souls of people who died during the night. *See also* POLYNESIAN MYTHOLOGY.

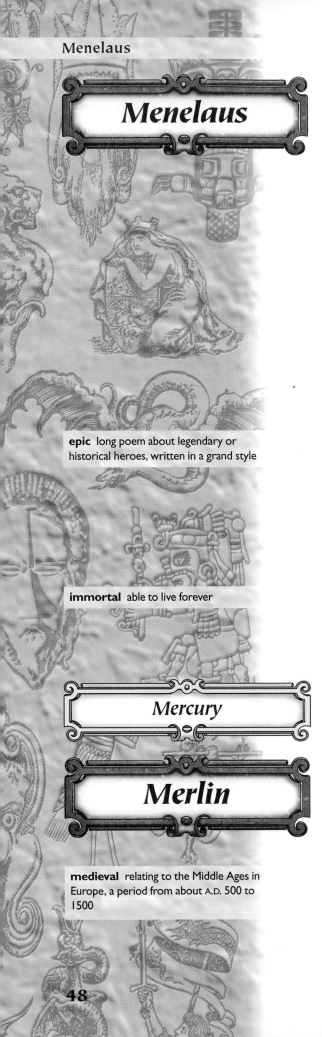

Menelaus

epic long poem about legendary or historical heroes, written in a grand style

immortal able to live forever

Mercury

Merlin

medieval relating to the Middle Ages in Europe, a period from about A.D. 500 to 1500

In Greek mythology, Menelaus, king of Sparta†, was the son of King Atreus of Mycenae and the brother of the great warrior Agamemnon†. Menelaus's beautiful wife, Helen, the daughter of Zeus† and a woman called Leda, was at the center of the events that led to the Trojan War.

Before her marriage to Menelaus, Helen lived with Leda and Leda's husband, King Tyndareus of Sparta. When the time came for Helen to marry, she had many suitors. To prevent any violence against her future husband, the Greek warrior Odysseus made his countrymen swear to protect the man she agreed to wed. Helen chose Menelaus, who later became king of Sparta.

The conflict with the Trojans was set in motion when Aphrodite, the goddess of love, took steps to win a beauty contest judged by Paris, a prince of Troy. If declared the most beautiful goddess, Aphrodite promised to give Paris the most beautiful woman in the world—Helen. Aphrodite won the contest; Paris went to Sparta and took Helen away with him to Troy. The Trojans refused to send her back. Agamemnon raised an army of Greek warriors to retrieve Helen, reminding them of their oath to her husband. The story of the war between Greece and Troy appears in Homer's† **epic** the *Iliad*.

During the war, Menelaus played a minor role in the fighting, but he did face Paris in single combat. Although Menelaus came close to killing Paris, Aphrodite intervened and saved Paris, her personal favorite.

After the Greeks defeated Troy, Menelaus returned to Sparta with Helen. However, the journey home was very difficult because he had neglected to offer sacrifices to the Trojan gods. The story of the voyage is told in Homer's *Odyssey*†. When Menelaus died, he became **immortal** because he had married a daughter of Zeus. He joined Helen in Elysium, a place of ideal happiness in the afterlife. *See also* AGAMEMNON; GREEK MYTHOLOGY; HELEN OF TROY; PARIS; TROJAN WAR.

See *Hermes.*

In the legends about King Arthur, the king had the help and advice of a powerful wizard named Merlin. Indeed this magician, who arranged for Arthur's birth and for many aspects of his life, can be seen as the guiding force behind the Arthurian legends†. Many stories about Merlin circulated in **medieval** times.

Origins and Sources. The figure of Merlin seems to be based on a magician named Myrddin, who appeared in the pre-Christian mythology of the Celtic† peoples. The writings of Nennius, a Welsh storyteller of about A.D. 800, include tales of a young magician named Ambrosius who became an adviser to Vortigern, a legendary king of early Britain.

†*See **Names and Places** at the end of this volume for further information.*

Related Entries
Other entries related to Merlin are listed at the end of this article.

When King Arthur was a young boy, the powerful wizard Merlin prepared him to become Britain's ruler. In later years, Merlin became King Arthur's trusted adviser and helper.

Some 300 years later, the British chronicler Geoffrey of Monmouth told a more elaborate story about the magician in his *History of the Kings of Britain* (1136). In this account, a sorcerer known as Merlin Ambrosius served as adviser to British king Uther Pendragon and, later, to his son Arthur. Geoffrey of Monmouth also wrote a work about Merlin that drew on old Celtic legends about a "wild man of the woods" with magical and fortune-telling powers.

Some early legends claimed that Merlin was the son of a demon and of a human woman. Only half human, Merlin was mysterious and unpredictable, sometimes helping the human race but sometimes changing his shape and passing long periods as a bird, a cloud, or something else. He also desired and seduced women. By the 1200s, however, the influence of Christianity was reshaping the Arthurian legends, and Merlin became a more respectable figure—a wise old man who supplied moral guidance as well as magic.

49

Merlin's Life and Works. In the legend of Vortigern, the king was trying to build a temple on Salisbury Plain, but it kept falling down. The boy Ambrosius told the king of a vision in which he had seen a red dragon and a white dragon fighting in a pool under the temple's foundation. From this, he predicted that the red dragon of Wales (King Vortigern) would be defeated by the white dragon of Britain (King Uther Pendragon), which later happened. The magician then built the temple himself, using his magic to bring standing stones from Ireland and to arrange them on the plain on a single night. That, according to legend, was how Stonehenge was built.

Merlin Ambrosius became the ally of Uther and used his magic to enable Uther to spend a night with another king's wife. The child born of that union was Arthur. Merlin predicted that he would be a great king who would one day unite all of Britain.

Entrusted with Arthur's upbringing, Merlin prepared the boy for kingship. Some accounts say that the wizard fashioned the magical sword Excalibur that proved that Arthur was the rightful king. According to other stories, Merlin also created the Round Table around which Arthur's knights sat. He was Arthur's helper and adviser in many things. Yet even Merlin could not prevent the final crumbling of the knights' fellowship and the fall of Arthur, as recounted in every version of the Arthurian legends.

As for Merlin's own fate, accounts vary. Some say that he lost his wits after Arthur's defeat and wandered into the woods. Most versions of the magician's story, however, end with his being tricked by a witch named Nimuë (or in some accounts by the Lady of the Lake), with whom he had fallen in love. Nimuë did not really care for Merlin but simply wanted to learn his secrets. When she had learned enough, she trapped him in an underground cave from which he could never escape. ***See also*** ARTHUR, KING; ARTHURIAN LEGENDS.

Mermaids

deity god or goddess

Female mermaids and male mermen are imaginary beings with the upper bodies of humans and the lower bodies of fish. Often mentioned in European legends, they also occur occasionally in the folklore of seagoing peoples from other regions of the world. Although mermaids are usually portrayed as being lovely, they are also associated with danger. Their dual nature reflects humankind's relationship with the sea, which can be either a beautiful and bountiful place or a realm of fear and disaster.

The idea of a **deity** or creature in which human features are combined with the bodies of fish is very ancient. Babylonian† texts mentioned a god named Oannes, who was part man and part fish and lived among humans. The Near Eastern god Dagon may have been portrayed as a merman, and the Syrian goddess Atargatis had the form of a mermaid. Ancient Greek and Roman sea gods and their attendants often appeared as human torsos rising from the waves with curved fish tails below. The Greeks called these beings nereids if they were female and tritons if they were

male. Japanese folklore features a mermaid called Ningyo, and Polynesian mythology includes a half-human and half-porpoise creator god called Vatea.

In European folklore, mermaids were associated with sirens, beautiful creatures whose singing lures sailors to their doom. Mermaids were commonly pictured as floating on top of the waves, singing or combing their long hair and gazing into mirrors. Seeing a mermaid was considered bad luck, as mermaids often appeared before storms or other disasters and were believed to carry drowned men away to their kingdom at the bottom of the sea. Although encounters with mermaids and mermen often ended badly for humans, in some legends, these sea creatures married human partners and took completely human form to live on land. *See also* SIRENS.

Metamorphoses, The

chaos great disorder or confusion

The *Metamorphoses,* a poem by the Roman author Ovid dating from around A.D. 8, tells many of the ancient myths and legends of Greece, Rome, and the Near East. All the stories have a common theme of change, or metamorphosis, hence the name of the work. Characters in each of the tales undergo some sort of transformation into other forms, including animals, plants, and stars. The changes usually come either as a reward for obeying or helping the gods or as a punishment for disobeying or challenging them.

The *Metamorphoses* is presented as a series of 15 books in which the tales are mostly told chronologically. The first story is about the creation of the universe, in which **chaos** changes into order. The last story concerns the transformation of Julius Caesar from the human emperor of Rome into a god. The *Metamorphoses* is one of the most important sources of myths and legends from the ancient world. Although many of its stories can be found in works by other authors, some are preserved only in the *Metamorphoses.*

medieval relating to the Middle Ages in Europe, a period from about A.D. 500 to 1500

The *Metamorphoses* had a profound impact on later works of literature. It was a strong inspiration for the **medieval** authors Geoffrey Chaucer and Giovanni Boccaccio. It also influenced Arabian tales such as the famous story collection *The Thousand and One Nights. See also* GREEK MYTHOLOGY; OVID.

Mexican Mythology

Mexico's mythology, like its population, reflects a blend of Native American and Spanish influences. Most people in modern Mexico trace their ancestry to Native Americans, to the Spanish who controlled Mexico for three centuries, or to both, in a mixed-race heritage called mestizo. In the same way, Mexican religion, myths, and legends are a blend of Indian traditions, European influences such as Christianity, and mixtures of the two. The Maya Indian villagers believe, for example, that the *chacs,* ancient rain spirits, are controlled by Jesus Christ and accompanied in their movement across the skies by the Virgin Mary, his mother. Mexican mythology is a product of syncretism—a process in which two belief

51

deity god or goddess
pantheon all the gods of a particular culture

pagan term used by early Christians to describe non-Christians and non-Christian beliefs

Many legends surround Emiliano Zapata, a man who fought for peasants' rights during the Mexican Revolution (1911-1917).

systems merge to form one that is different from either of the original systems or in which a new belief system overlies an older one that has not disappeared.

Background and Roots. Even before the Europeans arrived, Mexico was a land of varied cultures. Peoples who shared the Nahua family of languages dominated the north, while Mayan languages and culture were widespread in the south. Migration, trade, and war brought the different people and cultures of Mexico into contact with one another.

These contacts led to syncretism in religion and mythology. As the Aztecs of northern Mexico embarked on wars of conquest and built an empire in central Mexico, they absorbed the **deities** of conquered peoples into their own **pantheon.** In turn, myths and religious practices from central Mexico filtered south to influence the Maya. The Aztec influence boosted the importance of the god Quetzalcoatl—known as Kukulcan to the Maya—and of human sacrifices to the gods.

Spain conquered Mexico between 1519 and 1521 and governed it as a colony until 1821, when Mexico won its independence. During the three centuries of colonial rule, a new syncretism emerged, one that blended Indian and European beliefs. Spanish missionaries and priests strove to convert the Native Americans to Christianity and to stamp out their **pagan** religions. At the same time, some of the missionaries collected information about Indian beliefs, customs, and myths. Father Bernadino de Sahagun published accounts of the Aztecs that remain valuable sources of traditional lore; Father Diego de Landa did the same for the Maya.

Roman Catholic Christianity did take hold in Mexico, and 95 percent of Mexicans now practice it. Yet the old ways did not completely disappear. A few Native American groups, especially the Huichol and the Tarahumara, remained pagan. Many others, however, combined Catholicism with surviving forms of pre-Christian beliefs and mythologies. For example, they identified Roman Catholic saints, whose feast days are scattered throughout the year, with the ancient gods, traditionally honored with agricultural festivals at specific times.

Some myths and legends of Mexico have grown out of the events of the country's history. Parts of Aztec mythology, such as the legend of how the ancient Aztecs founded their capital of Tenochtitlán on the site where they saw an eagle fighting a serpent, have become part of the national heritage of modern Mexico. The Spanish conquest, the fight for independence, and the Mexican Revolution of 1910–1920

The Black Legend

The term *Black Legend* refers to a centuries-old view of Spain and its people as particularly cruel, prejudiced, and greedy. Some of the literature that promoted the Black Legend came from European Protestants hostile to Catholic Spain. But part of the Black Legend emerged from the writings of Bartolomé de Las Casas, a Spanish bishop who served in Mexico and wrote a vivid account of the conquistadors' brutality to the Indians. Although modern historical research has shown that other nations were guilty of similar cruelties, traces of the Black Legend linger on as negative images of the Spanish element in Latin American culture.

conquistador Spanish military explorer and conqueror

have also produced legends that have helped shape Mexico's image of itself as a nation and a people.

Major Deities and Figures. Perhaps the most widely recognized and honored figure of Mexican religious mythology is the Virgin of Guadelupe. Tradition says that in 1531 the Virgin Mary appeared before a peasant named Juan Diego on Tepeyac, a hill to the north of Mexico City, and told him that she wished to have a church built there. When the bishop of Mexico asked Juan for proof of what he had seen, the Virgin appeared again to the peasant and instructed him to gather roses in his cloak and take them to the bishop. Juan unfolded the cloak before the bishop, and a miraculous image of the Virgin could be seen where the roses had been.

Another tradition associated with the Virgin of Guadelupe says that a shrine to Tonántzin, an Aztec corn goddess, once stood at Tepeyac and that the Virgin replaced Tonántzin as the goddess mother of the Mexican people. However, there is no clear evidence of pre-Christian worship at that site.

The Mexican people have long regarded the Virgin of Guadelupe as a sign of divine favor. They have credited her with ending an epidemic of disease in the 1700s and later with inspiring movements toward independence and liberation. Mexicans of all regions and all racial backgrounds are united in their devotion to the Virgin as an emblem of both religious faith and national pride.

Among the historical figures who have acquired legendary status in Mexico are Hernán Cortés (1485–1547), the **conquistador** who overthrew the Aztecs and brought Mexico under Spanish rule, and Malinche, a Native American woman who assisted him as an interpreter of Indian languages. Malinche had a son by Cortés and later married one of his followers. In the past, Mexicans have condemned Malinche as a traitor, coining the term *malinchismo* to refer to favoring foreign things over those of one's own people or culture. In recent years, women writers and artists in Mexico have tried to create a more balanced image of Malinche.

Legends also cluster around Miguel Hidalgo y Costilla (1753–1811), a priest and leader of the independence movement who died before a firing squad; Francisco "Pancho" Villa (1878–1923), a bandit turned revolutionary general; and Emiliano Zapata (1879–1919), a peasant who fought for peasants' rights in the Mexican Revolution. It is said that Zapata is not really dead but only sleeping. One day, like King Arthur of British legend, he will return to help his people. Some speak of hearing the hoofbeats of his horse Lightning as he rides through their villages at night.

Major Themes of Myths and Legends. Myths and tales told in modern Mexico not only amuse and entertain but also preserve old traditions and offer lessons in good or wise behavior. Some stories reflect pre-Christian beliefs, mentioning Father Sun and Mother Moon, once regarded as deities. Legend says that eclipses—during which part or all of the sun or moon is hidden by shadow—are caused by evil creatures trying to devour the

53

This painting by Diego Rivera shows people celebrating the Day of the Dead, November 2. During this Mexican holiday, families prepare altars with offerings for dead relatives. Deceased family members are believed to visit the world of the living on this day.

heavenly bodies. One version identifies the evil creatures as ants, which cover Father Sun or Mother Moon with their huge colonies.

Some Mexican myths explain features of the natural world. One story tells how the basilisk, a type of lizard, acquired the crest on its head. The Lord of the Woods announced that he would give a special hat to the animal that won a race. Most of the animals refused to compete, protesting that Big Deer was bound to win. However, to the amusement of all, the little basilisk said that it would race on one condition: all the animals had to close their eyes at the start of the race. The Lord of the Woods agreed, and Big Deer and the basilisk took off toward the stone that was their goal. When Big Deer arrived, he slowed down, thinking that he must have passed the basilisk long before. But to his surprise, as he prepared to sit on the stone, he found the basilisk there before him. The Lord of the Woods awarded the hat to the basilisk because he knew that the little creature had cleverly grabbed Big Deer's tail at the starting point and ridden it to the stone.

Many Mexican tales contain, under their humor, criticisms of social injustice or of bad behavior by those in power. A legend about Pancho Villa, for example, says that he became a leader of men by selling his soul to the devil, who came accompanied by many kings, popes, generals, and cardinals of the church—all of whom had made similar deals. A myth about a hungry peasant tells of a poor man driven by desperation to steal a chicken and cook it. A stranger appeared and asked for some food. The peasant refused him. The stranger revealed that he was God, upon which the peasant declared that he would definitely not share with God, who favored the rich but was unkind to the poor. Another stranger appeared, asking for food. When this second stranger revealed that he was Death, the peasant gladly shared with him, explaining that Death was fair, taking the fat and thin, young and old, rich and poor equally.

Legacy of Mythology. Several aspects of modern Mexican culture show the importance of myths in national life. Religious fiestas or festivals often combine pagan traditions with the worship of Christian saints. Mourning and funeral practices are also a syncretistic blend of Native American and Christian ideas.

The ancient belief that people's personalities and needs continue unchanged after death leads to the custom of burying possessions and useful objects with the dead. A related belief is the notion that the dead can harm the living unless ceremonies are performed to keep them from doing so. On November 2, the people of Mexico celebrate a national holiday called the Day of the Dead. Images of death, such as skulls and skeletons, appear everywhere on toys, candies, breads, and masks; at the same time, families prepare altars with offerings for dead relatives, who are thought to visit the world of the living at that time.

Some of the best-known art of modern Mexico includes images drawn from Native American, Christian, and revolutionary myth. The most noted painters of the Mexican School, José Clemente Orozco (1883–1949), Diego Rivera (1886–1957), and David Alfaro Siqueiros (1896–1974), produced murals that glorified the Mexican past, the Indians and peasants, and revolutionary ideals. Rivera's painting *The Deliverance of the Peon* illustrates his use of mythic symbols: the figure of Christ being taken from the cross represents the peasants who gave their lives in the Mexican Revolution. *See also* AZTEC MYTHOLOGY; BASILISK; MAYAN MYTHOLOGY.

deity god or goddess

Micronesian Mythology

Micronesia, an area in the southwest Pacific Ocean containing thousands of islands, has no single mythology. The various islands and island groups—including the Caroline Islands, Marshall Islands, Mariana Islands, and Gilbert Islands—each have their own collection of legends and mythological beings. Micronesia is part of a vast region known as Oceania.

Europeans arrived in Micronesia in the 1520s and brought Christianity with them. As the new religion became established in many areas, traditional beliefs declined. In addition, the contact with European cultures led to changes in local myths and legends. Travelers and missionaries wrote down some of the original myths, but many were lost before they could be recorded. Although the myths and legends have changed over the years, reflecting developments in Micronesia, they remain an important part of the region's cultural heritage.

Religion and Myth. Before the arrival of Europeans, the peoples of Micronesia practiced a variety of forms of polytheism, a belief in more than one **deity.** These polytheistic religions resembled one another, but the gods and myths differed from island to island.

The Micronesian religions also included ancestral spirits (called Ani in the Caroline Islands) and numerous other spirits that performed specific functions and were associated with particular locations. Only certain people, such as priests, healers, and magicians, could communicate with these spirits. They usually did so through dreams and trances.

Spirits might be called on for a variety of reasons, including the diagnosis and cure of illness, success in fishing, control of weather,

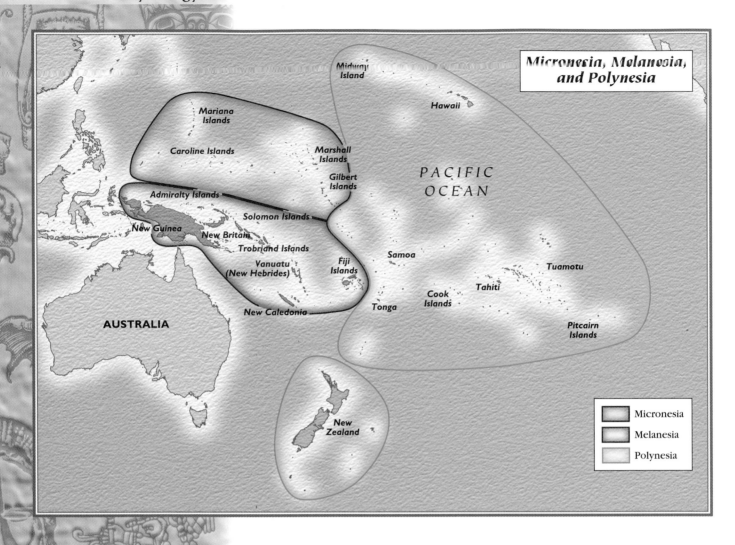

Micronesia, Melanesia, and Polynesia

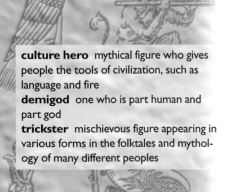

culture hero mythical figure who gives people the tools of civilization, such as language and fire
demigod one who is part human and part god
trickster mischievous figure appearing in various forms in the folktales and mythology of many different peoples

primeval from the earliest times

courage in battle, and skill in navigation. To ensure the goodwill of the spirits, people often entertained them by dancing and singing. In return, the spirits provided information about the cause of individual misfortunes and prescribed cures and magical spells.

Myths were often used to teach members of a group about particular beliefs or skills. Myths about Aluluei, a god of seafaring, included information useful for training navigators. In addition, legends told in the Marshall Islands dealt with forecasting weather and determining position at sea by observing natural phenomena. The Micronesians also had myths that expressed their beliefs about the earth and sky, the afterlife, and the roles of gods and **culture heroes.** The myths were passed from one generation to the next by professional storytellers.

Major Gods and Characters. Micronesian myths featured creator gods, **demigods, tricksters,** heroes, and ancestral spirits. Creation stories generally dealt with the origin of particular islands or groups of people. For this reason, there were numerous creation myths and a variety of creator deities.

Nareau, the Spider Lord, of the Gilbert Islands, was one of the best-known creator gods. After emerging from a **primeval** place—

consisting of darkness, endless space, or the sea—he created heaven and earth and two beings, Na Atibu and Nei Teukez. From these beings sprang many gods. One also called Nareau and known as Young Spider played an important part in separating the earth from the sky and in creating the stars, islands, trees, and creatures of the earth. Another creator deity was Loa, the supreme being of the Marshall Islands. From his leg emerged Wulleb and Limdunanij, the first man and woman.

Perhaps the most important trickster and culture hero in Micronesian mythology was Olifat (also called Olofat, Olofath, and Orofat). The son of the god Lugeilan and of a human woman, the mischievous Olifat was a contradictory figure torn between two worlds. He sometimes rose to heaven on a column of smoke and other times descended to earth on a bolt of lightning. He was often associated with fire. While in heaven, Olifat disturbed the gods by singing and making other noises. On earth, he played tricks on humans. Some tricks had unforeseen consequences, such as giving sharks sharp teeth and putting stingers on the tails of scorpions.

The Micronesians linked particular deities, spirits, and heroes with certain functions and skills. Aluluei, the god of seafaring, had numerous eyes that became the stars of the night sky used by sailors to navigate at sea. Bue, a culture hero of the Gilbert Islands, taught Micronesians how to sing and dance, build canoes and houses, and raise winds by magic. Naniumlap, the fertility god of the Caroline Islands, helped ensure that plants and animals grew and that women had children. Finally, Nei Tituaabine, the tree goddess of the Gilbert Islands, made sure that trees grew and bore fruit.

Major Themes and Myths. Despite the great variety of myths that existed on Micronesia's many islands, certain themes could be found throughout the region. Origin myths typically dealt with the creation of the earth and sky, gods, islands, heroes, features of the landscape, humans, and other creatures. A common theme in eastern Micronesia was the use of a creator god's body to form the earth, sky, sun, moon, and other features. In the Gilbert Islands, the work of creation was shared by the Spider Lord, Nareau, and the younger Nareau (Young Spider).

The main event in many creation myths was the separation of the earth from the sky. Stories about the older Nareau, for example, told how he ordered Sand and Water to mate. Two of their offspring then produced many beings, including Riiki, the eel. Riiki pushed up the sky, and Nareau created the sun, moon, stars, rocks, and a great tree. The ancestors of humans sprang from the branches of this ancestral tree.

Myths about travels between the sky and the earth were also quite common. Stories about the trickster Olifat often described his journeys up to heaven and his descents to earth. In addition, a mythical child named Thilefial traveled to the sky to escape mistreatment on earth and then returned to earth to take revenge.

Micronesians believed that the gods made humans mortal—subject to death—and various myths dealt with death and the

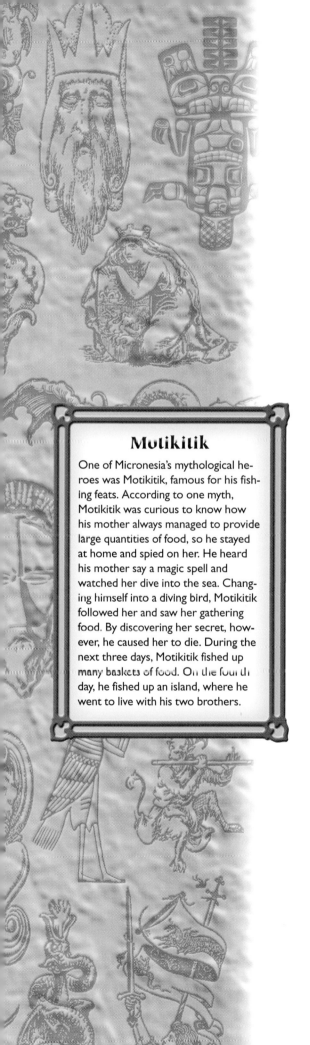

Motikitik

One of Micronesia's mythological heroes was Motikitik, famous for his fishing feats. According to one myth, Motikitik was curious to know how his mother always managed to provide large quantities of food, so he stayed at home and spied on her. He heard his mother say a magic spell and watched her dive into the sea. Changing himself into a diving bird, Motikitik followed her and saw her gathering food. By discovering her secret, however, he caused her to die. During the next three days, Motikitik fished up many baskets of food. On the fourth day, he fished up an island, where he went to live with his two brothers.

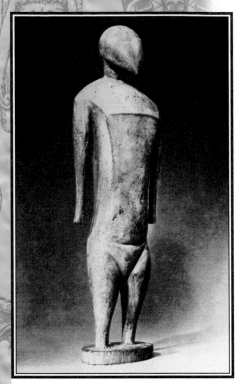

Micronesians worshiped ancestral spirits that were associated with particular purposes and places. Priests and healers communicated with these beings through dreams and trances. This wooden figure comes from the Caroline Islands.

ogre hideous monster

taboo prohibition against doing something that is believed to cause harm

afterlife. According to one myth, when gods first created humans, men and women lived separately under two different trees. The guardian spirit Na Kaa warned them not to leave their particular trees, but once during his absence, the men and women gathered under the same tree. When Na Kaa returned, he told them that they had chosen the Tree of Death. This was how humans became mortal. When humans died, their souls journeyed either to a paradise (underwater or in the sky) or to a gloomy underworld realm whose gates were guarded by evil spirits.

The adventures of tricksters were a common feature in Micronesian myths. The trickster Olifat annoyed the gods, made fools of men, and sometimes caused human injury or death. Many stories about him tell how he changed his form to a bird, an animal, or an object to escape detection or punishment. Despite his often harmful behavior, Olifat sometimes helped humans who sought his advice about love and other personal matters. He is also credited with introducing the art of tattooing to the people of Micronesia.

Many Micronesian myths featured animal tricksters. The stories usually revolved around three main characters, such as a rat, a crab, and either a turtle or an octopus, and recounted the pranks they played on other creatures. The myths also helped explain the relationships among various animals.

Some evil characters in Micronesian myths were cannibal spirits or **ogres.** Usually characterized by their strength and stupidity, these creatures could be frightened away by loud noises and were terrified of fire. A well-known mythological hero was the ogre-killing child who sometimes saved entire villages by destroying the evil creatures.

Tales about Pälülop, a great canoe captain, and members of his family were popular in the Caroline Islands. The stories were complex, included a bewildering array of characters, and dealt with many different subjects. One story told how Pälülop's sons Big Rong and Little Rong became jealous of their younger brother Aluluei and killed him. Pälülop brought Aluluei back in spirit form and gave him lots of eyes that shone like stars to help the boy protect himself.

Another well-known myth involved a porpoise girl, a mermaid-like creature who came to land either to steal something or to watch people dance. While she was on land, a man hid her tail, which prevented her from returning to the sea. The porpoise girl married the man and had children. Many years later she found her tail and returned to the sea after telling her children never to eat porpoise. Stories of this type, in which people learn not to eat certain foods, were often used to explain the origin of certain food **taboos.** In some versions of the myth, the girl came from the sky, and the man hid her wings.

The theme of an animal in human form who marries a mortal man and then leaves him to return to her home can be found in stories from India dating back more than 3,000 years. The presence of similar legends throughout Oceania suggests that a myth of this type may have originated in Asia and spread to the islands

† See **Names and Places** at the end of this volume for further information.

of the Pacific at a very early date. *See also* AFTERLIFE; ANIMALS IN MYTHOLOGY; CREATION STORIES; MELANESIAN MYTHOLOGY; POLYNESIAN MYTHOLOGY.

Midas

Midas, a legendary king of Phrygia†, was fabled for having the "golden touch." According to Greek and Roman mythology, Silenius, a companion of the god Dionysus†, became drunk while visiting Phrygia. Silenius was captured and brought to Midas, who ordered that he be released and returned safely to Dionysus. The god gratefully offered to grant Midas any wish as a reward. Midas asked that everything he touched turn to gold. Knowing the wish to be dangerous, Dionysus asked the king if he was sure that was what he wanted. Midas assured him that it was, and the god granted the wish.

At first Midas was overjoyed. He began accumulating wealth simply by touching things. However, when he tried to eat, each mouthful of food turned to gold as it touched his lips. When he went to hug his daughter, she turned to gold as well. Midas finally begged the god to release him from his wish. Dionysus instructed him to bathe in the River Pactolus. From that day forward, the sands of the river turned to gold dust. In fact, the Pactolus is a river in Turkey that was famous in ancient times as a source of gold.

In another tale, Midas acted as the judge of a music contest between the god Apollo† and either Pan, the god of the pastures, or the **satyr** Marsyas. Midas declared Pan (or Marsyas) the winner, and the angry Apollo gave the king the ears of a donkey. Midas wore a hat to hide the ears and made his barber swear never to tell anyone the embarrassing secret. Unable to keep the secret, the barber dug a hole and whispered into it, "King Midas has the ears of an ass." Reeds later grew from the hole, and whenever a breeze blew through them, they whispered the secret to anyone who was nearby. *See also* APOLLO; DIONYSUS; GREEK MYTHOLOGY; PAN; ROMAN MYTHOLOGY.

satyr woodland deity that was part man and part goat or horse

Mimir

In Norse† mythology, the giant Mimir was considered the wisest member of the group of gods known as the Aesir. He served as the guardian of Mimisbrunnr, the well of knowledge located at the base of the world tree Yggdrasill.

During the war between the Aesir and another group of gods called the Vanir, the Vanir took Mimir and a companion named Hoenir as hostages. Hoenir was treated as a chieftain by the Vanir, but without the wise Mimir he could not speak well. The Vanir felt cheated, therefore, and cut off Mimir's head and sent it back to Odin, the father of the gods, who kept it alive in a shrine near the base of Yggdrasill.

The well of knowledge sprang from the spot where Mimir's head was kept. Seeking wisdom, Odin rode to the well to drink its waters. However, Mimir allowed him to do so only after Odin left

one of his eyes in the well. From then on, when Odin wished to learn secrets from the well, he asked questions to Mimir's head, which gave him the answers. *See also* GIANTS; NORSE MYTHOLOGY; ODIN; YGGDRASILL.

Minerva

See *Athena.*

Minos

In Greek mythology, King Minos of Crete was best known for building the Labyrinth—a complicated network of passages—to imprison the monstrous Minotaur. Europa, the king's mother, had been carried away from her home in Tyre by Zeus†, disguised as a bull. He brought her to the island of Crete, where she gave birth to three sons. Europa later married Asterius, the king of Crete, who adopted her sons.

When Asterius died, a dispute arose over which of the sons should win the throne. Minos claimed the right to be king on the grounds that he could convince the gods to answer any prayer that he offered. He prayed to Poseidon† to send him a bull that he would sacrifice to the god, and a beautiful white bull emerged from the sea.

Minos became the new king. However, he decided that the bull was too magnificent to sacrifice and offered another bull instead. Angry with Minos for failing to keep his word, Poseidon caused the king's wife, Pasiphae, to fall in love with the white bull. She spoke of her passion to Daedalus, a master craftsman, and Daedalus created a lifelike model of a cow in which the queen could conceal herself. The bull mounted the cow, and in time Pasiphae gave birth to the Minotaur, a monstrous creature with the body of a man and the head of a bull. Minos then ordered Daedalus to build the Labyrinth in which to hide and imprison the Minotaur.

Minos's son was killed in Athens, and the king called on the gods to curse the city with famine and earthquake. To lift the curse, Minos required Athens to send him seven boys and seven girls each year to be fed to the Minotaur. One year this group included a youth named Theseus, with whom Minos's daughter Ariadne fell in love. With the assistance of Daedalus, she made it possible for Theseus to kill the Minotaur and escape with her. To punish Daedalus for helping Theseus, Minos imprisoned him and his son Icarus. However, the master craftsman created two sets of wings, which he and his son used to escape and fly out of Crete. Daedalus managed to reach Sicily, but Icarus fell from the sky to his death.

Minos began a search for Daedalus. He sent a challenge to the kings of neighboring lands, asking for someone who could pass a thread through a spiral seashell, knowing that only Daedalus could accomplish this feat. When King Cocalus of Sicily sent back a properly threaded shell, Minos went to Sicily to seize Daedalus.

†*See **Names and Places** at the end of this volume for further information.*

Cocalus greeted the Cretan king and offered him a bath. However, Daedalus had made the pipes that led to the bath, and while Minos was bathing, Daedalus burned him to death with boiling water. *See also* ARIADNE; DAEDALUS; MINOTAUR; THESEUS.

Minotaur

In Greek mythology, the Minotaur was a monstrous creature with the head of a bull on a man's body. Like many other mythological monsters, the Minotaur had a ravenous appetite for human flesh. He was eventually slain by a worthy hero with the help of a resourceful heroine.

The Minotaur—which means "Minos's bull"—was born in the palace of King Minos of Crete, a large island south of Greece. Some time earlier, the sea god Poseidon had sent Minos a pure-white bull to be sacrificed in his honor. When the king saw the magnificent creature, however, he refused to kill it. This angered Poseidon, who arranged for Minos's wife, Pasiphae, to fall in love with the bull. The offspring of their unnatural mating was the Minotaur. The king imprisoned the Minotaur in the Labyrinth, a maze built by a craftsman at his court named Daedalus.

In later years, after the people of the Greek city of Athens killed one of Minos's sons, the Cretan king called down a plague on their city. Only by agreeing to send seven young men and seven young women to Crete every year could the Athenians obtain relief. These youths and maidens were sent into the Cretan Labyrinth, where the Minotaur devoured them.

Theseus of Athens was determined to end the slaughter of young people. He volunteered to go to Crete as one of the sacrificial victims, vowing to slay the Minotaur. When the ship carrying the Athenians reached Crete, Ariadne, daughter of Minos and Pasiphae, fell in love with Theseus. She gave him a plan of the Labyrinth that she had obtained from Daedalus and a ball of string. He was to tie one end of the string to the exit as he went in and then to follow the string to find his way out. Deep in the Labyrinth, Theseus met the bellowing, bloodthirsty Minotaur and killed it with a blow of his fist. He and the other Athenians then fled Crete, taking Ariadne with them.

Some scholars suggest that the myth of the Minotaur arose out of ancient rituals in which a priest or king donned a bull mask before performing sacrifices. The Labyrinth may have represented the ancient palace at Knossos on Crete, which was a sprawling complex of chambers and hallways. *See also* ARIADNE; DAEDALUS; GREEK MYTHOLOGY; MINOS; MONSTERS; THESEUS.

A monstrous creature in Greek mythology, the Minotaur had the head of a bull and the body of a man. This vase painting dating from the 500s B.C. shows Theseus killing the Minotaur.

Mithras

deity god or goddess
cult group bound together by devotion to a particular person, belief, or god

sorcerer magician or wizard

subterranean under the earth

pagan term used by early Christians to describe non-Christians and non-Christian beliefs

Mixcoatl

deity god or goddess

Mithras—also called Mithra—was a **deity** from ancient Indo-Iranian† mythology. He became a major figure in the religion known as Zoroastrianism, which originated in ancient Persia†. The **cult** of Mithras spread into the Mediterranean world, where for a time it rivaled Christianity as the fastest-growing new religion.

Some scholars identify Mithras with Mitra, a mythic figure of the Aryan peoples who invaded northern India around the 1600s B.C. Mitra, the god of friendship, was associated with the sun and served as one of the judges of the dead. He was supposed to bring worthy people back to life after the universe ended. Some of Mitra's functions lingered in the developing mythology of Mithras.

The Persians saw Mithras as the principal assistant of Ahura Mazda, the god of goodness and light. Mithras battled demons, **sorcerers,** and other evildoers and helped the souls of worthy humans. In another role, as a god of war, he rode in a golden chariot pulled by four horses. Born from the earth, Mithras emerged from a broken rock with a torch in one hand and a sword in the other. These objects represented his two roles as sun god and war god.

In the Greek and Roman form of the cult, Mithras's most important mythic act was the slaying of a great bull, whose body and blood became the source of all life on earth. Images of Mithras usually show him killing a bull. Such sacrifices were central to his worship, which took place in shrines located in caves or cavelike buildings in honor of the god's **subterranean** origins.

Little concrete information about the Greek and Roman form of Mithraism survives. Most descriptions of how the religion was practiced in Greece and Rome come from later Christian writers. Among Romans, Mithraism became an all-male cult much favored by soldiers, and the army carried it to Britain, Germany, and other outposts of the empire. Several Roman emperors worshiped Mithras. One was Diocletian, who in A.D. 307 dedicated a temple on the Danube River to Mithras, "Protector of the Empire."

Mithraism bore many similarities to Christianity. For example, Mithras was said to have been born on December 25, to have performed miracles, and to have eaten a last supper with his 12 followers. After Christianity became the official religion of the empire in the 300s, Mithraism was suppressed along with other **pagan** beliefs. *See also* AHURA MAZDA; PERSIAN MYTHOLOGY.

Mixcoatl was a **deity** of the Aztecs and of a number of other Native American peoples in central Mexico. Like many mythological figures of this region, Mixcoatl possessed an identity that was both complex and changeable. The Aztecs saw him primarily as a form of Tezcatlipoca, the powerful night sky god. Other groups knew him as Camaxtli. He was often portrayed with a black face or mask, a red-and-white striped body, and long hair.

Scholars of mythology have identified Mixcoatl as a hunting god of the Otomi, Chichimec, and Toltec people and their descendants. The mythic figure may have been based on the real-life warrior Eight Deer, who achieved greatness as a leader of the Pioneer

Toltecs. Mixcoatl's name, which means "cloud serpent," came from his ability to change shape and take the form of clouds moving across the sky. He was also associated with the stars, particularly with the starry band known as the Milky Way.

Both a creator god and a destroyer, Mixcoatl's many roles included teaching humans the arts of hunting and fire making. He fathered 400 sons and 5 daughters to feed the sun. He was also the father of Quetzalcoatl†, an important Toltec and Aztec deity. The goddess Coatlicue was one of his wives. ***See also* Aztec Mythology; Coatlicue; Quetzalcoatl; Tezcatlipoca.**

Modern Mythology

chaos great disorder or confusion

Urban Legends

The urban legend is a story that is supposed to have happened recently, usually to someone remotely known to the teller, such as "a friend of a friend." Urban legends spread quickly, then die out, perhaps to reappear later in slightly different form. One of the first urban legends to be studied by folklore experts was a story about alligators living in New York City sewers. Rumor had it that children vacationing in Florida had brought home tiny alligators, which they flushed down toilets when the pets started to grow. This legend, although unfounded, has had a longer life than any alligator.

Not all mythology dates from the days of ancient cultures. People around the world continue to create new myths and to embroider or rework existing ones. Modern technologies such as publishing, movies, telecommunications, and the Internet allow folktales, rumors, and newly minted myths to travel faster and reach more people than ever before. One distinctive feature of some modern legends is that they originated as artistic creations, although their creators may have drawn on earlier themes.

Like all myths and legends, modern mythology springs from a sense of life's wonder, excitement, mystery, and terror. Modern legends offer images of the best and worst aspects of the human condition. They suggest that good behavior will be rewarded and evil, greedy, or foolish behavior punished. Some modern legends reflect people's fear of rapid social change or of science and technology; others appeal to their desire to find meaningful patterns beneath the confusing **chaos** of ordinary life.

More or Less than Human. A number of modern myths explore what it means to be human. In 1912 the American writer Edgar Rice Burroughs created the character Tarzan, the son of an English nobleman raised by apes in the African jungle. Like earlier myths about people raised by animals, the Tarzan story features animals with admirable "human" qualities and people with brutish "animal" qualities. Tarzan himself combines the virtues of animal strength and civilized honor.

Like the heroes of ancient myths, modern superheroes have extraordinary powers. The most famous superhero is Superman, created by American cartoonists Jerry Siegel and Joseph Shuster in 1938. In comics and on radio, television, and movie screens, he fights for "truth, justice, and the American way," using his powers of flight and incredible strength, powers he possesses because he is from another planet. Like most modern superheroes, Superman keeps his identity a secret and pretends to be an ordinary man. Such myths suggest that anyone can have unsuspected potential for heroism.

If Tarzan and Superman offer visions of the ideal human being, the legend of Frankenstein explores human flaws. The English writer Mary Wollstonecraft Shelley wrote *Frankenstein: or, the Modern Prometheus* in 1818. It tells the story of Victor Frankenstein,

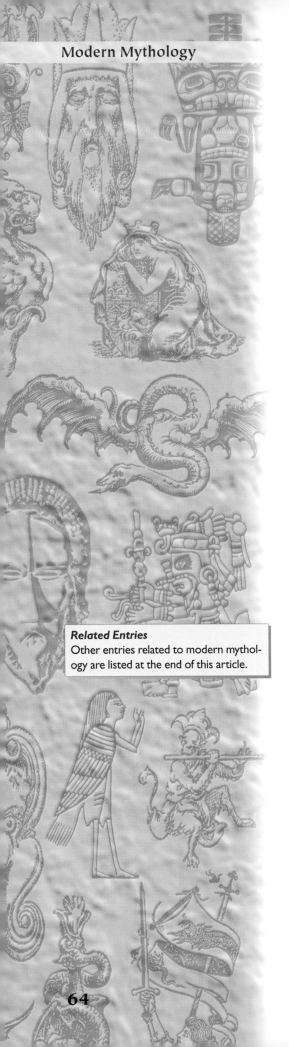

People around the world continue to create myths and legends. One of the most popular modern stories concerns UFOs, unidentified flying objects.

a scientist who builds an artificial creature from pieces of corpses and brings the creature to life. An element of the Frankenstein story that has been repeated in many modern books and movies is the theme of the "mad scientist" who crosses a moral boundary and unleashes forces beyond his control. The monster, who is intelligent and kind but so ugly that everyone fears and hates him, represents everyone who is misunderstood and cannot find a place in the world. He symbolizes both a fear of the unknown and the pain caused by prejudice.

Many ancient myths feature monstrous, frightening beings who are partly human and who prey on humans. Such figures continue to fascinate today. Among the most enduring monsters in modern mythology are werewolves and vampires. The werewolves represent the idea that a fearsome beast lurks inside a human being; vampires give form to humans' fears of darkness and death. One of the most famous vampires is Count Dracula from the 1897 novel *Dracula* by Irish writer Bram Stoker. A modern twist on the vampire legend emerged in the 1990s, when a few books, films, and television shows portrayed vampires as sympathetic characters battling against their bloodthirsty impulses.

Myths for Children. Some mythic characters appear mainly in stories for children. Santa Claus originated centuries ago as a Dutch folk character. Since the 1800s, he has developed into a universally recognized symbol of Christmas who is said to bring gifts to good children. Stories about his workshop at the North Pole, his elves, and the reindeer who pull his sleigh complete the modern Claus mythology. Another figure with links to ancient mythology is the Easter Bunny, said to bring candy eggs to children in the

spring. This modern myth has its roots in an ancient relationship between eggs, rabbits, and a Germanic fertility goddess named Eastre or Ostara.

Parents may call on other mythological figures to encourage good behavior in their children. They may warn disobedient children about scary beings such as the bogeyman, a goblin that originated in old English and Scottish folklore. On the other hand, the Tooth Fairy is said to bring gifts to children when they lose their teeth.

A World of Wonders. A great many modern myths attempt to paint the world in dramatic colors or find hidden meanings in random events. Once they have appeared in print a few times, such myths begin to seem like facts to some people. "The curse of King Tutankhamen's tomb," for example, was a fiction coined by newspaper writers, but it gave rise to a body of tales about ancient mummies coming to life to attack people who disturb their tombs.

One of the most widespread legends of modern times concerns UFOs, unidentified flying objects or flying saucers. Ever since pilot Kenneth Arnold reported seeing strange objects flying over the state of Washington in 1947, rumors and reports of spacecraft piloted by extraterrestrial beings have surfaced in the media. By the late 1990s, the UFO myth had grown into an elaborate set of stories about various kinds of aliens, some of which kidnap humans. UFO stories bear striking similarities to earlier myths, such as kidnappings by fairies and mysterious appearances of ghosts or demons. Ironically, the lack of reliable evidence to support UFO claims merely adds to the mythology, as people maintain that the absence of evidence points to a government conspiracy or cover-up. Conspiracies—secret forces that shape events and conceal the truth from the public—appear in a number of modern myths, perhaps reflecting a failure of trust in leaders and authority figures.

The search for the marvelous and strange lies behind many modern legends. Stories about mysterious unknown creatures, such as Sasquatch or Bigfoot in North America and the yeti or Abominable Snowman in the Himalayas, are survivors of ancient folklore taken seriously by some modern believers. Other myths—such as the notion that an unusually large number of deaths and disappearances have occurred in a region of the Atlantic Ocean known as the Bermuda Triangle—are modern inventions. Many such legends have mysterious and inexplicable elements in place of the gods and magic of earlier mythologies. ***See also*** DRACULA; LOCH NESS MONSTER; SANTA CLAUS; VAMPIRES; WEREWOLVES.

Moloch

Moloch, or Molech, was a god to whom some cultures of the ancient Near East sacrificed children. Some scholars have identified Moloch with Melqart, a god worshiped in the city of Tyre on the eastern coast of the Mediterranean Sea.

Roman sources state that a sculpture of Moloch stood in Carthage, a city in northern Africa. The people who performed

Monsters

the sacrifices there placed children on the outstretched hands of the statue, and the children fell through to fire below. According to the Bible, the law given to Moses by the supreme god Yahweh prohibited the Jews from sacrificing children to Moloch. Nevertheless, King Solomon introduced the **cult** of Moloch into Israel, but a later king banned worship of the god. Moloch's shrine was located at a site outside Jerusalem named Gehenna, which some Christians used as another name for hell. ***See also* SEMITIC MYTHOLOGY.**

Monsters peer and prowl, roar and ravage in myths and legends the world over. They are the stuff of nightmares, the looming presences outside the comforting circle of firelight, the menacing shapes glimpsed moving through the shadows of trees or in deep water. Monsters are creatures that represent everything that is fearful about the natural world and the darker corners of human nature. Mythological monsters inspire dread and embody evil. They challenge heroes and heroines to prove their worth in order to advance in their quests or simply to survive.

Types and Characteristics of Monsters. Monsters are by definition unnatural, something that should not exist. The word *monster* comes from the Latin *monstrum,* meaning a sign of future events. The Romans used the word to refer to bizarrely unusual events—such as a rain of mud or the birth of a two-headed calf—that were believed to show divine displeasure or a troubled future.

The world's mythmakers and storytellers have created hundreds of kinds of monsters, but all share two qualities. First, monsters are not human. Even those that look and act to some extent like people are not fully human. Second, monsters are hostile to people, enemies of the human world.

A monster may be a creature grown unnaturally large and strong. Fenrir, the immense world-devouring wolf of the Norse† gods, was so large that when he opened his mouth his jaws spanned the gulf between earth and sky. According to the Ambundu people of Angola, the hero Sudika-mbambi slew two giant creatures in the **underworld:** the great serpent Kinioka kia Tumba and the monstrous crocodile Kimbiji kia Malenda.

Many monsters are hybrids, the offspring of unions between **deities** or demons and animals or people. Hindu myths tell of Bhutas, monstrous beings born of unions between demons and ghosts. They hover over sleeping people and drop disease into their ears. In Chinese myth, Lei Jen Zu was the son of the thunder dragon and the earth. The egg from which he hatched was formed when lightning struck the earth. He started out as a human but then changed into a green-faced dragon with boars' tusks and an anteater's snout.

Monsters may be composites that combine the features of several kinds of beings. The Chimaera of Greek myth, for example, had the head of a lion, the body and legs of a goat, and the tail of a

†*See **Names and Places** at the end of this volume for further information.*

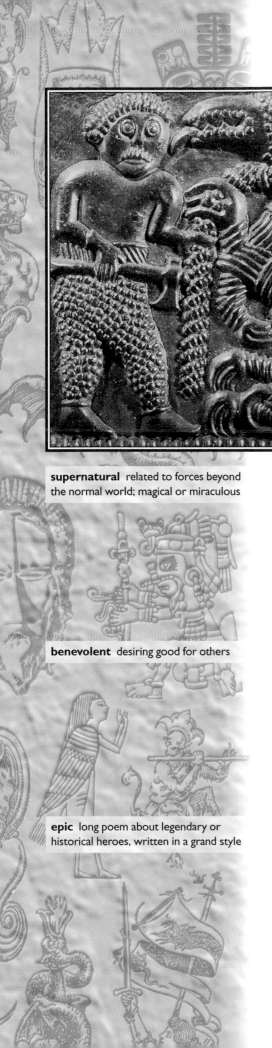

supernatural related to forces beyond the normal world; magical or miraculous

benevolent desiring good for others

epic long poem about legendary or historical heroes, written in a grand style

Fenrir, a monstrous wolf in Norse mythology, grew so large and powerful that the gods decided to capture him. They recruited the brave god Tyr to convince Fenrir to allow chains to be placed on him.

snake. Another Greek mythological monster, the Lamia, occurred in various forms, one of which was a mixture of woman, rabid dog, cow, and mule. Even monsters that are not hybrids are generally deformed or hideous. The Flying Head of the Native American Iroquois people is a huge, hungry head with wings of flapping hair, fiery eyes, and knife-blade teeth. Palraiyuk, an Eskimo water monster, has two faces, two spiked tails, and three stomachs. Roman mythology features Cacus, a creature with an enormous spider body and three fire-breathing heads, who hunts at night for anything warm-blooded.

Some monsters combine human and animal qualities. The *tengu* of Japanese mythology, mysterious and mischievous **supernatural** creatures, are part human and part bird. Eastern and northern European cultures have legends of werewolves, beings that look like humans but take wolf form when the moon is full. Such shape shifting, or shape changing, is a common feature of monster legends. The Chaga, a Bantu people of Tanzania, have a tale about a young woman who met a handsome man at a village dance. She married him, but after they left her village together, she discovered that he was really a werewolf.

Not all such beings are hostile to people, at least not all the time. For example, the centaurs of Greek myth, creatures half human and half horse, were sometimes warlike and sometimes friendly. Dragons, the fire-breathing serpents of myth and legend, also appear **benevolent** on occasion, as do giants. The term *monster* is generally reserved for the destructive and cruel creatures who attack and torment people.

Many mythic monsters prey on human beings. The Aborigines of northern Australia have stories about the Namorodo, skeletons that fly by night. They create more Namorodo by sucking the flesh from living people and turning them into arid skeletons. The vampires of European legend also feed on humans by sucking their blood. The fearsome Minotaur of Greek mythology had to be fed a steady diet of young humans. Grendel, one of the monsters in the Anglo-Saxon **epic** *Beowulf,* preyed on the warriors of Denmark. Native American mythology, too, includes many eaters of human flesh. Among these are the Hantceciitehi or cannibal dwarfs of the Arapaho people, the Dzoavits or cannibal giants of the Shoshone, and dozens of people-eating giants, babies, grandmothers, water monsters, and more.

Monsters and Myths. The Orokaiva people of the Pacific island of New Guinea have a myth that includes the themes of

How to Defeat a Flying Head

Intelligence and good fortune may be more useful than brute force against monsters. In a myth of the Iroquois Indians, a clever woman outwits the Flying Head. Knowing that the Head would see her, she roasted chestnuts in a fire and ate them with obvious enjoyment. The Head thought she was eating stones heated by the fire and decided to share the feast. It flew into her hut and gobbled up the hot stones of the hearth and the entire fire. But the Head could not swallow the fiery stones, because it was only a head with no stomach. It could not spit them out past the barrier of its teeth. It had to hold the hot stones in its mouth until they burned it up.

trickster mischievous figure appearing in various forms in the folktales and mythology of many different peoples

shape shifting, unnatural union, and cannibalism. A monster named Totoima married a human woman. He was in human form at first, but when his wife had children, he turned into a wild boar and devoured them. His wife got the help of a magician. After Totoima ate his baby son, the magician made the boy grow up at once in the boar's stomach. The son then burst forth, killing the boar. The wife married the magician and fed the boar's meat to her neighbors.

A Native American myth from eastern North America illustrates the hero's role in protecting the community from monsters. Gluskap, a **trickster** god and hero, created a village where life was perfect—until the spring that provided water dried up. A villager went to investigate and found a huge, grinning monster who had built a dam to hold all the water. Inside the monster's gaping mouth were the many things the monster had devoured, and the man did not like the way the monster was eyeing him. Gluskap saw what was happening and armed himself with a sharp knife made from a flint mountain. He fought the monster and slit its stomach open, causing a mighty river to flow forth. Then he seized the monster, squeezed it small, and tossed it into a swamp. It became no more than a croaking frog.

Greek mythology contains a great number of monsters. Heroes such as Odysseus† and Hercules† are frequently pitted against them. Sometimes the outcome depends as much on good luck and sharp wits as on strength. Odysseus, for example, outwitted a one-eyed Cyclops after blinding him. One of Hercules' tasks was to clear the Stymphalian Marshes of the monstrous, man-eating birds that infested them. Hercules tried shooting the birds out of their nests with arrows, but there were far too many of them. When he shook his weapons in frustration, the rattling sound drove the birds into flight. At this, Hercules ran about shaking his weapons and uttering a loud battle cry, and the birds kept flying until they left the human world altogether. *See also* BASILISK; BEOWULF; CENTAURS; CYCLOPES; DEVILS AND DEMONS; DRAGONS; FENRIR; FURIES; GIANTS; GOLEM; GORGONS; GRIFFINS; HARPIES; HYDRA; LEVIATHAN; LOCH NESS MONSTER; MANTICORE; MINOTAUR; NEMEAN LION; SATYRS; SCYLLA AND CHARYBDIS; SERPENTS AND SNAKES; SPHINX; THUNDERBIRD; TROLLS; UNICORN; VAMPIRES; WEREWOLVES.

Moon

The moon, the largest and brightest object in the night sky, has long inspired curiosity and wonder. It appears at night, the time of sleep and dreaming that sometimes seems to approach the borders of death and the afterlife. Radiating an air of mystery and magic, the moon is also associated with love and often serves as a symbol of unattainable beauty.

Unlike the sun, the moon does not present the same face every day. It waxes, or grows larger, until it becomes a glowing silver-white disk. Then night by night it wanes, or shrinks, to a curved sliver until it vanishes altogether. A few days later a slender new moon appears and begins to grow again in an endless cycle that

†*See **Names and Places** at the end of this volume for further information.*

sect religious group

repeats each month. In ancient times, people used these phases of the moon to measure time.

Themes and Beliefs. The moon's waxing and waning have made it a symbol of time, change, and repetitive cycles around the world. One such cycle is the constant alternation of birth and death, creation and destruction. People have linked the moon with both birth and death.

The Polynesian islanders of the Pacific Ocean said that the moon was a creator goddess named Hina and that women called wahines were her representatives on earth. In ancient Persia†, the moon was Metra, the world mother.

For some people the moon had a destructive aspect. The Aztecs of Mexico called it Mictecacuiatl and believed that it traveled through the night skies hunting out victims to consume. The Maori people of New Zealand referred to the moon as "man eater." Africans and Semitic† peoples of the ancient Near East also feared this terrifying aspect of the moon.

In certain cultures, the moon had a gentler association with death. Some ancient Greek **sects** thought that the moon was the home of the dead, and early Hindus believed that the souls of the dead returned to the moon to await rebirth. The moon could even symbolize birth and death at the same time. The Tartars of Central Asia called it the Queen of Life and Death.

In mythology the moon is often female, a goddess who may be paired with a sun god. The Incas of South America told of a brother and sister, the moon maiden and the sun man, who were the ancestors of the royal Incas. In the Mayan writing system, a symbol showing the moon goddess seated inside the moon was used before the names of noble women. The Greeks associated the moon with the goddess Artemis†, sister of Apollo. They also called it Hecate, Cynthia, and Selene. The Roman name for the moon was Luna. Native American names for the moon include the Old Woman Who Never Dies and the Eternal One.

Sometimes, however, the moon is male. The Inuit of Greenland picture the moon as a hunter sitting in front of his igloo. Norse† mythology speaks of a moon son and a sun daughter, and Mrs. Sun and Mr. Moon are part of German folklore.

Other legends explain the appearance of the moon, whose mottled surface has suggested various shapes and identities. The "man in the moon" is one common interpretation thought to have originated from the biblical book of Numbers, which describes a man carrying a load of sticks. People have also interpreted the shapes as frogs and toads, and rabbits

People of many cultures have created myths and legends about the moon. This pre-Columbian rattle depicts a moon goddess.

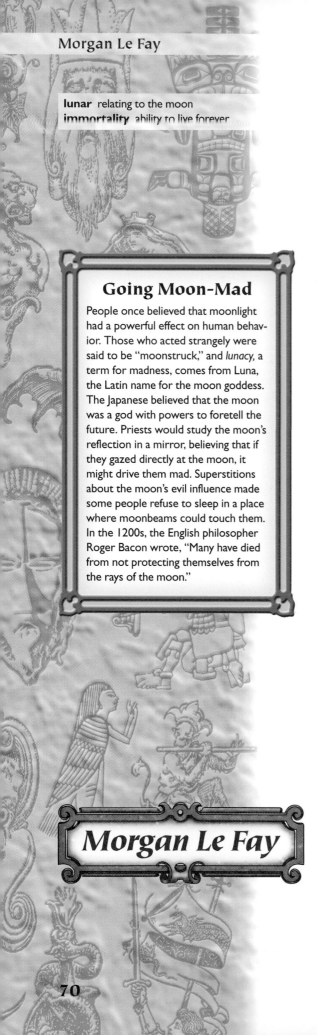

lunar relating to the moon
immortality ability to live forever

Going Moon-Mad

People once believed that moonlight had a powerful effect on human behavior. Those who acted strangely were said to be "moonstruck," and *lunacy*, a term for madness, comes from Luna, the Latin name for the moon goddess. The Japanese believed that the moon was a god with powers to foretell the future. Priests would study the moon's reflection in a mirror, believing that if they gazed directly at the moon, it might drive them mad. Superstitions about the moon's evil influence made some people refuse to sleep in a place where moonbeams could touch them. In the 1200s, the English philosopher Roger Bacon wrote, "Many have died from not protecting themselves from the rays of the moon."

Morgan Le Fay

in the moon occur in many mythologies. In China and Japan the **lunar** rabbit is said to mix a potion that gives **immortality.**

The Moon in Myths. A Native American myth says that the sun and moon are a chieftain and his wife and that the stars are their children. The sun loves to catch and eat his children, so they flee from the sky whenever he appears. The moon plays happily with the stars while the sun is sleeping. But each month, she turns her face to one side and darkens it (as the moon wanes) to mourn the children that the sun succeeded in catching.

The Efik Ibibio people of Nigeria in West Africa also say that the sun and the moon are husband and wife. Long ago they lived on the earth. One day their best friend, flood, came to visit them, bringing fish, reptiles, and other relatives. Flood rose so high in their house that they had to perch on the roof. Finally he covered the house entirely, so the sun and moon had to leap into the sky.

According to the Greek myth of Endymion and Selene, the moon (Selene) fell in love with a handsome young king named Endymion and bore him 50 daughters. One version of the story says that Selene placed Endymion in eternal sleep to prevent him from dying and to keep him forever beautiful.

In a myth of the Luyia people of Kenya in East Africa, the sun and moon were brothers. The moon was older, bigger, and brighter, and the jealous sun picked a fight with him. The two wrestled and the moon fell into mud, which dimmed his brightness. God finally made them stop fighting and kept them apart by ordering the sun to shine by day and the mud-spattered moon to shine by night to illuminate the world of witches and thieves.

A myth from the Indonesian island of Java tells how Nawang Wulan, the moon goddess, came to earth to bathe in a lake. A man stole her cloak of swan's feathers so she could no longer fly back up into the sky, and she stayed on earth and married him. Nawang Wulan used her magic powers to feed the household every day with just a single grain of rice. When her husband discovered her secret, she lost her magic power and had to gather and pound rice every day like all other wives. However, she did find her swan-feather cloak and used it to return to the sky. She stayed there at night but spent the daylight hours on earth with her husband and daughter. ***See also*** HECATE; SUN.

Morgan Le Fay appears in various identities—some helpful, some troublesome—in the legends of King Arthur and the Knights of the Round Table. In all her roles, she has the power to heal and the ability to change shapes at will.

According to some sources, Morgan Le Fay is Arthur's sister (or half sister). She opposes him and schemes to destroy his court by revealing the affair between his queen, Guinevere, and Sir Lancelot. Other stories identify Morgan Le Fay as the enchantress known as Nimuë or the Lady of the Lake. In this role, she tricks

*†See **Names and Places** at the end of this volume for further information.*

Arthur's magician Merlin to fall in love with her. After learning Merlin's secrets, she imprisons him behind invisible walls.

Morgan Le Fay has another side in some stories. As the leader of the nine women who guard the island of Avalon, she lives in a castle beneath a lake surrounding the magical island. She appears as a **benevolent** figure when she gives Arthur the magical sword Excalibur and takes him to Avalon when he is near death. ***See also*** **ARTHUR, KING; ARTHURIAN LEGENDS; AVALON; EXCALIBUR; LADY OF THE LAKE; MERLIN.**

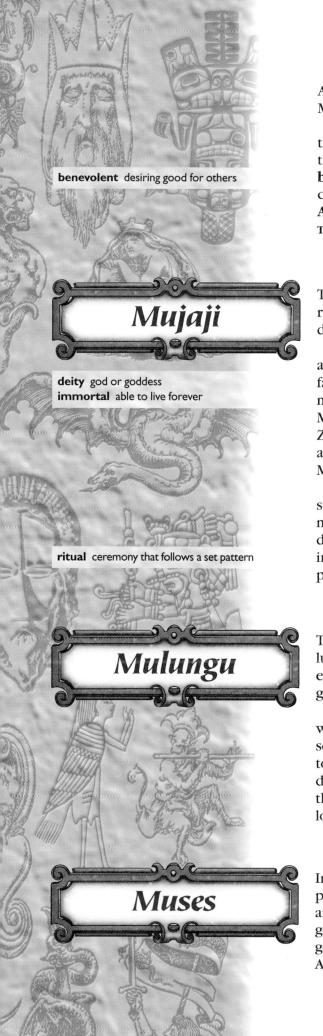

benevolent desiring good for others

Mujaji

deity god or goddess
immortal able to live forever

The mythology of the Lovedu people of South Africa includes a series of **deities** known as Mujaji. They are rain queens who send drought to their enemies but cause rain to fall on their people.

The original Mujaji, sometimes called Mujaji I, lived in isolation and was considered both wise and **immortal.** She mated with her father, Mugodo, and gave birth to Mujaji II, who succeeded her mother as queen. During the reign of Mujaji II and her daughter Mujaji III, the Lovedu homeland was invaded by Europeans and Zulus. Although the Europeans conquered the Lovedu, the tribe and its beliefs survived. These two rain queens were followed by Mujaji IV.

According to the Lovedu, Mujaji IV continues to oversee the supply of rainfall and the cycle of seasons in their land. People make offerings to Mujaji and perform dances to please her. A rain doctor assists by seeking the cause of any droughts and performing **rituals** to remove obstacles that block Mujaji's rainmaking powers. ***See also*** **AFRICAN MYTHOLOGY.**

ritual ceremony that follows a set pattern

Mulungu

The Nyamwezi people of Tanzania in East Africa worship Mulungu as the god who created all things and who watches over the earth. Although he created the world, Mulungu is a very distant god with no personal relationship with living beings.

According to legend, Mulungu once lived on earth. He left and went to live in heaven because some people set fire to the landscape, causing devastation and killing many other people. Unable to climb the tree that linked heaven and earth, Mulungu asked Spider to help him travel up to the sky. Spider climbed up, spun a thread, and let one end of the thread fall to earth. Mulungu followed the thread up to heaven. ***See also*** **AFRICAN MYTHOLOGY.**

Muses

In Greek mythology, the Muses were sister goddesses of music, poetry, and other artistic and intellectual pursuits. Poets and other artists often called on them for inspiration. Zeus, the king of the gods, was the father of the Muses. Their mother was Mnemosyne, goddess of memory. In his role as god of music, poetry, and dance, Apollo† was sometimes said to be their leader. The Muses also

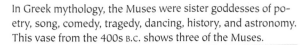

epic long poem about legendary or historical heroes, written in a grand style

figured in Roman mythology, although the Romans sometimes referred to them as the Camenae.

The Muses lived on two sacred Greek mountain peaks, Olympus† and Helicon. Originally they were three—Melete (Practice), Mneme (Memory), and Aoede (Song)—but the Greek poet Hesiod named nine Muses in his *Theogony* (History of the Gods). Ancient writers, particularly the Romans, often linked individual Muses with specific arts and sciences, but they did not agree on the functions of particular Muses. One widely reconized list identified Calliope as the Muse of heroic and **epic** poetry and associated Erato with lyric and love poetry, Polyhymnia with sacred songs and mime, Melpomene with tragedy, Thalia with comedy, Euterpe with music played on instruments, Terpsichore with dancing, Clio with history, and Urania with astronomy.

In myths, the Muses often punished or rewarded mortals. Hesiod claimed that they gave him knowledge and inspired him. The *Odyssey*† tells of Demodocus, a man who was blinded and then given the gift of song by one of the Muses. She claimed that song was even more precious than sight. Although the Muses could be generous, they resented mortals who questioned their supremacy in the arts. The *Iliad*† mentions Thamyris, a poet who challenged the Muses. They made him blind and took away his ability to sing. Another myth tells of the Pierides, nine sisters who lived in Macedonia, north of Greece. The Pierides challenged the Muses to a contest. The Muses won and then turned their challengers into chattering birds. Some of the Muses had famous offspring. Calliope was the mother of the great musician Orpheus†, and Clio was the mother of the beautiful Hyacinthus.

The word *museum* comes from the Muses. It means "place of the Muses" and was first used for the Museum of ancient Alexandria, Egypt, a center of scholarship and learning. **See also APOLLO; CALLIOPE; GREEK MYTHOLOGY.**

Mwindo

supernatural related to forces beyond the normal world; magical or miraculous
epic long poem about legendary or historical heroes, written in a grand style

In the mythology of the Nyanga people of central Africa, Mwindo was a hero with **supernatural** powers who had many adventures. His story is told in the **epic** of Mwindo.

Mwindo was the son of Shemwindo, a powerful chief who had seven wives. Shemwindo decreed that his wives should bear only female children and that he would kill any male child they produced. Six of his wives gave birth to females. Then his favorite wife, Nyamwindo, had a boy. The child emerged from her middle finger and could walk and talk immediately. She named him Mwindo. When Shemwindo found out about his boy, he tried to kill him with his spear. But Mwindo used magic to protect himself

†*See **Names and Places** at the end of this volume for further information.*

and to throw off his father's aim. Shemwindo then buried the child alive, but Mwindo escaped. Next the father sealed his son in a drum and threw him into a river to drown. Again, Mwindo used his magic powers to travel beneath the water.

Mwindo decided to visit his aunt Iyangura. Iyangura's husband tried to stop him by setting traps. But with the help of animal spirits, Mwindo escaped the traps and met his aunt. A guard called upon Master Lightning to strike Mwindo down, but Mwindo's magic made the lightning bolts miss.

Later Mwindo led his uncles to his father's village, intending to punish Shemwindo. They killed all of the villagers and destroyed the village. Shemwindo fled to the **underworld,** followed by Mwindo. There Mwindo met with the ruler of the underworld, Muisa, who promised to reveal Shemwindo's hiding place if Mwindo performed some tasks for him. Mwindo did so, but twice Muisa tried to kill Mwindo, and twice Mwindo used a magic **scepter** to save himself. Finally, Mwindo tracked down his father. Shemwindo apologized for trying to kill Mwindo and agreed to share his kingdom with his son. Mwindo then rebuilt the village and restored all the villagers to life.

Later Mwindo killed a dragon that was a friend of Master Lightning. As punishment, Mwindo was taken up to the sky, where he had to endure blazing heat from the sun and terrible cold and rain. After a year and after Mwindo promised never to kill another living thing, the spirits of the sky let him return to earth. From then on, Mwindo ruled his kingdom in peace, instructing his people to live in harmony, to avoid jealousy and hatred, to accept every child, and to be kind to the sick. *See also* AFRICAN MYTHOLOGY; DRAGONS; HEROES.

underworld land of the dead

scepter rod or wand that serves as a symbol of royal authority

omen sign of future events

epic long poem about legendary or historical heroes, written in a grand style

Myrmidons

According to Greek legend, the Myrmidons were a troop of fierce warriors who fought under the leadership of the hero Achilles† in the Trojan War†. Originally from the island of Aegina, they were created from a colony of ants to repopulate the island after a plague had killed nearly all of its inhabitants.

The plague had been sent by Hera, the jealous wife of Zeus†, because Aegina was named after one of her husband's lovers. After most of the island's population died, King Aeacus of Aegina prayed to Zeus to restore his people. Aeacus then heard a thunderclap, which he took to be a favorable **omen** from the gods. At that moment he saw a line of ants crawling up a tree, carrying grains in their mouths. He asked Zeus for as many subjects as the number of ants he saw, so that his kingdom would survive. That night he dreamed that the ants changed into human beings.

When Aeacus awoke the next morning, he found that the vision in his dream had come true. He named the new people Myrmidons from the Greek name of the ant from which they came, *myrmex.* Aeacus's grandson Achilles ultimately inherited command of the Myrmidons. The Greek **epic** the *Iliad*† tells the story of the role played by the Myrmidons under Achilles in the Trojan

War. Today the term *myrmidon* refers to an individual who carries out a command faithfully, regardless of how cruel or inhuman it might be. *See also* ACHILLES; ANIMALS IN MYTHOLOGY; HERA; ILIAD, THE; TROJAN WAR.

Nabu

cult group bound together by devotion to a particular person, belief, or god

patron special guardian, protector, or supporter

Nabu was the god of wisdom and writing in the ancient Near Eastern lands of Babylonia† and Assyria†. His **cult** was introduced to Babylonia shortly after 2000 B.C., and he became known as the son of Marduk, **patron** god of the city of Babylon†.

Nabu later became one of the principal gods in Assyria. He even surpassed Marduk in popularity, perhaps because of Marduk's association with Babylonia, which was Assyria's rival. The Assyrians addressed many prayers and inscriptions to Nabu and named children after him. As god of writing and scribes, Nabu was the keeper of the Tablets of Destiny, in which the fate of humankind was recorded. In addition, he was sometimes worshiped as a fertility god and as a god of water. *See also* MARDUK; SEMITIC MYTHOLOGY.

Nagas

supernatural related to forces beyond the normal world; magical or miraculous

dynasty succession of rulers from the same family or group

immortal able to live forever

prophet one who claims to have received divine messages or insights

Nagas are a race of semidivine serpent creatures in Hindu and Buddhist mythology. Female Nagas are called Nagis or Naginis. Usually depicted as human above the waist and snake below the waist, Nagas can also change shape to appear fully human or snake. Nagas and Nagis are known for their strength, **supernatural** wisdom, and good looks. When Nagis take human form, they can marry mortal men, and some Indian **dynasties** claim descent from them.

According to legend, Nagas are children of Kadru, the granddaughter of the god Brahma†, and her husband, Kasyapa. Nagas lived on earth at first, but their numbers became so great that Brahma sent them to live under the sea. They reside in magnificent jeweled palaces and rule as kings at the bottom of rivers and lakes and in the underground realm called Patala.

Like humans, Nagas show wisdom and concern for others but also cowardice and injustice. Nagas are **immortal** and potentially dangerous. Some are demons; others seem friendly and are worshiped as gods. Nagas also serve as protectors and guardians of treasure—both material riches and spiritual wealth.

One famous Naga named Muchalinda spreads his cobra hood to shelter the **prophet** Buddha while he meditates. When the god Vishnu† sleeps, he is protected by Shesha, king of the Nagas. Shesha's seven snake heads cover the god. As servants of the god Indra, Nagas oversee the distribution of rain. Sometimes they withhold the rain until forced to release it by the eagle god Garuda. *See also* BRAHMA; BUDDHISM AND MYTHOLOGY; HINDUISM AND MYTHOLOGY; INDRA; SERPENTS AND SNAKES.

†*See **Names and Places** at the end of this volume for further information.*

Naiads

See *Nymphs.*

Nala and Damayanti

epic long poem about legendary or historical heroes, written in a grand style

In Hindu mythology, Nala and Damayanti were lovers who overcame various obstacles to marry and live happily. Their story appears in the Hindu **epic** the *Mahabharata* and in the *Naiadhiyacarita,* a poem written by the poet Shriharsha.

According to legend, Nala was the young, handsome, and skillful king of Nishadha in central India. Damayanti, said to be the most beautiful girl in the world, was the daughter of King Bhima of Vidarbha, a neighboring country. One day Nala captured a swan. In return for freedom, the swan flew to Vidarbha and praised the virtues of Nala to Damayanti. After hearing about him, Damayanti hoped that he would fall in love with her.

Soon after, Damayanti's father decided to find a suitable husband for his daughter and invited many princes to his palace. Several of the gods also sought her hand in marriage. On the way to the palace, the gods met Nala and told him to serve as messenger and announce their intentions to Damayanti. When he arrived at the palace, Damayanti marveled at Nala's good looks. Nala relayed the message from the gods, but Damayanti told him that she wanted only him and vowed to wed him or die.

On the day that Damayanti was supposed to choose her future husband, the royal court was full of men. Among them were the gods, who each appeared as the handsome Nala. Unable to distinguish among them, Damayanti announced that she had pledged

In Hindu mythology, Nala and Damayanti were lovers who overcame many obstacles to marry and live happily together. This colorful drawing shows their marriage.

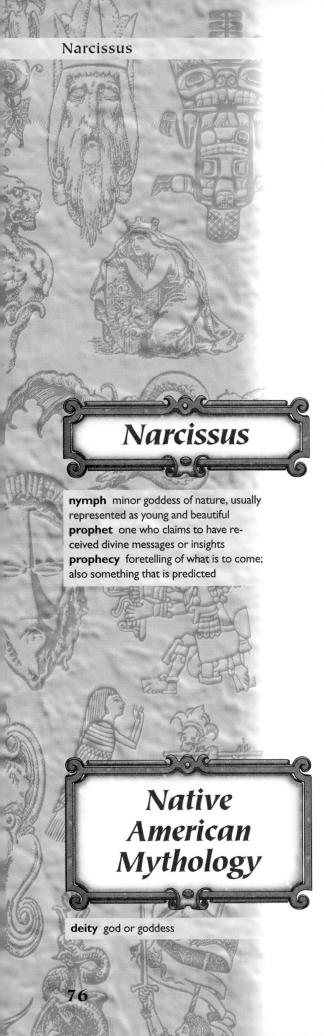

herself to Nala and began to pray. As she prayed the gods assumed their own forms. Damayanti chose Nala, and the two were married.

Angered that Damayanti had married a mortal, the demon Kali vowed to take revenge and tricked Nala into gambling away the royal treasury. Having lost everything, Nala advised his wife to leave him. She refused. Kali lured Nala away from Damayanti. Nala wandered the world. During his travels, a Naga, or serpent god, changed Nala into Vahuka, the charioteer of King Rituparna of Ayodhya.

Uncertain whether Nala was alive, Damayanti announced that she would marry again within a day. Rituparna sped with the charioteer Vahuka to claim her. When they arrived, Damayanti did not recognize the charioteer as Nala. Yet she suspected that the man was Nala because only he could reach her so quickly. After she questioned him, the charioteer changed back into Nala. The two lovers were reunited and lived together in Nishadha. *See also* HINDUISM AND MYTHOLOGY; INDRA; MAHABHARATA, THE; NAGAS.

Narcissus

Narcissus, the son of the river god Cephissus and the **nymph** Leiriope, was an extremely good-looking Greek youth. His beauty ultimately led to his death. A **prophet** named Tiresias told Leiriope that her son would enjoy a long life as long as he never knew himself or saw his reflection. Although Leiriope did not understand the **prophecy** at the time, its meaning eventually became clear.

Narcissus was so handsome that many women and men fell in love with him. He rejected all of them. One of his admirers was the nymph Echo, who had been cursed by Hera† to repeat only the last words spoken to her. Ameinias, another admirer, was so devastated by Narcissus's indifference toward him that he killed himself. Before doing so, however, Ameinias called on the gods to punish Narcissus. They caused the beautiful youth to gaze into a pond at his reflection. He fell in love with his own image and drowned trying to touch it. In other accounts of the story, Narcissus killed himself out of sorrow and frustration. The gods then changed him into the flower that bears his name. *See also* ECHO; GREEK MYTHOLOGY; TIRESIAS.

Native American Mythology

The Native American or Indian peoples of North America do not share a single, unified body of mythology. The many different tribal groups each developed their own stories about the creation of the world, the appearance of the first people, the place of humans in the universe, and the lives and deeds of **deities** and heroes. Yet despite the immense variety of Native American mythologies, certain mythic themes, characters, and stories can be found in many of the cultures. Underlying all the myths is the idea that spiritual forces can be sensed through the natural world—including clouds, winds, plants, and animals—that they shape and sustain. Many stories explain how the actions of gods, heroes, and ancestors gave the earth its present form.

†*See Names and Places at the end of this volume for further information.*

Background and Sources

According to the mythologies of most Native American cultures, their people originated in the places where their ancestors traditionally lived. Some tales speak of ancient migrations. However, Native Americans are descended from hunting and gathering peoples of northeastern Asia who traveled across the Bering Sea into North America during the most recent Ice Age. During that Ice Age, which ended around 8000 B.C., the level of the oceans was much lower, and a bridge of land linked Siberia and Alaska. Some groups may also have reached Alaska from Siberia by boat or by walking on ice. Over thousands of years, the population of North America grew and diversified into the peoples and cultures that Europeans encountered when they began to colonize the continent in the A.D. 1500s.

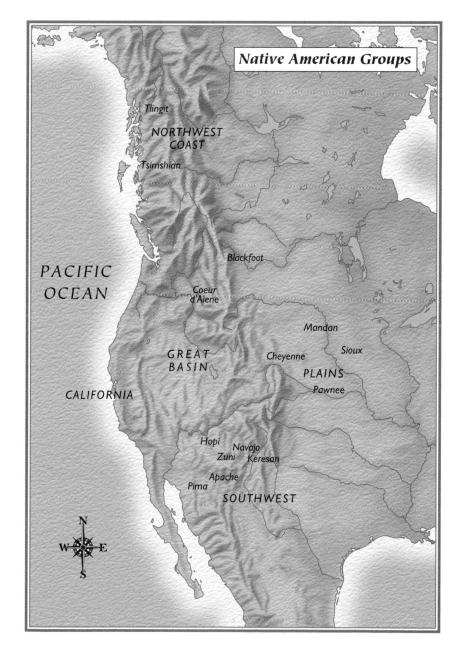

Native American Groups

Tlingit

NORTHWEST COAST

Tsimshian

PACIFIC OCEAN

Blackfoot

Coeur d'Alene

Mandan

Sioux

GREAT BASIN

Cheyenne

PLAINS

CALIFORNIA

Pawnee

Hopi

Navajo

Zuni Keresan

Apache

Pima

SOUTHWEST

N W E S

trickster mischievous figure appearing in various forms in the folktales and mythology of many different peoples

clan group of people descended from a common ancestor or united by a common interest

culture hero mythical figure who gives people the tools of civilization, such as language and fire

ritual ceremony that follows a set pattern

Regions and Types. Scholars have divided North America into different regions based on patterns of Native American mythology. Although each region contains many different peoples and languages, some elements of mythology are shared across the region, and certain kinds of stories are particularly important.

In the eastern part of the Arctic region, the myths of the Inuit or Eskimo people focus on Sedna, a deity known as the mistress or mother of sea animals. In the western Arctic, tales about Igaluk, the moon god, and **trickster** stories are common. The peoples of the Subarctic region of inland Alaska and western Canada have myths about tricksters and heroes who transform, or change, the world into its present state. Such characters also play an important role in the Coast-Plateau region of the Pacific Northwest. Stories about the origins of **clans,** found in many regions, are widespread among peoples of the northwest coast from Puget Sound to southern Alaska.

In addition to trickster and "transformer" myths, the California region produced various myths about animals and about the deities who started the process of creation. The Great Basin region, located east of California, has a number of myths about female heroes and about gods who die and are reborn. Myths about a "dying god" also appear in the Midwest region, which stretches into central Canada. Clan and trickster myths are important in the Midwest as well.

Between the Great Basin and the Midwest is the Plains region, where legends of heroes and tricksters predominate. Such tales appear also in the Southeast region, along with stories about councils of animals. Myths from the Northeast cluster around **culture heroes.**

Stories about dying gods appear among peoples of the Southwest, such as the Hohokam, as well. The tales are similar to Aztec and Mayan legends from Central America. Myths about migrations, heroes who rid the world of monsters, and the origins of humans within the earth are also important in the Southwest.

The Oral Tradition. Before the arrival of Europeans and the spread of European influence, Native Americans did not use written languages. As a result, their myths and legends were passed from generation to generation in oral form, usually by special storytellers who sometimes used objects such as stone carvings, shells, rugs, or pottery to illustrate the tales.

Mythology, religion, history, and **ritual** were not separate things for Native American peoples. They were strands woven together in the various tales and stories that defined peoples' identity and gave order and meaning to their lives. The most serious of these were myths about how the gods created and ordered the universe and about the origins of important things such as humans, landforms, food, and death.

Certain myths could not be told lightly. They formed the basis of sacred rituals, including ceremonies in which participants acted out traditional sacred stories. Many Native Americans believed that some myths could be told only at certain times, often during winter nights. A dire fate—such as an attack by snakes—awaited those who told the stories at the wrong time. Other myths resembled folktales. They could be told for fun or to teach a lesson about proper behavior, and those who told them were free to change or add elements to the basic story. Many such tales involved tricksters.

Major Deities and Figures

Native American mythology contains a great many gods, tricksters, heroes, and other mythical beings. The creator gods and heroes usually establish or restore order. Characters such as tricksters and animals can have either positive or negative qualities. Sometimes they are helpful and entertaining; at other times, they are unpredictable, deceptive, or violent. Mythic figures do not always fall into the same category. A trickster may act as a culture hero, a culture hero may be an animal, an animal may be a creator figure, and a creator may have a capacity for destruction.

personification presenting in human form or with human qualities

Creators, Gods, and Spirits. Many Native American mythologies have a high deity—sometimes referred to as the Great Spirit—who is responsible for bringing the universe or the world into existence. Often, however, the Great Spirit merely begins the process of creation and then disappears or removes itself to heaven, leaving other gods to complete the detailed work of creation and to oversee the day-to-day running of the world.

In many Native American mythologies, Father Sky and Mother Earth or Mother Corn are important creative forces. The high god of the Pawnee people, Tirawa, gave duties and powers to the Sun and Moon, the Morning Star and Evening Star, the Star of Death, and the four stars that support the sky. The Lakota people believe that the sun, sky, earth, wind, and many other elements of the natural, human, and spiritual worlds are all aspects of one supreme being, Wakan Tanka. The secondary gods are often **personifications** of natural forces, such as the wind. In the mythology of the Iroquois people, for example, the thunder god Hunin is a mighty warrior who shoots arrows of fire and is married to the rainbow goddess.

Not all creators are universally good. Napi, the creator god of the Blackfoot people in the Plains

For many centuries, Native Americans have passed their myths from generation to generation though oral stories and artistic repesentations. This mural painting shows a scene from the Hopi people's snake legend.

region, appears as both a wise sky god in creation stories and as a trickster in his actions toward humans. The character Coyote figures in some tales as a trickster and in others as a creator whose actions benefit humankind.

Kachinas, spirits of the dead who link the human and spiritual worlds, play an important role in the mythologies of the Pueblo peoples of the American Southwest, including the Zuni and Hopi Indians. In Hopi mythology, the creator deity is a female being called Spider Woman. Among the Zuni, the supreme creator is Awonawilona, the sun god. The mythology of the Navajo Indians—who live in the same area as the Hopi and Zuni but are not a Pueblo people—focuses on four female deities called Changing Woman, White Shell Woman, Spider Woman, and First Woman.

Culture Heroes and Transformers. Central to many Native American myths is the culture hero who makes the world a suitable place for humans and teaches people how to live. Such a character might form the earth and sky, create people and animals, or kill monsters or turn them into stones. These figures might also release animals that evil spirits have imprisoned, establish social structures for humans, or teach people crafts, arts, and ceremonies.

In the mythologies of some Indian groups of the Northeast, the culture hero Gluskap creates humans, returns from death to defeat evil, and protects people from natural and magical disasters. In Navajo mythology, warrior twins named Monster Slayer and Child of Water—sons of Sun and of Water, respectively—play a similar role. The myths of some California Indians tell of the Attajen, who teaches the first people how to make rain and how to fill the earth with plants and animals, and of Chinigchinich, who teaches the wise men how to perform ceremonial dances that will summon him when they have need of help in the future.

Tricksters. Tricksters appear in nearly all Native American mythologies, but they generally have a greater place in the folklore of hunter-gatherer peoples than of settled agricultural groups, possibly because people who lived on wild resources were more keenly aware of the uncertain nature of life. The trickster, who is almost always male, represents uncertainty. He loves to upset things and spread confusion.

Sometimes the trickster's acts are comic pranks, but they often have a cruel side as well. They might involve sexual trickery, as when the trickster disguises himself as a woman so that he can marry a man or marries his own daughters while in disguise. A trickster can also be a devilish figure who eats babies or leads other creatures to harm themselves. His behavior often stems from impatience or from uncontrollable appetites.

Occasionally, the trickster ends up being tricked himself. The Eye-Juggler story, for example, tells how the trickster saw birds tossing their own eyes into the air and then putting them back in their heads. He tried to do the same thing, but once he had taken out his eyes, he could not put them back.

Why People Die

A number of Native American myths explain how death came into the world, usually to prevent the earth from becoming overcrowded. The Shoshone people say that long ago Wolf and Coyote got into an argument. Wolf said that people could be brought back to life after they died. Coyote argued that if people returned from death, there would soon be too many of them. Wolf agreed that Coyote was right, but then he arranged for Coyote's son to be the first to die. Coyote asked Wolf to bring his son back to life. However, Wolf reminded Coyote that he had insisted on death, and so his son must remain dead.

Native American groups of the Northwest Coast of the United States and Canada create carved and painted logs of wood called totem poles. The animals and spirits on these poles often come from Native American myths and folktales.

The trickster appears as a culture hero when his pranks—such as stealing fire or the sun—benefit humans. Stories from the Northwest Coast region tell how a distant chief had stolen all the light, leaving the earth in darkness. The trickster Raven flew to the chief's land and turned himself into a tiny seed in water, which the chief's daughter swallowed. In time the girl gave birth to the chief's grandson, who was really Raven in disguise. The boy begged the chief to give him the stars and moon as toys, and when the chief gave them to him, the boy released them into the sky. Finally the young boy tricked the old man out of his dearest possession, the sun. He then turned back into Raven and flew away, taking the sun with him.

Animals. Tricksters are often animals. Common trickster figures in Native American mythology include Rabbit in the Eastern regions, Coyote and Spider in the Plains and the Southwest regions, and Raven in the Pacific Northwest.

Although animals appear in many myths and legends, they seldom have purely animal characteristics. They talk and interact with people and often change between human and animal form. According to tradition, in the "myth age"—before people and animals became fixed in their present forms—animals could change their appearance whenever they wished.

Some stories tell of an Animal Wife or Animal Husband, as when a human marries a deer who is disguised as a person. Often the animal spouse is a bear. Many Native American cultures regarded bears as close relatives of people or as people wearing bear coats. A myth from the Northwest Coast region tells of Rhpisunt, a chief's daughter who met two young men while gathering berries. She went with them to the home of the bear chief and married his son. Some time later, Rhpisunt's brothers found their sister in the den of her bear husband and took her and her twin cubs back to their home village. Under the cubs' bear coats were two fine boys, who lived with the people until Rhpisunt died. They then returned to bear life. However, Rhpisunt's family never forgot their kinship with the bears, who brought them good luck in the hunt.

Major Themes and Myths

Despite the great number and variety of Native American myths and legends, certain themes and subjects occur again and again. One of the key concepts of Native American mythology

primeval from the earliest times

is creation, the steps by which the world and everything in it took on their present forms.

Creation Myths. Native American creation stories fall into several broad categories. In one of the oldest and most widespread myths, found everywhere but in the Southwest and on the Arctic coast, the earth is covered by a **primeval** sea. A water creature—such as a duck, muskrat, or turtle—plunges to the depths of the sea and returns with a lump of mud that becomes the earth, which is often supported on the back of a turtle. This Earth Diver myth also exists in northern Europe and Asia, which suggests that the Native American versions may be survivals of ancient myths shared with distant Asian ancestors.

The creation myth of the Iroquois peoples combines elements of the Earth Diver story with the image of a creator who descends from the heavens. Creation begins when a sky goddess named Atahensic plummets through a hole in the floor of heaven. This Woman Who Fell from the Sky lands in the primeval sea. To support her and give her room to move about, the animals dive deep into the sea for bits of earth. The goddess spreads this earth on Great Turtle's back to create the land, and the daughter she bears there becomes known as Earth Woman.

The Navajo and Pueblo peoples, as well as some Plains groups, have a different image of creation, one in which life emerges from the earth like a sprouting plant rising from the soil. The Navajo emergence myth tells how insects climbed up from their First or Red World to the Second or Blue World, the realm of birds. When the Second World became too crowded, the insects and birds flew up to the Third or Yellow World, where they found animals and people. All lived together until food became scarce. Then the people, animals, birds, and insects flew up again into the Fourth or Black and White World of day and night. They found people created by the gods already living there, and these people taught the newcomers how to farm and live in their new world.

The Hopi emergence myth centers on Spider Woman, a powerful earth goddess and creator who is the mother of life. Together with Tawa, the sun god, Spider Woman sang the First Magic Song. This song brought the earth, light, and life into being. She then shaped and wove Tawa's thoughts into solid form, creating birds, fish, and other creatures. After people were created, Tawa rose into the sky. However, Spider Woman moved among humans, dividing them into groups, leading them to their homelands, and teaching them how to live and worship the gods. Spider Woman then disappeared from the people's sight, drawn back down into the earth in a whirlpool of sand.

Pairs and Opposites. A number of Native American mythologies feature paired or opposing characters or qualities. Twins or sets of brothers appear in many myths and legends. For example, in Iroquois mythology, Earth Woman gives birth to the twin brothers Good Twin and Evil Twin. Good Twin creates light, forests,

Native American Mythology

Other entries relating to Native American mythology include

Changing Woman	Hiawatha	Masewi and Oyoyewi	Thunderbird
Dekanawida	Igaluk	Old Man	Wakan Tanka
First Man and First Woman	Kachinas	Sedna	White Shell Woman
Gluskap	Kokopelli	Spider Woman	Woman Who Fell From the Sky

and food plants, while Evil Twin creates impassable mountains, mosquitoes, and a toad that drinks all the water. After a long struggle, Good Twin finally kills Evil Twin. However, Evil Twin's soul and his creations survive to make life difficult for the people that Good Twin brings into being.

The principal heroes of Navajo myth are the warrior twins Monster Slayer and Child of Water. Monster Slayer is associated with bright light and Child of Water with rain clouds. While traveling to see Sun, the warrior twins notice smoke rising from a hole in the ground. Climbing down, they find themselves in the home of Spider Woman. She warns them of dangers they will face on their travels and gives them magic feathers for protection. After many adventures, the brothers reach the house of Sun, who tests them by trying to spear them, boil them, and poison them. With the help of their magic feathers and a friendly caterpillar that provides magic stones to protect them from the poison, the twins survive these ordeals. Sun finally recognizes them as his sons and gives them weapons to use to protect the Navajo people.

Legacy

Although many early European explorers noted the beliefs of the Native Americans they met, Americans and Europeans did not begin recording and collecting Indian myths in earnest until after the 1820s. By that time, many Indian societies had already been disrupted and some of the ancient traditions lost. Between the 1880s and the 1930s, scholars made great efforts to record the words of Native Americans who still knew traditional myths, legends, and folktales. Modern scholars, both Indian and non-Indian, are still studying those texts as well as gathering old lore and exploring new interpretations of familiar myths.

Today Native American myths and legends occupy a significant place in the study of world mythology. More importantly, they remain a living spiritual foundation for Native Americans who practice their traditional religions. The stories help explain the origins of ceremonies and customs, provide tribal and clan histories, and inspire Native American artworks, such as the sand paintings of the Navajo and the totems and other carved wooden objects of the Northwest peoples. *See also* ANIMALS IN MYTHOLOGY; BIRDS IN MYTHOLOGY; CORN; CREATION STORIES; FIRE; HEROES; TRICKSTERS; TWINS.

Near Eastern Mythology

See *Egyptian Mythology; Persian Mythology; Semitic Mythology.*

Nemean Lion

oracle priest or priestess or other creature through whom a god is believed to speak; also the location (such as a shrine) where such words are spoken

invulnerable incapable of being hurt

In Greek mythology, the Nemean Lion was a fearsome beast slain by Hercules† as one of his 12 Labors. The hero had killed his wife and children in a fit of madness and was told by an **oracle** to go to the city of Tiryns for his punishment. There King Eurystheus could present him with 12 seemingly impossible challenges or labors.

Hercules' first task was to slay the Nemean Lion, the offspring of the monsters Typhon and Echidna. Twice as large as a normal lion, the animal had skin so tough that no weapons could penetrate it. After tracking the lion to its cave in the land of Nemea, Hercules tried to kill it with arrows given to him by the god Apollo†. However, the arrows simply bounced off the lion. Hercules struggled with the beast using only his bare hands and strangled it to death. He then used the lion's own razor-sharp claws to remove its skin. Afterward, he wore the skin as a cloak to make him **invulnerable.**

After killing the beast, Hercules took the skin back to Eurystheus, but the king was so terrified when he saw the lion that he hid himself inside a storage jar. He told Hercules that, from then on, the hero should present his trophies to a messenger outside the city. To honor the lion's struggle against Hercules, Zeus† (or Hera† in some accounts) transformed the lion into the constellation, or group of stars, called Leo. *See also* GREEK MYTHOLOGY; HERCULES.

Neptune

deity god or goddess
trident three-pronged spear, similar to a pitchfork

patron special guardian, protector, or supporter

In Roman mythology, Neptune was an early Italian water **deity** who became identified with the Greek god Poseidon after about 400 B.C. Unlike Poseidon, who appeared in many Greek myths and legends, Neptune played a relatively minor role in Roman mythology. In ancient Roman art, he is generally shown holding a **trident,** a traditional weapon of fishermen in the Mediterranean region.

Possibly called Nethunus by the Etruscans of ancient Italy, the early Neptune was linked to freshwater rivers, lakes, and springs. After identification with Poseidon, he also became the god of the sea. His wife, Salacia, a goddess of springwater, became associated with Amphitrite, the wife of Poseidon and queen of the sea.

The ancient Romans held an annual festival to honor Neptune in July, a time when the hot, dry weather of Italy made water scarce. The purpose of the festival was probably to appease the god and help ensure that water would soon be abundant again. Closely associated with horses, as was Poseidon, Neptune may also have been worshiped by the Romans as a god of horses and **patron** of horse racing. *See also* POSEIDON; ROMAN MYTHOLOGY.

Nereids

See *Nymphs.*

†*See Names and Places at the end of this volume for further information.*

Nibelungenlied

epic long poem about legendary or historical heroes, written in a grand style

vassal individual who swears loyalty and obedience to a superior lord

The *Nibelungenlied* (Song of the Nibelungs) is a German **epic** poem of the Middle Ages. Based on old Norse† legends, it tells the story of Siegfried (Sigurd), a German prince. The Nibelungs of the poem's title were originally evil dwarfs who had a magical but cursed treasure of gold. In time, people who possessed the gold were also identified as Nibelungs.

Tales of the Nibelungs. The dwarfs known as the Nibelungs lived in Nibelheim, an underground land of darkness or mist. Many stories about their treasure appear in Norse and Germanic mythology. The *Nibelungenlied,* written in about A.D. 1200 by an unknown Austrian, combines a number of these myths with tales of legendary rulers, princes, princesses, and heroes. Some of these stories may have been based on events of an earlier age. The work had a tremendous impact on later Germanic art and literature. Most notably, it provided the characters for a series of operas, *Der Ring des Nibelungen* (The Ring of the Nibelung), written by German composer Richard Wagner between 1853 and 1873.

The Nibelungenlied Story. The story begins in the city of Worms on the Rhine River, where Princess Kriemhild (Gudrun) of Burgundy has a vision in which two eagles attack and kill a falcon. Her mother, a skilled interpreter of dreams, explains that this means that Kriemhild's future husband will be attacked.

Meanwhile, farther west on the Rhine, Prince Siegfried hears of Kriemhild's great beauty and decides to woo her. When Siegfried arrives in Worms, he is recognized in the court as a great hero who possesses some of the famed Nibelungen gold. Kriemhild notices the prince while gazing from her window and falls in love with him.

Siegfried wins the favor of Kriemhild's brother, King Gunther (Gunnar) of Burgundy, when he helps the Burgundians defeat their enemies in Saxony and Denmark. After meeting Kriemhild at a victory tournament, Siegfried asks for her hand in marriage. Gunther agrees, on one condition. He asks Siegfried to help him win the hand of Brunhilde of Iceland, a queen of outstanding strength and beauty who has vowed to marry only a man who can match her athletic skills.

Disguised as Gunther's **vassal,** Siegfried accompanies the king on his quest. When they arrive in Iceland, Brunhilde warns Gunther that he and his men will all die if he does not match her skills. Gunther becomes fearful when he sees the spear he must hurl, a spear that can barely be lifted by 12 men. But Siegfried reassures the king, telling him to pretend to lift and throw the spear. Meanwhile, Siegfried puts on a magic cloak, which makes him invisible, and hurls the great spear farther than Brunhilde can. He also throws an enormous stone and beats the queen as well. Defeated, Brunhilde agrees to marry Gunther.

The adventurers return to the Rhine, where in a double wedding ceremony, Gunther marries Brunhilde and Siegfried marries Kriemhild. However, Brunhilde wonders why the king's sister is

This painting shows an episode from the German poem the *Nibelungenlied:* King Etzel enters the city of Vienna on horseback.

invulnerable incapable of being hurt

marrying Siegfried, a mere vassal. Later that night, she questions Gunther about the apparent mismatch and refuses to sleep with him until he explains. When Gunther refuses to answer, she angrily picks her husband up and hangs him from a peg on the wall.

When Siegfried hears what has happened, he again uses his magic cloak to make himself invisible. The next evening, he follows Gunther and Brunhilde to their room and wrestles with Brunhilde in the dark. Believing that it is her husband who is overpowering her, Brunhilde submits to Gunther, and in doing so she loses her miraculous strength. Before leaving their room, Siegfried takes Brunhilde's belt and gold ring. These he gives to his wife after explaining what happened. Siegfried then returns to his own country with Kriemhild.

After many years, Siegfried and Kriemhild visit Gunther and Brunhilde. During a ceremonial feast, the two women quarrel. Brunhilde ridicules Kriemhild for marrying a mere vassal, and in retaliation, Kriemhild suggests Brunhilde has been unfaithful to her husband and allowed Siegfried to sleep with her. She produces Brunhilde's belt and ring as proof. Siegfried denies the charge, but the matter is not settled. Brunhilde persuades Gunther's friend Hagen that Siegfried has wronged her, and Hagen promises to avenge her.

Siegfried had become **invulnerable** after he bathed in the blood of a dragon. However, Hagen discovers that one spot between the hero's shoulders is vulnerable. While out hunting one day, Hagen thrusts a spear through that spot, killing Siegfried. At her husband's funeral, Kriemhild discovers the identity of Siegfried's murderer and curses Hagen.

Kriemhild stays on in Burgundy. Three years after Siegfried's death, Hagen suggests to Gunther that Kriemhild should be persuaded to bring Siegfried's Nibelungen treasure to Burgundy. When the treasure arrives, Hagen sinks it in the Rhine, hoping to recover it for himself and Gunther one day.

In time, Kriemhild marries King Etzel of Hungary, who agrees to help her avenge Siegfried's death. After several years, Etzel invites the Burgundians to Hungary. Guided by Hagen, they reach the banks of the Danube River but find no ships to carry them across. Hagen meets three swan maidens and forces them to help him. After telling Hagen about a ferryman, they warn him that only one person from his group, a priest, will return home.

Hagen tricks the ferryman into bringing his boat ashore and then kills him. Then while ferrying the Burgundians across the river, Hagen throws a priest overboard, hoping to prove the swan maidens wrong. But when the priest swims safely to shore, Hagen knows that their **prophecy** will come true.

When the Burgundians arrive in Hungary, Kriemhild demands her gold. Hagen tells her it will remain at the bottom of the Rhine. Vicious fighting later breaks out between the Hungarians and Burgundians. Hagen kills the child of Etzel and Kriemhild, and Kriemhild promises a reward to anyone who captures and brings Hagen to her.

After more fighting, Hagen and Gunther are captured and taken to Kriemhild. Once again she asks Hagen to reveal the location of the treasure. Again Hagen refuses, explaining that he promised never to reveal the secret while his lord was alive. Insane with fury, Kriemhild orders the execution of Gunther, her own brother, and then carries Gunther's head to Hagen as proof that his lord is dead. When Hagen still refuses to reveal the hiding place, she cuts off his head with a sword that belonged to Siegfried. In the end, a hero named Hildebrand, outraged at Kriemhild's actions, kills the queen. *See also* BRUNHILDE; DWARFS AND ELVES; HEROES; NORSE MYTHOLOGY; SIGURD.

An Age of Heroism and Honor

Though based on legendary characters, the *Nibelungenlied* expresses ideals of heroism and chivalry that were very important in the period when the work was written. Moreover, while the roots of the Nibelungen legends are found in pre-Christian Scandinavia, the *Nibelungenlied* presents a Christian view of European courtly life and traditions. The work also strongly illustrates the Germanic ideas of fate and loyalty to the chief or king.

prophecy foretelling of what is to come; also something that is predicted

Nicholas, St.

patron special guardian, protector, or supporter

relics pieces of bone, possessions, or other items belonging to a saint or sacred person

One of the most popular saints in Christianity, St. Nicholas is the **patron** of children, unmarried women, sailors, and merchants, as well as the patron saint of Russia. He has long been associated with winter and served as the basis for Santa Claus.

Little is known for certain about the life of St. Nicholas. According to tradition, he was born in the seaport of Patara in Asia Minor (present-day Turkey) and became bishop of Myra in the A.D. 300s. He was persecuted and imprisoned for his Christian faith.

After his death around A.D. 350, St. Nicholas was buried in the church at Myra. In about 1087, the **relics** of the saint were moved to Bari, Italy, which became a popular pilgrimage site in the Middle Ages. The church of San Nicola in Bari remains the main shrine to St. Nicholas.

St. Nicholas had a reputation for kindness and generosity, especially to the poor, and these traits became the basis for various legends. According to one story, St. Nicholas helped three poverty-stricken girls escape a life on the streets by giving them

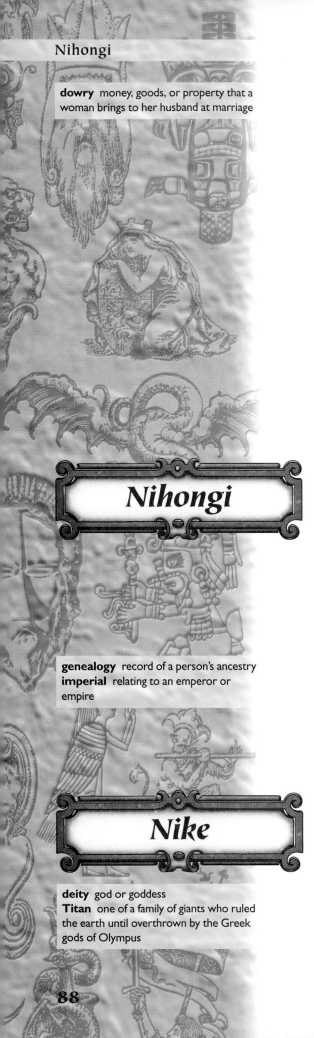

dowry money, goods, or property that a woman brings to her husband at marriage

bags of gold to serve as **dowries.** In another tale, he miraculously brought back to life three young children who had been chopped up and put in a barrel of saltwater to serve as bacon. In yet another legend, St. Nicholas saved the lives of three drowning sailors by stopping a violent storm that threatened to overwhelm them.

During the Middle Ages, devotion to St. Nicholas spread throughout Europe, and it became customary to give gifts to children on the saint's feast day, December 6. The people of Holland called the saint Sinte Klaas, and when Dutch settlers came to North America, they brought the traditions associated with him to the New World.

When the English took over the Dutch colony of New Netherland, they adopted the tradition of Sinte Klaas. But to avoid celebrating the feast day of a Catholic saint, English Protestants transformed him into a nonreligious figure based on both Sinte Klaas and the Germanic god Thor, a figure also associated with winter. In addition, they moved the feast day from December 6 to Christmas. The name Sinte Klaas was eventually transformed into Santa Claus, the jolly figure who brings gifts to children on Christmas Eve. *See also* SANTA CLAUS; THOR.

Nihongi

genealogy record of a person's ancestry
imperial relating to an emperor or empire

The *Nihongi,* or *Nihonshoki* (Chronicles of Japan), is one of the earliest and most important sources of Japanese mythology. Along with the *Kojiki* (Records of Ancient Matters), it provides most of the myths and legends from the early periods of Japanese history up to the death of Empress Jitô in A.D. 697.

Written in Chinese and strongly influenced by both Chinese and Korean mythological traditions, the *Nihongi* was completed by Prince Toneri in A.D. 720. Based on the work of a number of earlier scholars, it provides much useful information about ancient Japan.

Both the *Nihongi* and the *Kojiki* contain stories that trace the **genealogy** of the Japanese **imperial** family back to the creation of the world and to the sun goddess Amaterasu, said to be the divine ancestor of Japanese emperors. Besides linking the imperial family to divine authority, these myths also served to strengthen the authority of the Japanese ruling class. *See also* AMATERASU; JAPANESE MYTHOLOGY; KOJIKI.

Nike

deity god or goddess
Titan one of a family of giants who ruled the earth until overthrown by the Greek gods of Olympus

Nike, the Greek goddess of victory, may originally have been considered an aspect of the goddess Athena† rather than a **deity** in her own right. According to the Greek writer Hesiod†, Nike was the daughter of the river Styx and the **Titan** Pallas. Zeus† honored her for helping him win the battle of the gods against the Titans. The Romans knew Nike as Victoria and considered her the protector of the Roman senate.

Nike was usually shown as a small figure carried in the hands of Zeus or Athena. As the goddess of victory, she appeared as a winged figure holding a laurel wreath above the heads of those

† *See **Names and Places** at the end of this volume for further information.*

who won competitions. However, in her identity as Athena Nike, she was portrayed without wings. *See also* ATHENA; GREEK MYTHOLOGY; ROMAN MYTHOLOGY.

Nimrod

invincible too powerful to be conquered

According to Jewish legend, Nimrod was a powerful king of a land called Shinar, who built a great tower to challenge God's authority. The only direct mention of Nimrod in the Bible calls him "a mighty hunter before the Lord." He supposedly acquired immense strength by wearing animal skins that Adam and Eve had received from the Hebrew god Yahweh. The clothing gave Nimrod power over all animals and made him **invincible** in combat.

Although people worshiped Nimrod as a god, he wished for even greater glory. He had his subjects build the Tower of Babel from which he could attack heaven. However, Yahweh blocked Nimrod's plans by causing the people to speak different languages so they could not understand one another. Disputes arose among the people, dividing them and destroying Nimrod's power. Some scholars have related this story to a earlier myth that tells how the civilization of Sumer† came to an end when the god Enki created many different languages among the Sumerians. *See also* BABEL, TOWER OF; SEMITIC MYTHOLOGY.

Noah

In the book of Genesis in the Bible, Noah was the hero chosen by God to survive a great flood on earth. The biblical story was probably based on similar accounts of a flood in myths from Mesopotamia†.

According to the story in Genesis, the human race had become so wicked that God was sorry he ever created it. He decided to wash away all the creatures of the earth in a great flood. However, God saw that Noah was a righteous man so he decided to save him. God told Noah of his plans and instructed him to build a great ark in which he could ride out the storm with his wife and children. Then he commanded Noah to find male and female specimens of every type of animal on the earth and bring them into the ark and also to gather plants and seeds. Noah followed God's instructions and entered the ark as the rain began to fall.

It rained for 40 days and 40 nights, until the waters covered even the tops of the highest mountains. After the rain ended, Noah released a raven and a dove to find out whether there was any dry land on earth. Both birds returned, indicating that water still covered the planet. Seven days later, Noah sent the dove out again. This time it returned with an olive branch, which meant that dry land had finally appeared. According to later Jewish legend, the ark came to rest on the top of Mount Ararat (in what is now Turkey), and Noah and his family emerged with all the animals.

Noah built an altar and made a sacrifice to God. God then made a covenant, or agreement, with Noah, promising never again to devastate the earth because of the wickedness of humans. He placed a rainbow in the sky as a reminder of this covenant. *See also* FLOODS; GILGAMESH; SEMITIC MYTHOLOGY; UTNAPISHTIM.

Norse Mythology

cosmic large or universal in scale; having to do with the universe

medieval relating to the Middle Ages in Europe, a period from about A.D. 500 to 1500

saga story recounting the adventures of historical and legendary heroes; usually associated with Icelandic or Norse tales of the Middle Ages

Norse mythology comes from the northernmost part of Europe, Scandinavia: Sweden, Norway, Denmark, and Iceland. The mythology of this region is grim, shadowed by long, sunless winters. But the darkness is laced with gleams of grandeur and sparks of humor. The myths depict a universe in which gods and giants battle among themselves in a **cosmic** conflict fated to end in the destruction of the world.

Background and Sources

Norse mythology developed from the myths and legends of northern peoples who spoke Germanic languages. It shares many features with the mythology of pre-Christian Germanic groups. When some of these groups spread into England and Scandinavia, they carried their myths with them. As they converted to Christianity, their traditional beliefs faded. But Christianity did not take hold in Scandinavia until a later date, and the Norse version of Germanic mythology remained vigorous through the Viking era, from about A.D. 750 to 1050. Modern knowledge of Norse mythology stems from **medieval** texts, most of them written in Iceland. Descendants of Norse colonists in that country maintained a strong interest in their heritage even after becoming Christian.

A major source of information about Norse mythology is a book called the *Poetic Edda,* sometimes known as the *Elder Edda.* It consists of mythological and heroic poems, including *Voluspa,* an overview of Norse mythology from the creation to the final destructive battle of the world, called Ragnarok. The unknown author who compiled the *Poetic Edda* in Iceland around 1270 drew on materials dating from between 800 and 1100.

Around 1222, an Icelandic poet and chieftain named Snorri Sturluson wrote the *Prose Edda,* or *Younger Edda,* which interprets traditional Icelandic poetry for the audiences of Snorri's time. Part of the *Prose Edda* describes a visit by Gylfi, a Swedish king, to the home of the gods in Asgard. There the king questioned the gods about their history, adventures, and fate.

Norse mythology is known from other Scandinavian texts as well. Many Norse poems refer to mythic events or figures. In the early 1200s, Icelanders started writing family **sagas** about their ancestors and heroic sagas about their legendary heroes. Many of these sagas contain references to mythological subjects. Also in the 1200s, a Danish scholar named Saxo Grammaticus wrote a history of the Danish people that begins with an account of

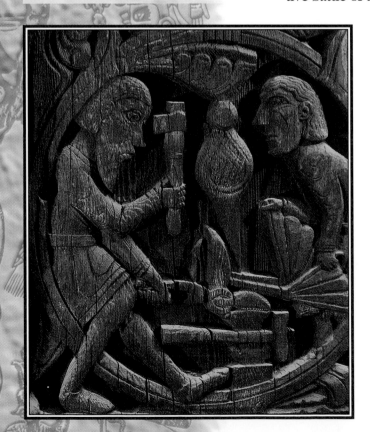

One story from Norse mythology tells of Sigurd, a hero who used a special sword to slay the dragon Fafnir. When Sigurd roasted and ate the beast's heart, he was able to understand the language of the birds. They warned him that he was going to be killed.

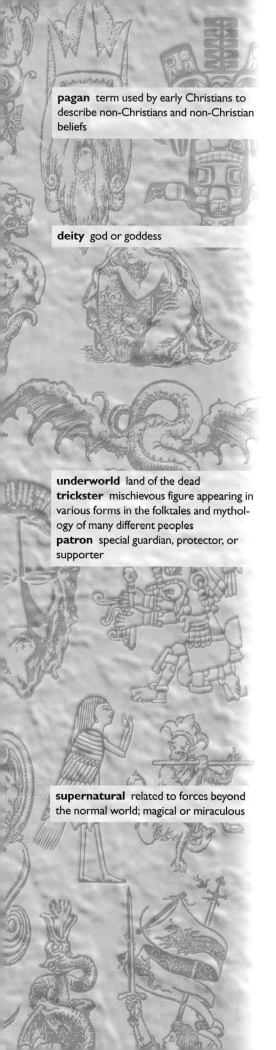

pagan term used by early Christians to describe non-Christians and non-Christian beliefs

deity god or goddess

underworld land of the dead

trickster mischievous figure appearing in various forms in the folktales and mythology of many different peoples

patron special guardian, protector, or supporter

supernatural related to forces beyond the normal world; magical or miraculous

their **pagan** gods and ancient heroes. Works by earlier Roman and medieval historians also include information about Germanic and Norse myths. In A.D. 98, for example, the Roman historian Tacitus wrote *Germania*, a description of the Germanic tribes that mentions some of their religious beliefs and customs.

Major Deities and Figures

Like the Greek **deities,** the Norse gods and goddesses have all the characteristics of larger-than-life human beings. Unlike the Greek deities, however, they seldom interact with human beings. The world of Norse mythology includes two groups of gods, the Aesir and the Vanir, as well as giants, trolls, elves, dwarfs, and heroic human warriors.

The Aesir. The Aesir were gods of war and of the sky. Chief among them was Odin, god of battle, wisdom, and poetry, who was regarded by the Vikings as the ruler of the deities and the creator of humans. The mighty Thor, warrior god of thunder, ranked as the second most important Norse deity. Tiwaz, an early Germanic sky god who became Tyr in Norse mythology, appears in some accounts as a son of Odin. Balder, also Odin's son, was a gentle, beloved god. Murdered, he descended to the **underworld,** to return after a new world had been created. Loki, a cunning **trickster,** sometimes helped the other gods but more often caused trouble because of his spiteful, destructive nature. The sky goddess Frigg was Odin's wife and the **patron** of marriage, children, and households.

The Vanir. The Vanir were associated with the earth, fertility, and prosperity. In the beginning, the Aesir and Vanir waged war against each other, perhaps reflecting an actual historical conflict between two cultures, tribes, or belief systems. Realizing that neither side could win, the two groups of gods made peace and together fought their common enemy, the giants. To ensure a lasting peace, some of the Vanir came to Asgard, the home of the Aesir, as hostages. Among them were Njord, the patron of the sea and seafaring. His twin children, Freyr and Freyja, were the most important Vanir and represented love, sexuality, and fertility. The giants' desire to capture Freyja was one cause of strife between the gods and the giants.

Other Mythological and Legendary Beings. The **supernatural** beings who inhabited the Norse mythic world included elves, creatures related to humans; and dwarfs, skilled crafts workers who made many of the finest treasures of gods and humans. The most powerful and dreaded mythological beings were the giants, huge beings associated with ice, snow, and paralyzing cold. They were descended from Ymir, the frost giant, who was killed by Odin and his brothers. Although the giants were generally enemies of the gods, many marriages took place between deities and giants. Both the mother and the wife of Freyr, for example, were giantesses.

Norse Deities and Other Supernatural Beings

Deity	Role
Balder	Odin's son, gentle and handsome god
Bragi	god of poetry and music
Fenrir	monstrous wolf, child of Loki
Freyja	goddess of love and fertility, twin of Freyr
Freyr	god of fertility and prosperity, twin of Freyja
Frigg	wife of Odin, goddess of the sky, marriage, and childbirth
Heimdall	god who guards Asgard, the home of the gods
Hel	goddess of the dead, child of Loki
Idun	goddess of fertility, spring, and rebirth
Jormungand	giant serpent
Loki	trickster figure, companion to the gods
Mimir	giant who guards the well of knowledge
Njord	sea god, father of Freyr and Freyja
Odin	god of wisdom, battle, and poetry, and ruler of the gods
Thor	god of the sky and thunder, associated with the weather, crops, and warriors
Tyr	god of war, justice, and order
Valkyries	female spirits, servants of Odin
Ymir	frost giant whose body was used to form the world

epic long poem about legendary or historical heroes, written in a grand style
destiny future or fate of an individual or thing
chaos great disorder or confusion

Although human beings appear rarely in Norse myths about the gods, Norse literature is filled with legends of heroic warriors, kings, and ancestors. The most important is the *Volsunga Saga*, written around 1300. The Norse version of the German **epic** the *Nibelungenlied*, it tells the story of Sigurd, a hero who slays a dragon, acquires a magical ring, awakens a sleeping beauty (the Valkyrie† Brunhilde), and bravely meets his **destiny.** Like Beowulf, another Germanic hero, Sigurd triumphs over the forces of evil and **chaos** by slaying a monster.

† *See **Names and Places** at the end of this volume for further information.*

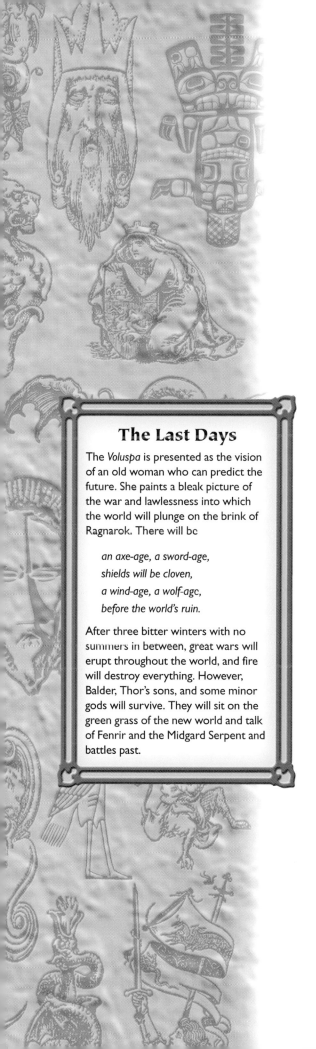

Major Themes and Myths

Bravery in the face of a harsh fate is one of the main themes of Norse mythology. Even the gods were ruled by an unalterable fate that doomed everything to eventual destruction. A hero who strove to accept his destiny with reckless courage, honor, and generosity might win lasting fame, regarded as the only true life after death.

Creation. Various accounts of the creation of the world and of human beings appear in Norse mythology. All begin in Ginnunga-gap, a deep empty space between realms of heat and ice. Frost formed and became a giant, Ymir. A cosmic cow named Aud-humla also appeared. Licking the cliffs of ice, she revealed a man who had three grandsons. One of them was Odin. With his two brothers, Odin killed the frost giant Ymir and formed the earth from his body, the seas and rivers from his blood, and the sky from his skull, which was held suspended above the earth by four strong dwarfs.

The *Voluspa* says that Odin and his brothers made the first man and first woman out of an ash tree and an elm tree. They gave the humans life, intelligence, and beauty. A poem called "The Lay of Vafthrudnir," however, says that the first man and first woman grew out of Ymir's armpits before he was killed.

The Universe. Once they had killed Ymir, Odin and the other gods created an orderly universe in three levels. Although journeys between the different levels of the universe were possible, they were difficult and dangerous, even for the gods. The top or heavenly level contained Asgard, the home of the Aesir; Vana-heim, the home of the Vanir; and Alfheim, the place where the light or good elves lived. Valhalla, the hall where Odin gathered the souls of warriors who had died in battle, was also located on this level.

Connected to the upper level by the rainbow bridge Bifrost was the middle or earthly level. It contained Midgard, the world of men; Jotunheim, the land of the giants; Svartalfaheim, the land of the dark elves; and Nidavellir, the land of the dwarfs. A huge serpent called Jormungand encircled the middle world. The bottom level consisted of the underworld of Niflheim, also known as Hel after Loki's daughter Hel, who ruled there.

Running through this universe from bottom to top, holding it all together and linking the three worlds of heaven, earth, and underworld, was a great ash tree called Yggdrasill. Its branches spread over the heavens, and its roots stretched into all three worlds. Springs rose from these roots. One, the Well of Urd, was guarded by the Norns, the three goddesses of fate. A serpent or dragon named Nidhogg gnawed endlessly at the Yggdrasill's roots, and an eagle perched on its topmost branch. Goats, deer, and other animals ate the tree's shoots and lived in it, and a squirrel named Ratatosk ran up and down its trunk, carrying messages and insults between the eagle and Nidhogg.

The Last Days

The *Voluspa* is presented as the vision of an old woman who can predict the future. She paints a bleak picture of the war and lawlessness into which the world will plunge on the brink of Ragnarok. There will be

> *an axe-age, a sword-age,*
> *shields will be cloven,*
> *a wind-age, a wolf-age,*
> *before the world's ruin.*

After three bitter winters with no summers in between, great wars will erupt throughout the world, and fire will destroy everything. However, Balder, Thor's sons, and some minor gods will survive. They will sit on the green grass of the new world and talk of Fenrir and the Midgard Serpent and battles past.

This illustration shows Odin's son Hermod on his father's eight-legged horse at the gates of Hel. Hermod has come to ask for the return of his brother Balder.

Good Against Evil. The gods represented order in the universe, but their enemies the giants tried constantly to return to the state of formless chaos that had existed before the creation. Although the gods sometimes displayed treachery, cowardice, or cruelty, in general they stood for good against evil.

Myths describe the gods' interactions with one another and with the giants. One story, for example, tells how Loki helped a frost giant kidnap Idun, the goddess who tended the golden apples that kept the gods young. Without the magic apples the gods began to age, and they demanded that Loki rescue Idun. Donning a feathered cloak, he flew to Jotunheim, changed the goddess into a nut, and brought her back to Asgard. The giant took the form of an eagle and pursued Loki. But the gods lit a fire on the walls of Asgard that burned the giant's wings, causing him to drop to the ground, where the gods killed him. The giant's daughter was furious. However, Loki the jokester made her laugh, and she made peace with the gods.

Related Entries
Other entries related to Norse mythology are listed at the end of this article.

Another myth tells of Fenrir, a wolf who was one of several monstrous children that Loki fathered. Fenrir grew up in Asgard among the gods, but he was so fierce that only Odin's son Tyr could feed him. Fearing what Fenrir might do, the gods tried to chain him down. The wolf, however, broke every metal chain as though it were made of grass. Odin ordered the dwarfs to produce an unbreakable chain. The suspicious Fenrir would not let the gods put it around his neck until Tyr placed his hand in the wolf's mouth. Once he discovered that he could not break this new chain, the enraged Fenrir bit Tyr's hand off. The gods left Fenrir bound on a distant island, from which his howls could be heard. When the final battle of Ragnarok approaches he will break free.

Ragnarok. The twilight of the gods and end of the earth began when Loki used trickery to kill Balder, whose death was a sign that the orderly universe was falling apart. The gods chained Loki to a rock, but eventually he will break loose and lead the giants in a last bitter battle against the gods and the greatest heroes from Valhalla. The bridge Bifrost will shatter, cutting Midgard off from Asgard, and all monsters will run free. Fenrir will kill Odin, while Thor will perish in the process of slaying the serpent Jormungard. In the end, all worlds will be consumed by fire and flood. One man and one woman will survive, sheltering in the World Tree Yggdrasill, to become the parents of a new human race.

Legacy

Norse mythology inspired the stirring poems and sagas that were written down during the late Middle Ages, and it has inspired more recent artists as well. German composer Richard Wagner used the legend of Sigurd as the basis for his cycle of four operas, known collectively as *Der Ring des Nibelungen* (The Ring of the Nibelung). Some modern writers of fantasy have drawn on Norse stories and creations such as elves and dwarfs in their work. The best known of these is J.R.R. Tolkien, whose *Lord of the Rings* features many themes from Norse mythology, such as dragon slaying and enchanted rings. High-spirited and muscular Thor, the subject of many of the most popular myths, has even been the subject of a comic-book series called *The Mighty Thor.* In one form or another, the Norse gods have managed to survive Ragnarok. *See also* BALDER; BEOWULF; BERSERKS; DWARFS AND ELVES; FENRIR; FREYJA; FREYR; FRIGG; HEIMDALL; HEL; IDUN; LOKI; MIMIR; NIBELUNGENLIED; ODIN; RAGNAROK; SAGAS; SIGURD; THOR; TROLLS; TYR; VALHALLA; VALKYRIES; YGGDRASILL; YMIR.

Nummo

Divine twins called the Nummo figure prominently in the creation stories of the Dogon people of Mali in West Africa. The Nummo were the offspring of the union of Amma, the supreme god who represents the male spirit, and the earth, a female spirit.

Lonely, Amma wanted to have a child with the earth. However, their first attempt did not produce a child but a jackal. Amma went to the earth a second time. This time their union had the perfect result: twins called the Nummo, one male and one female. The top half of each twin was human, and the bottom half resembled a serpent. They each had green skin and hair, red eyes, forked tongues, and wavy arms without joints.

The Nummo represented light and water, the life force of creation. When the twins looked down from heaven, they saw that the earth was naked. They went down to earth bearing plants and wove the fibers of the plants around the bare earth. The first wind arose as a result of the twins' activity, and language began.

The jackal, however, became jealous that the earth had language. By stealing the earth's clothing, which contained language, the jackal received the power of speech. Amma was so upset by this attack on the earth that he decided to create living things without her help. The Nummo realized Amma's decision meant that no more twins would be born. To make sure that the birth of twins would continue, they drew on the ground a picture of a male and a female. According to tradition, all humans have both a male and a female soul at birth. *See also* AFRICAN MYTHOLOGY; AMMA.

Nut

In Egyptian mythology, Nut was the sky goddess and the mother goddess of ancient Egypt. Egyptian artists often portrayed her as a woman arched over the earth god Geb, her twin brother and husband, with her fingers and toes touching the ground. Typically, her body was painted blue and covered with stars.

Nut and Geb, the children of the god Shu (Air) and goddess Tefnut (Moisture), were born locked together in a tight embrace. The sun god Ra ordered Shu to separate them, so Shu held his daughter high above the earth, creating room between Nut and Geb for other creatures to live. In another version of the myth, Ra climbed onto Nut's back and asked her to lift him into the heavens. As Nut rose higher, she became dizzy, but four gods steadied her legs, and Shu held up the middle of her body. In this way Nut's body became the sky, and Ra attached stars to her.

Angered by the marriage of Nut and Geb, Ra decreed that Nut could not bear children during any month of the year. Thoth, the god of wisdom, took pity on Nut and played a game with the moon—the regulator of time—that allowed him to create five extra days in the year. Because these days were not covered by Ra's decree, Nut was able to give birth to five children: Osiris†, Isis†, Set†, Nephthys, and Horus.

Nut's body divided the **cosmos** and helped keep the forces of **chaos** from breaking through the sky and overwhelming the earth. During the day, Ra sailed

This painting from the tomb of King Tutankhamen in Thebes shows the Egyptian ruler with the sky goddess Nut.

†See **Names and Places** at the end of this volume for further information.

cosmos the universe, especially as an orderly and harmonious system
chaos great disorder or confusion
underworld land of the dead

along Nut's body in a boat. When he reached her mouth, she swallowed him, bringing on the night. After traveling through Nut's body at night, Ra emerged again at dawn and brought on the day. In some myths, Nut plays an important role in the **underworld,** providing fresh air for the souls of the dead. *See also* EGYPTIAN MYTHOLOGY; ISIS; OSIRIS; RA (RE); THOTH.

Nu Wa

In Chinese mythology, Nu Wa is the goddess of order who created humans and saved the world from destruction. According to legend, Nu Wa came to earth before there were any people.

Nu Wa became lonely and decided to make copies of herself from mud in a pool. The figures she created came to life and wandered off to populate the earth. After a while, Nu Wa realized that it would take too long to fill the earth with people if she made each one by hand. So she took a rope, dipped it into the mud, and flung the drops of mud in all directions. Each drop became a separate human being. The people Nu Wa created by hand became the rich and powerful people in the world; those she flung as drops from the rope became the poor and the weak.

Another popular story recounts how Nu Wa saved the earth. The water god Gong Gong had tried to overthrow the fire god Zhu Rong. When Gong Gong failed, he became angry and rammed Imperfect Mountain with his head. The mountain, which supported the heavens, crumbled, tearing a hole in the sky and causing the ends of the earth to give way. The disorder that followed included fires and floods. Selecting several stones from a river, Nu Wa shaped them to repair the hole in the sky. She also slew a giant tortoise and used its legs to support the heavens. Nu Wa's actions restored the order of the universe and saved the world from destruction. *See also* CHINESE MYTHOLOGY.

Nyame

Nyame is the supreme being and creator **deity** worshiped by the Ashanti and Akan people in the West African country of Ghana. In mythology, Nyame appears in both male and female forms.

deity god or goddess

Often identified with the sun and the moon, Nyame is also associated with storms. In his role as the sun, he appears as a king known as Nyankopon. As the moon, Nyame represents the queen mother. Lightning that flashes during a storm is considered to be Nyame's thunderbolts, also called God's Axes. To honor the god, people often place stone axes in forked posts beside doorways. Near the posts, they keep pots that hold special offerings for Nyame. *See also* AFRICAN MYTHOLOGY.

Nymphs

In Greek mythology, nymphs were minor female **deities** associated with nature. Typically pictured as beautiful girls or young women, they could live for a very long time but were not **immortal.** Most nymphs were the daughters of Zeus† or of other gods. They generally had gentle natures and acted with kindness toward

In Greek mythology, different types of nymphs were associated with particular parts of the natural world. Nereids, such as the one seen in this fresco painting, lived in both saltwater and freshwater.

deity god or goddess
immortal able to live forever

satyr woodland deity that was part man and part goat or horse

underworld land of the dead

humans. However, some stories tell of nymphs who lured unsuspecting mortals to their deaths.

Different kinds of nymphs were associated with particular parts of the natural world. The Oceanids were sea nymphs, daughters of the sea god Oceanus. One of the Oceanids married the sea god Nereus, and their daughters became the Nereids, nymphs who dwelled in both freshwater and saltwater. Another group of water nymphs, the Naiads were freshwater spirits associated with fountains, streams, rivers, and other forms of running water. Forest nymphs were divided into Dryads, originally linked specifically with oak trees but later known as nymphs of woods and forests in general, and the Hamadryads, who dwelled inside particular trees and perished when the trees died. Other types of nymphs included the Orestiads or Oreads (mountain nymphs), Meliae (nymphs of ash trees), and Leimoniads (meadow nymphs).

Nymphs rarely had a central role in Greek myths. Usually they played supporting parts as the companions of gods and **satyrs.** The goddess Artemis†, for example, often had nymphs attending her when she went hunting. Nymphs also became the lovers or wives of gods or heroes. The Dryad Eurydice married the poet and musician Orpheus. After Eurydice died from a snakebite, Orpheus tried to retrieve her from the **underworld** but failed to meet the conditions set for her return.

Another nymph who gained mythic status as a wife was Oenone. Married to Paris, prince of Troy, Oenone predicted that if Paris left on a journey to Greece, the trip would be disastrous for Troy. During that trip, Paris eloped with Helen, the wife of the Spartan king, setting in motion the events that led to the Trojan

†See **Names and Places** at the end of this volume for further information.

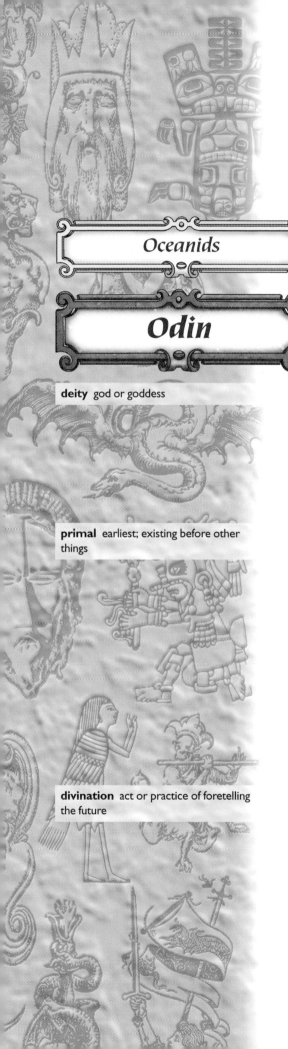

deity god or goddess

primal earliest; existing before other things

divination act or practice of foretelling the future

War† and the eventual destruction of Troy. When Paris lay wounded from fighting, Oenone refused to help him, even though she had the gift of healing. Eventually she relented and rushed to Troy to save her husband, but she arrived too late. Upon discovering that Paris had died, Oenone committed suicide. *See also* CALYPSO; ECHO; EURYDICE; PARIS; THETIS.

Oceanids

See *Nymphs.*

Odin

Odin was the ruler of the Aesir, a group of **deities** in Norse† mythology. Sometimes called Allfather, Odin played a central role in myths about the creation and destruction of the world. He was the god of battle and also of wisdom, magic, and poetry. His name means "fury" or "frenzy," the quality of fierce inspiration that guided warriors and poets alike. Odin probably originated in the myths of early Germanic peoples, who called him Woðanaz. The name of the fourth day of the week, Wednesday, comes from Woden's-day, the god's Old English name. Odin was married to Frigg, the guardian of marriage.

Myths. Odin spanned the history of the Norse mythic world from its creation to its destruction. Before the world existed, he and his two younger brothers, Vili and Ve, killed the **primal** frost giant Ymir. They used Ymir's bones, blood, and flesh to form the universe. Odin arranged the heavens for the gods, the middle world for humans and dwarfs, and the underworld for the dead. He then created the first man and woman from an ash tree and an elm tree.

Among the deities said to have been Odin's children were Balder and Thor†. Odin—the favorite deity of princes, nobles, and warriors—came to be seen as the supreme Norse god, the one to whom the other deities turned for help and advice. He ruled them from his palace Valhalla† in the heavenly realm called Asgard. As the god of war, Odin watched over warriors who fell in battle. Valkyries† carried the fallen ones straight to Valhalla. There Odin feasted them and prepared them for Ragnarok, the final battle in which the gods and the world were doomed to perish.

Odin was credited with great wisdom, including knowledge of magic and **divination.** He had paid a high price for this gift, however, giving one of his eyes in exchange for a drink from the well of Mimir. The waters of this well, which seeped from among the roots of the World Tree Yggdrasill, contained great wisdom. Another myth says that Odin stabbed himself with his magical spear, called Gungnir, and hung from Yggdrasill for nine days and nights in a living death. This self-sacrifice gave him knowledge of the runes, the Norse symbols used for writing and fortune-telling. Yet although Odin was wise, he could also be sly and treacherous. It was not unusual, for example, for him to break his word or to turn people against each other to start conflicts.

This engraved stone from the A.D. 700s shows the Norse god Odin on horseback in front of the great hall Val-halla. Spirits called the Valkyries conduct the bravest warriors to this place after they are slain in battle.

Odin had the power to change his appearance, and this shape shifting played a part in the myth that explains Odin's connection with poetry. The wisest being who ever lived was Kvasir, whom the gods had formed from their own saliva. Dwarfs killed Kvasir and mixed his blood with honey to form a potion that granted wisdom and the gift of poetry. A giant hid the potion in the middle of a mountain and set his daughter to guard it. Odin changed himself into a snake and slithered through a tiny hole in the mountain. Then taking the form of a handsome giant, he charmed the daughter into letting him drink the potion. Once Odin had swallowed it, he changed into an eagle and flew to Asgard, where he vomited the potion into three sacred vats. A few drops of the potion fell to the earth during his flight and became the inspiration of lesser human poets.

Another myth reveals Odin as both a treacherous figure and the enforcer of divine justice. He observed two young princes, Agnar and Geirrod. On Odin's advice, Geirrod sent Agnar out to sea in a boat and then reported that his brother had drowned. After Geirrod grew up and became king, he was tested when a man named Grimnir appeared in his court. Fearing that the man was a **sorcerer,** Geirrod had him tortured. However, the king's son showed pity on Grimnir and helped him. After predicting that Geirrod would kill himself with his own sword, Grimnir revealed that he was Odin. The king grabbed his sword to attack him but tripped and stabbed himself. Odin then set the kindly son on the throne.

Odin liked to wander the earth in the form of an old man wearing a blue cloak and a wide-brimmed hat that hid his one-eyed face. Often he was accompanied by wolves and ravens, flesh eaters that haunt battlefields. His ravens Hugin (Thought) and Munin (Memory) traveled around the world and the underworld each day, returning to tell their knowledge-loving master what they had seen. Odin occasionally rode an eight-legged horse named Sleipnir, who could travel at great speed through the air and across water.

sorcerer magician or wizard

cult group bound together by devotion to a particular person, belief, or god

patron special guardian, protector, or supporter
ritual ceremony that follows a set pattern

Worship. The **cult** of Odin flourished across much of northern Europe and gained strength in the A.D. 700s and 800s, the age of the Vikings. These Norse warriors and raiders, especially the fearsome fighters called the Berserks, regarded Odin as their special **patron.** Their ceremonies in his honor included human sacrifice. Some victims died by the spear or by fire. However, **ritual** hangings were especially important in the worship of Odin, who was sometimes called the Lord of the Gallows or the Hanging God

†*See **Names and Places** at the end of this volume for further information.*

because of his own mythic hanging on the tree Yggdrasill. When the Vikings raided Nantes, a town in northwestern France, in 842, they hanged many of the inhabitants, perhaps as an offering to Odin. *See also* BERSERKS; FRIGG; MIMIR; NORSE MYTHOLOGY; RAGNAROK; THOR; VALHALLA; YGGDRASILL; YMIR.

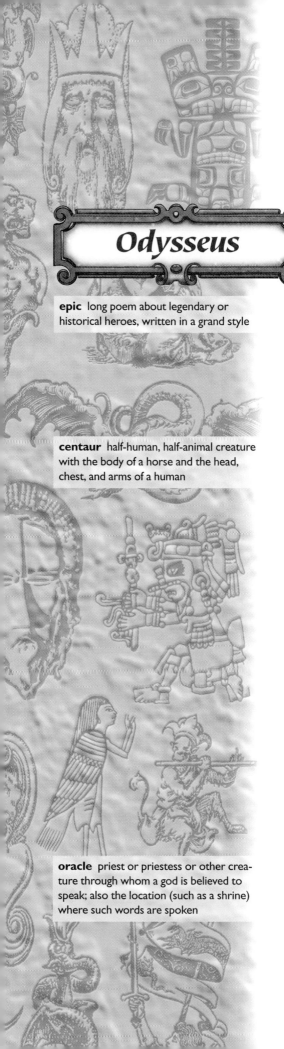

epic long poem about legendary or historical heroes, written in a grand style

centaur half-human, half-animal creature with the body of a horse and the head, chest, and arms of a human

oracle priest or priestess or other creature through whom a god is believed to speak; also the location (such as a shrine) where such words are spoken

Odysseus

In Greek mythology, Odysseus was a celebrated hero, best known for his role in the Trojan War† and for his ten-year journey home after the war. Odysseus (also known as Ulysses) appears as the central character in the *Odyssey,* an **epic** by the ancient Greek poet Homer, and he also plays a role in the *Iliad,* Homer's other major epic.

Early Life. Odysseus was generally said to be the son of Anticlea and of King Laertes of Ithaca. However, some stories maintain that his father was Sisyphus, founder of the city of Corinth and a cunning man who outwitted the god Hades†. This version says that Sisyphus seduced Anticlea before her marriage to Laertes and that Odysseus inherited his cleverness from Sisyphus.

Educated by the **centaur** Chiron, Odysseus began to display great strength and courage at an early age. While out hunting with his uncles and his grandfather, the young hero saved the adults by killing a wild boar. Before the creature died, however, it wounded Odysseus on the leg with its sharp tusk, leaving a permanent scar.

When Odysseus reached manhood, King Laertes stepped aside and let his son rule Ithaca. Around the same time, Odysseus began thinking of marriage. Like other young rulers and heroes in Greece, he desired Helen†, the beautiful daughter of King Tyndareus of Sparta. But Ithaca was a poor kingdom, and Odysseus had little hope of winning her. Nevertheless, he went to Sparta as a suitor.

While in Sparta, Odysseus displayed some of the cunning for which he became famous. Crowds of men had come to Sparta to seek the hand of Helen, and King Tyndareus feared what might happen when he chose one of them to marry his daughter. Odysseus advised the king to make all the suitors swear an oath to protect Helen and the man she married. The suitors agreed and thus accepted Menelaus when he was chosen to be Helen's husband. To show his gratitude, Tyndareus helped Odysseus win the hand of his niece Penelope, with whom the young hero had fallen in love. The couple returned to Ithaca, and Penelope bore Odysseus a son named Telemachus.

The Trojan War. When the Trojan War began, Odysseus tried to avoid participating. An **oracle** had told him that if he went to war, he would be away for 20 years and would return a beggar. So Odysseus pretended to be mad and sowed his fields with salt instead of seeds. When officials came to fetch him, they suspected a trick so they placed the infant Telemachus in the field. Odysseus stopped the plow to avoid killing the child, something a madman would not have done.

According to the *Iliad,* Odysseus's role in the Trojan War was mainly as an adviser and speaker rather than as a warrior. He helped discover the whereabouts of Achilles† and convince the great hero to join the war. He tricked Clytemnestra, wife of Agamemnon†, into sending her daughter Iphigenia to be sacrificed to the goddess Artemis† so that the Greek ships would have good winds for their voyage to Troy†. When a go-between was needed to settle quarrels between Agamemnon and Achilles, Odysseus stepped in. He also spied on the Trojans and discovered their plans.

Renowned for his eloquent and persuasive speaking, Odysseus was called upon many times to give advice. Although he fought bravely, he preferred strategy to heroics. When the Greeks captured the Trojan **prophet** Helenus and asked what they must do to capture Troy, it was Odysseus who accomplished the three tasks that were set. He persuaded Neoptolemus, the son of Achilles, to join the Greeks in battle. He used trickery to get Philoctetes, keeper of the bow and arrows of Hercules†, to join the fighting. He also used cunning to sneak into Troy and steal the Palladium, a statue of Athena believed to protect the city and bring it good fortune. Finally, Odysseus came up with the idea of pretending to sail away from Troy and leaving behind an enormous wooden horse—in which Greek soldiers were hidden. This trick enabled the Greeks to enter Troy at night and defeat the Trojans.

The Journey Home. After the fall of Troy, Odysseus set sail for Ithaca, but his voyage took ten long years because he incurred the anger of the sea god Poseidon†. His journey and adventures, described fully in the *Odyssey,* took the hero to many wondrous and dangerous places. Along the way, he lost all his companions and the treasure he had gotten from Troy. Arriving home at last after an absence of 20 years, Odysseus had to defeat rivals trying to take possession of his wife and his kingdom. Then he had to prove his identity to his wife, Penelope.

There are several different accounts of Odysseus's final years. Some stories say that he was accidentally killed by Telegonus, his son by the enchantress Circe. Other tales tell that he married Callidice, the queen of Thesprotia, and ruled there for a time while Penelope was still alive. Still other versions of the story report that Odysseus was forced into exile by relatives of the rivals he killed upon his return to Ithaca. ***See also*** **ACHILLES; CIRCE; GREEK MYTHOLOGY; HELEN OF TROY; HOMER; ILIAD, THE; ODYSSEY, THE; PENELOPE; TROJAN WAR.**

Odyssey, The

One of the great **epics** of ancient Greece, the *Odyssey* tells the story of the struggles and triumphs of the hero Odysseus as he made his way home after the Trojan War†. Pursued by the sea god Poseidon†, but aided both by his own cunning and by the goddess Athena†, Odysseus overcame countless obstacles during his long journey home. Along the way, he lost his ships, his crew, and the riches he had gained at Troy. The *Odyssey* is believed to be the work of the Greek poet Homer, who also composed the *Iliad.*

This mosaic from the A.D. 300s illustrates an episode from the *Odyssey*. Nearing an island, Odysseus and his men prepare to meet the Sirens, sea nymphs who lure sailors to death with beautiful singing.

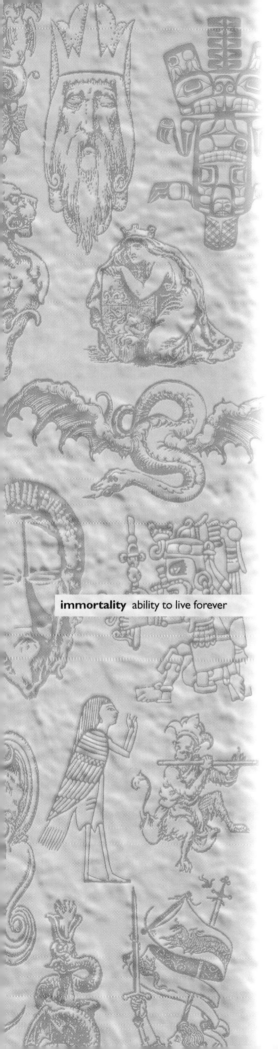

immortality ability to live forever

The Story Begins.

The *Odyssey* opens with Odysseus stranded on Ogygia, the island home of the enchantress Calypso. Almost ten years had passed since the end of the Trojan War. All the other Greek heroes were either dead or safely back in their homelands. Only Odysseus had yet to return home. Calypso was holding the hero captive, hoping that her beauty and offer of **immortality** would make him forget his wife, Penelope, and marry her.

Finally the gods took pity on Odysseus. Athena encouraged his son Telemachus to go on a quest in search of his father. The young man traveled to Pylos and then to Sparta, where he met Helen and Menelaus. Telemachus was proud when he learned of his father's fame. Meanwhile Zeus† sent Hermes† to command Calypso to let the hero leave. She reluctantly agreed, and Odysseus sailed from the island on a raft. While the hero was at sea, Poseidon sent a great storm that destroyed the raft. Saved by a sea goddess, Odysseus finally reached the land of the Phaeacians. The Phaeacians welcomed the stranger and treated him as an honored guest. In return, Odysseus revealed his name and told the Phaeacians about the adventures he had had since leaving Troy many years before.

Odysseus's Tale.

When the Trojan War ended, Odysseus set sail for his homeland of Ithaca with a number of companions in several ships. They first stopped in the land of the Cicones. After sacking the city there, they were driven off and suffered significant losses. Next they arrived at the land of the lotus-eaters, so named because the people there ate the honey-sweet fruit from the lotus plant. This fruit acted like a drug, and when some of the Greeks ate it,

103

they lost all desire to return home. Odysseus had to drag them to the ships and tie them down before he could set sail again.

The Greeks next arrived at the land of the Cyclopes, a race of one-eyed savage giants. When Odysseus and some of his men went into a large cave, the Cyclops Polyphemus trapped them inside by rolling a huge stone across the entrance. Polyphemus, a son of Poseidon, proceeded to kill and eat several of Odysseus's men, and the survivors lost nearly all hope of escaping. Odysseus came up with a plan. After blinding Polyphemus with a stake, he and his men escaped the cave by clinging to the undersides of the giant's sheep as they were let out to graze. The Greeks ran to their ships and set sail. Polyphemus hurled rocks at them and called on Poseidon to take revenge against Odysseus.

The Greeks landed next on the island of Aeolus, the keeper of the winds. Aeolus listened eagerly to Odysseus's tales of the Trojan War and gave the hero a bag containing all the storm winds. With these winds, Odysseus would be able to sail safely and quickly to Ithaca. After setting sail, however, his men became curious about the bag. Thinking that it might contain gold and jewels, they opened it and released the winds. The winds tossed the ships about and blew them back to the island of Aeolus. Aeolus refused to help Odysseus again and ordered the ships to leave.

After sailing for some time, Odysseus came to the land of the Laestrygonians, a race of cannibal giants. The giants destroyed all but one of his ships and ate many of his men. Barely escaping these dreadful creatures, Odysseus and his surviving companions traveled on to the island of Circe, a powerful enchantress. Circe cast a spell on some of Odysseus's men and turned them into pigs. Protected by a magical herb given to him by Hermes, Odysseus forced the enchantress to reverse her spell, and his men resumed their human form. Circe then invited Odysseus and his men to remain as her guests.

The Greeks stayed with Circe for a year. She told Odysseus that he must visit the **underworld** and consult the blind **prophet** Tiresias before returning to his homeland. Reluctantly and full of dread, Odysseus went to the kingdom of the dead. While there, he met his dead mother, Anticlea, and the spirits of Agamemnon†, Achilles†, and other Greek heroes. Tiresias told Odysseus what to expect and do during the rest of his journey and after he returned home to Ithaca.

After leaving the underworld, Odysseus went back to Circe's island for a short stay. Before he set sail again, the enchantress warned him about some of the dangers he still faced and advised him how to survive them. The first of these dangers was the Sirens, evil sea nymphs who lured sailors to their deaths with their beautiful singing. Odysseus ordered his men to plug their ears with wax so they would not hear the Sirens' song. Wanting to hear their songs himself, he had his men tie him to the ship's mast so that he could not be lured away.

Odysseus and his men next faced the monsters Scylla and Charybdis, who guarded a narrow channel through which their

underworld land of the dead
prophet one who claims to have received divine messages or insights

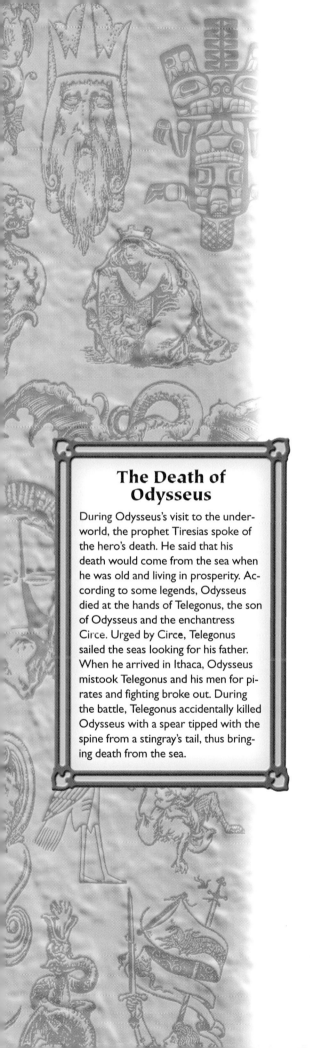

ship had to pass. Odysseus barely escaped the monsters, and he lost some of his men to them. The survivors reached the island of Helios with its herds of sacred sheep and cattle. Both Tiresias and Circe had warned Odysseus not to harm any of these animals, but his men ignored the warning and killed some of them as a sacrifice and for food. When Helios complained to the gods, Zeus sent a storm that destroyed Odysseus's ship and drowned all his remaining companions. Alone, the hero reached the island of the enchantress Calypso, the point at which the *Odyssey* began.

Return to Ithaca. After hearing the story of Odysseus's adventures, the Phaeacians gave him a ship, and he set sail for Ithaca. This time Poseidon put aside his anger and allowed Odysseus to reach home, but he punished the Phaeacians for helping him. In Ithaca, the goddess Athena appeared before Odysseus and reassured him that his wife, Penelope, had been faithful. She had resisted the attentions of many suitors who desired both her and his kingdom and were occupying his house. Disguised as a beggar by Athena, Odysseus stayed with a loyal swineherd while the goddess went to fetch his son Telemachus from Sparta.

When Telemachus returned, Odysseus revealed himself to his son, and together they plotted the undoing of Penelope's suitors. Still disguised as a beggar, Odysseus went to the palace and walked among the suitors. Later that night, Penelope asked to speak with the beggar, whom she did not recognize as her husband. She asked what he knew of Odysseus and told him how she had fended off the suitors. She had refused to marry until she finished weaving a shroud for Odysseus's father, Laertes. She would weave the shroud by day and then unravel her work at night. This worked until her trick was discovered. While they were talking, an old nurse came in to wash the beggar's feet. Recognizing a scar on his leg, she knew him to be Odysseus, but he swore her to secrecy.

Penelope announced to the suitors that she would marry the man who could string the bow of Odysseus and shoot an arrow through 12 axes placed in a row. The suitors all failed. Telemachus then demanded that the beggar be allowed to try. The beggar accomplished the feat. Then throwing off his disguise, he and Telemachus fought and killed all the suitors.

At first Penelope could not believe that this man was truly her long-absent husband. Only when Odysseus revealed a secret that only they knew—that their bed was carved from a tree and remained rooted in the ground—did she acknowledge and embrace him.

On the day following this reunion, Odysseus visited his father, Laertes, and learned that the families of the dead suitors were planning to attack. When the battle was about to begin, Athena frightened the attackers away. She then assured Odysseus that his reign would be long and would bring lasting peace to Ithaca. The *Odyssey* ends with this promise of peace and happiness. ***See also*** AEOLUS; ATHENA; CALYPSO; CIRCE; CYCLOPES; GREEK MYTHOLOGY; HOMER; ILIAD, THE; ODYSSEUS; PENELOPE; POSEIDON; SCYLLA AND CHARYBDIS; SIRENS; TIRESIAS; TROJAN WAR.

The Death of Odysseus

During Odysseus's visit to the underworld, the prophet Tiresias spoke of the hero's death. He said that his death would come from the sea when he was old and living in prosperity. According to some legends, Odysseus died at the hands of Telegonus, the son of Odysseus and the enchantress Circe. Urged by Circe, Telegonus sailed the seas looking for his father. When he arrived in Ithaca, Odysseus mistook Telegonus and his men for pirates and fighting broke out. During the battle, Telegonus accidentally killed Odysseus with a spear tipped with the spine from a stingray's tail, thus bringing death from the sea.

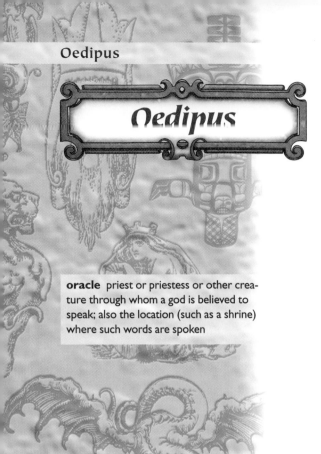

Oedipus

oracle priest or priestess or other creature through whom a god is believed to speak; also the location (such as a shrine) where such words are spoken

destiny future or fate of an individual or thing

Oedipus was a tragic hero of Greek mythology, a king doomed to a dire fate because he unknowingly killed his father and married his mother. His story is the tale of someone who, because he did not know his true identity, followed the wrong path in life. Once he had set foot on that path, his best qualities could not save him from the results of actions that violated the laws of gods and men. Oedipus represents two enduring themes of Greek myth and drama: the flawed nature of humanity and an individual's powerlessness against the course of destiny in a harsh universe.

The Myth. The story begins with a son born to King Laius and Queen Jocasta of Thebes†. The **oracle** at Delphi† told them that their child would grow up to murder Laius and marry Jocasta. Horrified, the king fastened the infant's feet together with a large pin and left him on a mountainside to die.

However, shepherds found the baby—who became known as Oedipus, or "swollen foot"—and took him to the city of Corinth. There King Polybus and Queen Merope adopted him and raised him to think that he was their own son. When Oedipus was grown, however, someone told him that he was not the son of Polybus. Oedipus went to Delphi to ask the oracle about his parentage. The answer he received was, "You are the man fated to murder his father and marry his mother."

Like Laius and Jocasta, Oedipus was determined to avoid the **destiny** predicted for him. Believing that the oracle had said he was fated to kill Polybus and marry Merope, he vowed never to return to Corinth. Instead, he headed toward Thebes.

Along the way, Oedipus came to a narrow road between cliffs. There he met an older man in a chariot coming the other way. The two quarreled over who should give way, and Oedipus killed the stranger and went on to Thebes. He found the city in great distress. He learned that a monster called the Sphinx was terrorizing the Thebans by devouring them when they failed to answer its riddle and that King Laius had been murdered on his way to seek help from the Delphic oracle. The riddle of the Sphinx was "What walks on four legs in the morning, two at noon, and three in the evening?" Oedipus gave the correct answer: "A human being, who crawls as an infant, walks erect in maturity, and leans on a staff in old age." With this answer, Oedipus not only defeated the Sphinx, which killed itself in rage, but won the throne of the dead king and the hand in marriage of the king's widow, Jocasta.

This painting on the base of an ancient cup shows Oedipus and the Sphinx, a winged monster with the body of a lion and the head of a woman. To rescue the people of Thebes from the monster's terror, Oedipus had to answer its riddle.

† *See **Names and Places** at the end of this volume for further information.*

prophet one who claims to have received divine messages or insights

epic long poem about legendary or historical heroes, written in a grand style

Oedipus and Jocasta lived happily for a time and had two sons and two daughters. Then a dreadful plague came upon Thebes. A **prophet** declared that the plague would not end until the Thebans drove out the murderer of Laius, who was within the city. A messenger then arrived from Corinth, announcing the death of King Polybus and asking Oedipus to return and rule the Corinthians. Oedipus told Jocasta what the oracle had predicted for him and expressed relief that the danger of his murdering Polybus was past. Jocasta told him not to fear oracles, for the oracle had said that her first husband would be killed by his own son, and instead he had been murdered by a stranger on the road to Delphi.

Suddenly Oedipus remembered that fatal encounter on the road and knew that he had met and killed his real father, Laius. At the same time, Jocasta realized that the scars on Oedipus's feet marked him as the baby whose feet Laius had pinned together so long ago. Faced with the fact that she had married her own son and the murderer of Laius, she hanged herself. Oedipus seized a pin from her dress and blinded himself with it.

Some accounts say that Oedipus was banished at once from Thebes, while others relate that he lived a miserable existence there, despised by all, until his children grew up. Eventually he was driven into exile, accompanied by his two daughters, Antigone and Ismene. After years of lonely wandering, he arrived in Athens, where he found refuge in a grove of trees called Colonus. By this time, warring factions in Thebes wanted him to return to that city, believing that his body would bring it luck. However, Oedipus died at Colonus, and the presence of his grave there was said to bring good fortune to Athens.

Legacy. Thus runs the best-known account of the myth of Oedipus, preserved in *Oedipus the King* and *Oedipus at Colonus,* two dramas by the ancient Greek playwright Sophocles. Most versions of the story have followed the pattern that Sophocles set down, although an earlier version, mentioned by Homer in the Greek **epics** the *Iliad* and the *Odyssey,* says that after Oedipus's identity was revealed, Jocasta hanged herself. Oedipus, however, continued to rule Thebes, died in battle, and was buried with honor.

The story of Oedipus has inspired artists and thinkers since ancient times. The Roman philosopher Seneca wrote a tragedy entitled *Oedipus* that influenced writers such as England's John Dryden and Alexander Pope and France's Voltaire and Pierre Corneille. Later artistic treatments of the Oedipus story include a translation of Sophocles' work by Irish poet William Butler Yeats, a play entitled *The Infernal Machine* by Jean Cocteau of France, music by Russian composer Igor Stravinsky, and the movie *Oedipus Rex* by Italian filmmaker Pier Paolo Pasolini. Sigmund Freud, one of the founders of modern psychiatry, used the term *Oedipus complex* to refer to a psychological state in which boys or men experience hostility toward their fathers and are attracted to their mothers. ***See also*** ANTIGONE; GREEK MYTHOLOGY; HOMER; JOCASTA; SPHINX.

Ogun

Ogun, or Ogun Onire, is the god of war and iron of the Yoruba people of West Africa. In Yoruba lore, Ogun and the other gods climbed down to earth on a spiderweb. When creation was completed, the gods realized that people needed to clear more land in the forest where they lived. Unfortunately, the only tools available were made of soft metal, a material not suitable for cutting down trees. However, Ogun had been given the secret of iron by Orunmila, son of the supreme god Olorun, and he used an iron ax to clear the forest. Ogun later shared the secret of iron with the other gods and with humans. He also showed them how to shape the iron into weapons.

Though a fierce god, Ogun is not evil and will help those who pray to him. Yoruba blacksmiths have traditionally sacrificed dogs to Ogun, and each year they hold a three-day festival in his honor. ***See also*** AFRICAN MYTHOLOGY; OLORUN.

Ohrmazd

See *Ahura Mazda.*

Oisin

In Celtic† mythology, Oisin (or Ossian) was a great warrior poet and the son of Finn, leader of a warrior band known as the Fianna. Legend says that an enchanter had changed Finn's lover, the goddess Sadb, into a deer. One day while looking for Sadb, Finn came upon Oisin. He realized the boy was his son after Oisin told him that his mother was a gentle deer. Finn raised Oisin and trained him to be a warrior, but Oisin also inherited his mother's gift of eloquent speech. He became a great poet as well as one of the fiercest warriors of the Fianna.

As a man, Oisin met Niamh, daughter of the sea god Manannan Mac Lir. She invited him to visit her father's kingdom of Tir Na Nog, the Land of Ever Young. Oisin stayed there for 300 years, although it seemed like only a few weeks. Lonely for home, he asked if he might visit Ireland. Niamh agreed and sent him back on horseback, warning him not to touch the ground or he would never return to Tir Na Nog. However, Oisin slipped and fell to the ground, instantly becoming a blind old man who never saw his beloved Niamh again. In 1761, a writer named James Macpherson published what was claimed to be a translation of Ossian's poems. Their authenticity was disproved by Samuel Johnson 14 years later. ***See also*** CELTIC MYTHOLOGY; FINN.

Old Man

Old Man, also known as Napi, is a creator god and **trickster** figure in the mythology of the Blackfoot Indians of North America. He is said to have created the world and all the creatures in it.

To make humans, Old Man fashioned figures out of clay and breathed life into them. The first man he created was satisfied with the world, but the first woman was not. She wanted to know

† See **Names and Places** at the end of this volume for further information.

trickster mischievous figure appearing in various forms in the folktales and mythology of many different peoples

if people would ever die and if life would be the same forever as it was now. The question surprised Old Man, who had not really thought about whether humans would live forever.

To answer the question, Old Man threw a piece of wood into the river. If the wood floated, he said, humans would die and come back to life after four days. If it sank, they would die and never live again. The wood floated, but the woman was still not satisfied. She decided to try the test herself. However, instead of a piece of wood, she threw a stone into the water. The stone sank, so Old Man decreed that death for humans would last forever. Similar stories, in which a trickster throws an object into water to determine whether humans will live forever, appear in the mythologies of other Native American cultures.

Another story says that after the world was filled with people, Old Man decided to experience life for himself. He lured a woman to a nest of rattlesnakes, and she mated with one of them. When her husband found out, he cut off her head. But the woman's headless body chased her two children. They saved themselves by throwing a piece of magic moss on the ground. A river formed, and the body drowned. One of the children was Old Man, who continued to live on earth before he died and disappeared behind the mountains.

The Blackfoot identify Old Man with the sun, which also disappears behind the mountains every evening. Like the sun returning in the morning, Old Man is also supposed to come back to earth one day. ***See also*** NATIVE AMERICAN MYTHOLOGY; TRICKSTERS.

Olorun

deity god or goddess
pantheon all the gods of a particular culture
chaos great disorder or confusion

In the mythology of the Yoruba people of West Africa, Olorun is the most powerful and wisest **deity**. The all-knowing god takes an active role in the affairs of both heaven and earth. Head of the Yoruba **pantheon**, Olorun is also known as Olofin-Orun (Lord of Heaven), Oba-Orun (King of the Sky), and Olodumare (Almighty).

According to Yoruba legend, Olorun was one of two original creator gods. The other was the goddess Olokun. In the beginning, the universe consisted only of sky and a formless **chaos** of marshy water. Olorun ruled the sky, while Olokun ruled the vast marshy waters below. There were thousands of other gods, but none had as much knowledge or power as Olorun.

Although Olokun was content with her watery kingdom, a lesser god named Obatala had ideas about improving her kingdom. He went to Olorun and suggested the creation of solid land, with fields and forests, hills and valleys, and various living things to populate it. Olorun agreed that this would be good and gave Obatala permission to create land.

Obatala went to Orunmila, the eldest son of Olorun, and asked how he should proceed. Orunmila told Obatala to gather gold to make a chain that could be lowered from the sky to the waters below. When the chain was finished, Orunmila gave Obatala a snail's shell filled with sand, a white hen, a black cat, and a palm nut.

chameleon lizard that can change color

oracle priest or priestess or other creature through whom a god is believed to speak; also the location (such as a shrine) where such words are spoken

Obatala lowered himself on the chain and poured the sand on the waters. He then released the hen, which scratched at the sand and scattered it in all directions. Anyplace the sand fell became dry land. Stepping onto the land—known as Ife—Obatala built a house, grew palm trees from the palm nut, and lived with the black cat as his companion.

Obatala later became lonely and built clay figures. Olorun made these figures into humans by breathing life into them. Many gods descended from the sky to live on earth, and Olorun told them to listen to the prayers of humans and protect them.

Not pleased by these acts of creation, the water goddess Olokun tried to flood the land to regain the area she had lost. However, Orunmila used his powers to make the waters recede. Angry that the sky god's son had defeated her, Olokun challenged Olorun to a weaving contest to see who was the more powerful.

Olokun was a weaver of unequaled skill and knowledge, but every time she made a beautiful cloth, Agemo the **chameleon**— who carried messages for Olorun—changed the color of its skin to match her weaving. When Olokun saw that even Olorun's messenger could duplicate her finest cloths, she accepted defeat and acknowledged Olorun as the supreme god. **See also** AFRICAN MYTHOLOGY; ILE-IFE.

Orestes

In Greek mythology, Orestes was the prince who avenged the murder of his father, King Agamemnon of Mycenae, by killing his own mother, Clytemnestra. Orestes' sisters Iphigenia and Electra play important roles in his story. A number of ancient writers and artists, including Greek playwrights Aeschylus and Euripides, have been inspired by the myth of Orestes.

Orestes was still a child when Agamemnon sailed off to fight in the Trojan War†. While the king was away, Clytemnestra took a lover, Aegisthus. She may have been driven to infidelity by a desire for revenge. To obtain favorable winds to carry his ships to Troy, Agamemnon had sacrificed their young daughter Iphigenia to the goddess Artemis†.

When Agamemnon returned to Mycenae at the end of the war, he was murdered by his wife and her lover. Aegisthus seized the throne. Electra feared that her young brother Orestes, the true heir to the throne, might be in danger, and she took him to stay with their father's old friend King Strophius of Phocis. Strophius raised Orestes with his own son Pylades, and the two boys became close friends.

When he grew up, Orestes visited Delphi† and asked the **oracle** of Apollo† what he should do to avenge his father's murder. The oracle replied that Orestes must kill his mother and her lover. So Orestes and his friend Pylades went to Mycenae disguised as messengers, and they met secretly with Electra to plan the murders. Then with the help of Electra and Pylades, Orestes killed Aegisthus and Clytemnestra, despite her pleas that a son should not kill his own mother.

†See **Names and Places** at the end of this volume for further information.

There are various versions of what happened next. In some accounts, Orestes received praise for avenging his father's murder. In others, the crime of matricide—the murder of one's mother—was seen as a great sin that deserved great punishment. In these stories, Orestes was pursued relentlessly by the Furies, female spirits of justice and vengeance who drove men mad.

In the version of the story told by Aeschylus, Orestes sought refuge from the Furies at Delphi, home of the oracle that had ordered him to avenge his father's death. Through the oracle, Apollo instructed Orestes to go to Athens and present his case to the Areopagus, an ancient court of elders. During the trial that followed, Orestes received the support of Apollo as well as that of the goddess Athena†, who cast the deciding vote in his favor. The angry Furies were eventually calmed, and they stopped pursuing Orestes.

In another version of Orestes' story, told by the Greek playwright Euripides, the verdict of the Areopagus did not soothe the Furies. Apollo told Orestes that he could put an end to their torment if he went to Tauris, a land of dangerous barbarians, and recovered a sacred statue of Artemis. Orestes and Pylades journeyed to Tauris but were captured by the barbarians. They were brought before the head priestess, who happened to be Orestes' sister Iphigenia. Iphigenia had been rescued from the sacrifice at Aulis before the Trojan War. She helped Orestes and Pylades escape with the statue, and she returned with them to Greece.

Upon returning to Greece, Orestes became ruler of Mycenae and Argos. Eventually he married Hermione, the daughter of Menelaus and Helen† of Sparta. **See also** AGAMEMNON; APOLLO; ATHENA; CLYTEMNESTRA; ELECTRA; FURIES; GREEK MYTHOLOGY; IPHIGENIA.

Orion

Orion was a giant hunter in Greek mythology. Some stories say he was the son of Zeus†, Poseidon†, or Hermes†. Others claim that he was born from a bull's hide that was buried after the king of Boeotia urinated on it.

Orion went to the island of Chios, where King Oenopion asked him to drive all the wild beasts from the land. In return, Oenopion promised Orion his daughter Merope in marriage. However, the king later refused to honor the agreement. Orion got drunk and raped Merope, and Oenopion blinded him. After recovering his vision, Orion went to Crete to live and hunt with the goddess Artemis†.

There are several accounts of his death. One story says that Eos, the goddess of the dawn, fell in love with Orion and that Artemis killed him out of jealousy. According to another version, Orion and Artemis were considering marriage, but she was tricked into killing him by her brother Apollo†. In still another myth, Orion pursued seven sisters known as the Pleiades. To save them from Orion's attentions, Zeus turned them into stars. Orion, too, became a constellation, which appears to chase the Pleiades through the heavens. **See also** PLEIADES.

Oro

patron special guardian, protector, or supporter

cult group bound together by devotion to a particular person, belief, or god

Orpheus

Muse one of nine sister goddesses who presided over the arts and sciences

lyre stringed instrument similar to a small harp

nymph minor goddess of nature, usually represented as young and beautiful

underworld land of the dead

In Polynesian mythology, Oro is the war god of the Pacific island of Tahiti. Oro enjoys fighting and demands human sacrifices during wartime. However, in peacetime he becomes a god of peace and is worshiped as Oro-i-te-tea-moe ("Oro of the spear laid down").

According to legend, Oro was the son of Hina-tu-a-uta and the creator god Ta'aroa. When Oro decided to marry, he created a rainbow between the heavens and the earth and traveled across it to a place known as the Red-ridged Mountain. There he met Vai-raumati, the daughter of Ta'ata, the first man. Vai-raumati became Oro's wife and bore him a son, Hoa-tabu-i-te-ra'i, who became a great ruler. Oro also had three daughters: Toi-mata, Ai-tupuai, and Mahu-fatu-rau.

Oro created and serves as **patron** of a Tahitian **cult** called the Areoi, whose members are known for their artistic skills and talents as performers and entertainers. Priests of the Areoi honor Oro with public festivals that include offerings of red feathers and the sacrifice of young pigs. *See also* POLYNESIAN MYTHOLOGY; TA'AROA.

In Greek mythology, Orpheus was a musician who sang and played so beautifully that even animals, rocks, and trees danced to his tunes. He was the son of Calliope, the **Muse** of epic poetry, and of the god Apollo†. It was Apollo who gave Orpheus his first **lyre,** the instrument that he always played.

Orpheus accompanied Jason† and the Argonauts on their quest for the Golden Fleece† and used his music several times to ease their journey. On one occasion, he calmed the sea with his playing; another time, he saved the Argonauts from the deadly Sirens by playing so loudly that they could not hear the Sirens' songs. He also stopped the Argonauts from quarreling with a song about the origins of the universe.

Orpheus fell in love with the **nymph** Eurydice. Shortly after their marriage, Eurydice was bitten by a snake and died. The grieving Orpheus refused to play or sing for a long time. Finally he decided to go to the **underworld** to find Eurydice. His playing enchanted Charon, the ferryman who carried the souls of the dead across the river Styx into the underworld. Charon agreed to take Orpheus across the river, even though he was not dead. Orpheus's music also tamed Cerberus, the monstrous three-headed dog who guarded the gates of the underworld. Even Hades and Persephone, king and queen of the underworld, could not resist his playing. They agreed to let him take Eurydice back to earth—on one condition. He was not to look back at her until they had both reached the surface. Orpheus led his wife from the underworld, and when he reached the surface, he was so overjoyed that he looked back to share the moment with Eurydice. Immediately she disappeared into the underworld.

Orpheus spent the rest of his life grieving for his lost wife. In time his grief infuriated the Maenads, a group of women who worshiped the god Dionysus†. To punish Orpheus for neglecting their

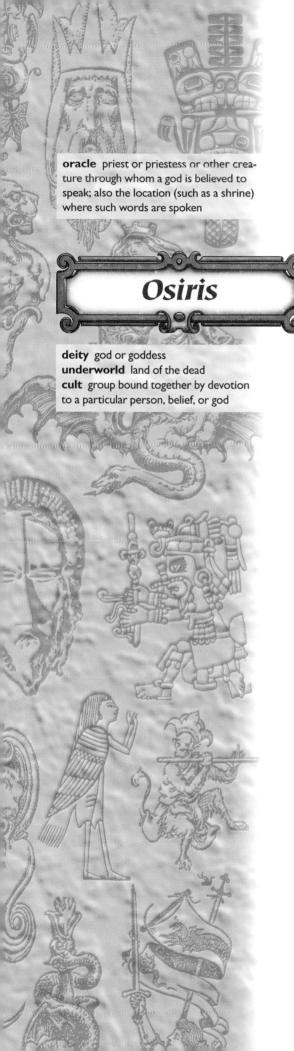

oracle priest or priestess or other creature through whom a god is believed to speak; also the location (such as a shrine) where such words are spoken

Osiris

deity god or goddess
underworld land of the dead
cult group bound together by devotion to a particular person, belief, or god

attentions, they tore him to pieces. The Muses gathered up the pieces of his body and buried them, but the Maenads threw his head and his lyre into the river Hebrus. The head continued to sing, and the lyre continued to play, and both eventually floated down to the sea, finally coming to rest on the island of Lesbos. The head became an **oracle** that rivaled the oracle to Apollo at Delphi†. The gods placed the lyre in the heavens as a constellation. *See also* ARGONAUTS; CALLIOPE; EURYDICE; MUSES.

One of the most important **deities** of ancient Egypt, Osiris was god of the **underworld** and judge of the dead. He also represented the idea of renewal and rebirth in the afterlife. Osiris appears in many Egyptian myths and legends, and his **cult** spread beyond Egypt.

Little is known about the origin of Osiris in Egyptian mythology. In very ancient times, he may have been a local god of the city of Busiris in Lower Egypt. It is possible that he was originally an underworld or fertility deity or a legendary hero. By about 2400 B.C., his cult had become firmly established and began to spread throughout much of Egypt.

In Egyptian mythology, Osiris was the son of the sky goddess Nut and the earth god Geb, brother and husband of Isis† and father of Horus. He supposedly served as a ruler of early Egypt, where his followers honored him as both god and man. Credited with civilizing the country, Osiris introduced agriculture and various crafts, established laws, and taught Egyptians how to worship the gods.

Osiris traveled to other parts of the world to civilize people there as well. Upon his return to Egypt, his jealous brother Set†

Osiris, the Egyptian god of the underworld and the judge of the dead, stands in the center of this piece of jewelry.

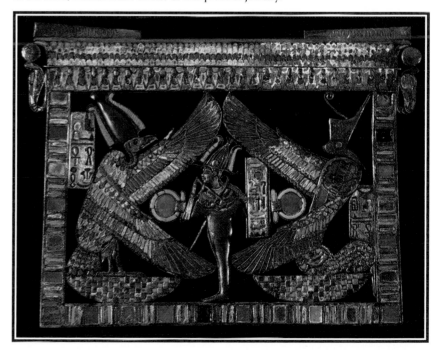

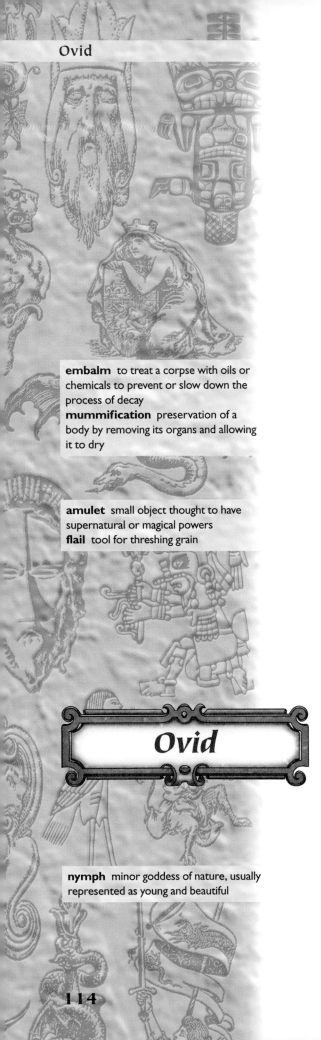

embalm to treat a corpse with oils or chemicals to prevent or slow down the process of decay
mummification preservation of a body by removing its organs and allowing it to dry

amulet small object thought to have supernatural or magical powers
flail tool for threshing grain

Ovid

nymph minor goddess of nature, usually represented as young and beautiful

plotted with others to kill him. They built a beautifully decorated box, tricked Osiris into getting into it, sealed the box, and then threw it into the Nile River. The box floated into the Mediterranean Sea and to the land of Byblos in Phoenicia†.

Overcome with grief at the loss of her husband, Isis searched high and low for his body. Eventually she found it. Bringing the body back to Egypt, she magically restored Osiris to life long enough to conceive a son, Horus. Isis then hid the body in a secluded spot. Set discovered it, cut it into pieces, and scattered them throughout Egypt. Isis gathered up the pieces, reassembled them, and restored Osiris to life once again.

Instead of staying on earth, he chose to become lord of the Egyptian underworld. As king of the dead, he sat in judgment of dead souls, measuring the worth of their lives and determining their punishment or reward. The gods Anubis and Thoth assisted him. In his role as god of the dead, Osiris became associated with the Egyptian practices of **embalming** and **mummification** and was the object of intense worship.

When Osiris became lord of the underworld, his son Horus became ruler of Egypt. The Egyptians believed that when a pharaoh, or king, died, he became the god Osiris. The new pharaoh represented Horus, the god of the living.

In ancient Egyptian art, Osiris is usually portrayed as a bearded king wrapped in cloth like a mummy. He generally wears the crown of Upper Egypt, has an **amulet** around his neck, and holds a crook and a **flail,** symbols of his powers as god of fertility and the underworld. Although Osiris's main cult center was at the city of Abydos, the god was worshiped intensely throughout Egypt. The appeal of a god who offered the promise of life after death was so strong that worship of Osiris also spread to other parts of the ancient world, most notably Greece and Rome. ***See also*** AFTERLIFE; ANUBIS; BOOK OF THE DEAD, THE; EGYPTIAN MYTHOLOGY; HORUS; ISIS; NUT; RA (RE); SET; THOTH; UNDERWORLD.

Born in 43 B.C. to a respectable Roman family, Ovid was a poet best known for his collection of myths and legends titled the *Metamorphoses.* As expected of a young man of his station, he studied rhetoric—oratory—in both Rome and Athens and served in several minor government posts. However, writing poetry was his first love, and he quickly gave up public life to pursue this art.

The *Metamorphoses* tells many of the ancient myths and legends of Greece, Rome, and the Near East. All the stories have a common theme: change, or metamorphosis. For example, when the **nymph** Daphne is pursued by Apollo†, she escapes by being turned into a tree. Other works by Ovid also present myths and legends. The *Heroides* is a collection of fictional letters from mythical women to the men they love, such as letters from Penelope to her long-absent husband, Ulysses (Odysseus†). The *Fasti* describes stories connected with ancient Roman religious festivals.

In A.D. 8, the Roman emperor Augustus exiled the poet to the city of Tomis on the Black Sea. Though never really explained, Ovid's exile appears to have been connected to a poem he wrote that was considered immoral and to a scandal in the **imperial** family. Ovid died nine years later in Tomis. Ovid's work with stories from Greek and Roman mythology influenced writers and artists centuries later. *See also* APOLLO; METAMORPHOSES, THE.

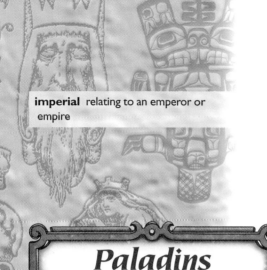

imperial relating to an emperor or empire

Paladins

medieval relating to the Middle Ages in Europe, a period from about A.D. 500 to 1500

In **medieval** European legend, the paladins were 12 brave knights who were loyal followers of Charlemagne, the king of the Franks and founder of the Holy Roman Empire. The name *paladin*—from a word meaning a person attached to the court—implies that the knights may have resided at the royal palace.

The paladins appear primarily in a series of legends surrounding Charlemagne, his adventures, and the history of the Frankish kingdom. Many were said to play important roles in the Crusades and battles against the Muslims. Among the most famous works in which some of the paladins appear is the *Chanson de Roland* (Song of Roland), a French poem written in the 1000s. A number of paladins also appear in Italian legends, though under slightly different names.

Perhaps the most famous paladin was Roland, the nephew of Charlemagne and main character in the *Chanson de Roland.* The other paladins included Roland's cousin, Rinaldo of Montalban; Namo, the duke of Bavaria; Salomon, the king of Brittany; Astolpho, an English duke; Fierambras, son of the king of Spain; Turpin, an archbishop; Ogier, a Danish prince; Florismart, a friend of Roland; Malagig, a magician; Olivier, a close friend of Roland; and Ganelon, a Frankish count who eventually betrayed the other paladins and became their enemy. *See also* CHARLEMAGNE; HEROES; ROLAND.

The paladins, 12 brave knights who served King Charlemagne, appear in many medieval legends.

Pan

nymph minor goddess of nature, usually represented as young and beautiful

Pan was a Greek fertility god associated with flocks and shepherds. From his waist down, he looked like a goat, but above the waist, he had human features, except for goat's ears and horns. Most often considered the son of Hermes†, he was abandoned by his mother at birth and raised by **nymphs.**

An accomplished musician, Pan played a reed pipe called a syrinx, named after a nymph that Pan had pursued. The nymph asked the gods to change her into a group of reeds to save her from the attentions of Pan. Pan then gathered these reeds and fashioned them into the instrument.

Titan one of a family of giants who ruled the earth until overthrown by the Greek gods of Olympus

Pandora

Titan one of a family of giants who ruled the earth until overthrown by the Greek gods of Olympus

Pan Gu

chaos great disorder or confusion
cosmic large or universal in scale; having to do with the universe

Although Pan was a playful figure who enjoyed chasing nymphs, he could be very ill-tempered if his sleep was disturbed. He could also cause irrational fear, hence the origin of the English word *panic.* In Greek mythology, Pan helped Zeus† and the other gods of Olympus† overthrow the early gods called **Titans.** He did this by blowing into a shell and making a loud roar that frightened the Titans. *See also* GREEK MYTHOLOGY.

In Greek mythology, Pandora was the woman who brought evil into the world and caused humankind's downfall. She was sent to earth by Zeus, king of the gods, who wanted to take revenge on the **Titan** Prometheus†. Prometheus had created men and had stolen fire from the gods and given it to the men. Zeus ordered the divine crafts worker Hephaestus† to form the first woman, Pandora, from clay. Athena† gave life to this creation, Aphrodite† made her beautiful, and Hermes† taught her to be cunning and deceitful.

Zeus sent Pandora down to earth, but Prometheus—whose name means "forethought"—would have nothing to do with her. However, his brother Epimetheus—afterthought—married Pandora, who brought with her a sealed jar or box as a gift from the gods. Some accounts say that Epimetheus opened Pandora's box; others maintain that Pandora herself opened it. Inside the container were disease, old age, poverty, evil, war, and all the other ills that have plagued humans ever since. When the box was opened, they flew out into the world, leaving only Hope at the bottom of the box to give people a scrap of comfort. A few accounts say that the box contained all the good things that Prometheus planned to give the human race, but when Pandora gave in to curiosity and opened the box, she let all the blessings escape.

Pandora and Epimetheus had a daughter, Pyrrha, who appears in a Greek myth about a great flood. Pyrrha and her husband, Deucalion, were the flood's sole survivors and became the parents of a new human race. *See also* ADAM AND EVE; GREEK MYTHOLOGY; PROMETHEUS.

In Chinese mythology, Pan Gu was the first living creature and the creator of the world. Among his acts of creation were the separation of the earth and sky, the placement of the stars and planets in the heavens, and the shaping of the earth's surface.

At the beginning of time, the universe consisted only of dark **chaos,** in the form of a **cosmic** egg. Within the egg lay a sleeping giant named Pan Gu. One day Pan Gu awoke and stretched, causing the egg to split open. After Pan Gu emerged, the light, pure parts of the egg became the sky, while the heavy parts formed the earth. This separation of the earth and sky marked the beginning of yin and yang, the two opposing forces of the universe.

Already gigantic in size, Pan Gu grew 10 feet taller each day. This went on for 18,000 years, and as Pan Gu became taller, he

†*See* **Names and Places** *at the end of this volume for further information.*

pushed the earth and sky farther apart and shaped them with his tools until they reached their present position and appearance. Exhausted by his work, Pan Gu finally fell asleep and died.

When Pan Gu died, parts of his body were transformed into different features of the world. According to some stories, his head, arms, feet, and stomach became great mountains that help to anchor the world and mark its boundaries. Other stories say that Pan Gu's breath was transformed into wind and clouds; his voice became thunder; and his eyes became the sun and moon. Pan Gu's blood formed rivers and seas; his veins turned into roads and paths; his sweat became rain and dew; his bones and teeth turned into rock and metal; his flesh changed into soil; the hair on his head became the stars; and the hair on his body turned into vegetation.

Some myths say that humans developed from fleas and parasites that fell from Pan Gu's body and beard. Other stories, however, tell how Pan Gu created humans by shaping them from clay and leaving them in the sun to dry. When a sudden rain began to fall, Pan Gu hastily wrapped up the clay figures, damaging some in the process, which explains why some humans are crippled or disabled.

Although a giant, Pan Gu is usually portrayed in Chinese art as a little person clothed in a bearskin or leaves, holding a hammer and chisel or the cosmic egg of creation. Sometimes he is shown working with his tools to create the world, accompanied by four **supernatural** creatures: a unicorn, tortoise, phoenix, and dragon. The earliest known myths of Pan Gu date from the A.D. 200s to 500s. Though primarily a figure in Taoist belief, he also appears sometimes in Chinese Buddhist mythology. *See also* BUDDHISM AND MYTHOLOGY; CHINESE MYTHOLOGY; CREATION STORIES; DRAGONS; GIANTS; PHOENIX; UNICORN; YIN AND YANG.

supernatural related to forces beyond the normal world; magical or miraculous

Papa

See *Rangi and Papa.*

Paris

seer one who can predict the future

In Greek mythology, Paris was a handsome young prince who eloped with the most beautiful woman in the world and caused the Trojan War†. The son of King Priam and Queen Hecuba of Troy†, Paris seemed destined for disaster from birth. Shortly before he was born, his mother dreamed that she gave birth to a flaming torch that destroyed Troy. Priam consulted a **seer,** who warned the king that the dream foretold disaster for the city. He advised Priam to have the baby killed.

When Paris was born, Priam ordered a shepherd named Agelaus to take the infant and abandon him on Mount Ida. Agelaus followed the instructions, but when he returned to the mountain after several days, he found the infant still alive. Moved by pity, the shepherd took the baby home and raised him as his own son. Paris grew into a very handsome young man. In time he married Oenone, a mountain **nymph,** and lived with her in the mountains, where he tended cattle.

nymph minor goddess of nature, usually represented as young and beautiful

117

Paris, a young Trojan prince, had to choose which goddess—Hera, Aphrodite, or Athena—was most beautiful. His decision, known as the judgment of Paris, is depicted on a vase from the 500s B.C.

prophecy foretelling of what is to come; also something that is predicted

One day Priam sent servants to the mountains to fetch a bull as a prize for a festival. When the men chose Paris's favorite bull, Paris decided to go to Troy, enter the festival contests, and win the animal back. The young man won all the events, defeating Priam's other sons. Agelaus revealed Paris's true identity to Priam and, forgetting the **prophecy,** Priam welcomed Paris and restored him to his rightful place in the royal household.

Some time later, Zeus† chose Paris to decide which of three goddesses was the most beautiful. Eris, the goddess of strife or discord, had tossed a golden apple inscribed with the phrase "For the Fairest" into the midst of the guests at a wedding. Hera†, Aphrodite†, and Athena† all claimed the prize. Each goddess promised Paris a special gift if he decided in her favor. Hera promised to make him a powerful ruler. Athena promised him wisdom and victory in battle. Aphrodite offered Paris the love of the most beautiful woman in the world, Helen of Sparta. Paris awarded the golden apple to Aphrodite. His decision, known as "the judgment of Paris," enraged Hera and Athena, who began to plan their revenge.

Paris abandoned his wife, Oenone, and went to Sparta. King Menelaus welcomed Paris and introduced him to Helen, his wife. Aided by Aphrodite, Paris won the beautiful queen's heart. While Menelaus was away, Paris sailed off with Helen, taking part of Sparta's treasure with him. According to some stories, Hera sent a storm that nearly destroyed their ship, but Aphrodite protected them until they reached Troy.

In the war that followed, Paris played only a minor role. As a warrior, Paris was greatly inferior to his brother Hector†, and his cowardly nature won little respect. At one point, Hector forced Paris to fight a single-handed combat with Menelaus after the Trojans and Greeks agreed that this would end the war. When Menelaus came close to winning, Aphrodite stepped in and rescued Paris, and the war continued.

Paris later killed the Greek hero Achilles† by shooting an arrow into his heel, the only spot where Achilles could be wounded. Then Paris himself was struck by a poisoned arrow. He was carried off the battlefield and taken to his wife, Oenone, who had the gift of healing. Angry that Paris had abandoned her, Oenone refused to help him. When she relented shortly afterward, it was too late. Paris was dead. ***See also*** ACHILLES; APHRODITE; HECTOR; HECUBA; HELEN OF TROY; ILIAD, THE; MENELAUS; PRIAM; TROJAN WAR; ZEUS.

†*See **Names and Places** at the end of this volume for further information.*

Patrick, St.

patron special guardian, protector, or supporter

pagan term used by early Christians to describe non-Christians and non-Christian beliefs

St. Patrick, the **patron** saint of Ireland, was born in Britain around A.D. 389. He was the son of a Roman official. At the age of 16, Patrick was captured by raiders from Ireland and carried back to their homeland. After working as a shepherd for six years, he had a dream in which he was told that a ship was prepared for him to escape his captivity.

The accounts of his journeys at this time differ. He either traveled back to Britain or sailed to Gaul (present-day France). In any event, it seems likely that he visited France, where he joined a monastery and was ordained as a priest. According to his autobiography, the *Confessio,* he had another dream, in which the Irish asked him to return to their island. St. Patrick left his monastery to travel among the **pagan** Irish chieftains, converting them and their people to Christianity.

Several legends have sprung up around St. Patrick, the most famous one claiming that he drove all the snakes out of Ireland and into the sea. A popular myth holds that he used the shamrock to explain to a pagan Irishman the Holy Trinity, the idea that God consists of three persons: Father, Son, and Holy Spirit. The shamrock is now Ireland's national flower, worn by the Irish on St. Patrick's feast day, March 17.

Pecos Bill

In the legends of the American West, Pecos Bill was a larger-than-life cowboy known for his amazing exploits. Created by journalists in the late 1800s, Pecos Bill was supposed to have been born in Texas and raised by coyotes after his parents lost him while crossing the Pecos River.

While still a child, Bill grew to be much bigger than most men. He wrestled and rode mountain lions, used rattlesnakes as lassos, and fought grizzly bears with his bare hands. When he was about ten, he discovered that he was a human and not a coyote. He decided to live among people and become a cowboy. He invented the rope lasso and six-shooter and gained a reputation for killing bad guys. However, he never harmed women or children.

Eventually Pecos Bill started ranching. After his cows ate all the grass in Texas, he moved to New Mexico, where he dug the Rio Grande to get water for his cattle. While living in New Mexico, Bill had a horse called Widow-maker that only he could ride. He invented fence posts, ten-gallon hats, and the bucking bronco.

One day a tornado appeared on the horizon. When the twister approached, Bill jumped on it and rode it like a bucking bronco. In an effort to shake Bill, the tornado rained so hard that it carved out the Grand Canyon. Bill finally fell off in California, hitting the ground with such force that he formed Death Valley.

One day when he was getting on in years, Pecos Bill was walking down the street in Laredo, Texas. He saw a man from Boston wearing a fancy cowboy suit and asking stupid questions about the West. Bill took one look at the man, lay down on the sidewalk, and laughed until he died. Another story, however, says

Pegasus

Gorgon one of three ugly monsters who had snakes for hair, staring eyes, and huge wings

Muse one of nine sister goddesses who presided over the arts and sciences

Pele

deity god or goddess

According to Polynesian stories, the powerful and destructive fire goddess Pele lives in the volcano of Kilauea on the island of Hawaii.

that he died after eating a meal of barbed wire washed down with nitroglycerin. In any event, that was the end of Pecos Bill. *See also* HEROES; MODERN MYTHOLOGY.

A winged horse in Greek mythology, Pegasus was supposedly the offspring of the sea god Poseidon and the **Gorgon** Medusa. According to legend, Pegasus was born from the blood that spurted from Medusa's neck when the hero Perseus killed her. Pegasus served Perseus until his death and afterward went to the home of the **Muses.** The water that gave the Muses their inspiration had dried up, so Pegasus stamped his hoof and created a spring.

With the help of the goddess Athena†, the hero Bellerophon later tamed Pegasus and rode the horse when he slew the monster called the Chimaera. Later Bellerophon tried to ride Pegasus to the top of Mount Olympus† so that he could join the Greek gods. However, Zeus† caused a fly to bite Pegasus, and the horse threw Bellerophon to earth, crippling him for life. *See also* BELLEROPHON; MEDUSA; MUSES; PERSEUS.

In Polynesian mythology, Pele is the fire goddess of Hawaii. A powerful and destructive **deity,** she is said to live in the crater of the volcano of Kilauea on the big island of Hawaii. Perhaps the best-known deity of Hawaii, Pele appears in many myths and legends.

Like many figures in Polynesian mythology, Pele is a great traveler. She came to Hawaii from the island of Tahiti, but the reasons for her trip vary. Some myths say that she fled Tahiti to escape the anger of her older sister, whose husband she had stolen. In other stories, she was driven from Tahiti by a great flood or went to Hawaii simply because she wished to travel.

Pele's arrival in the Hawaiian Islands was accompanied by mighty volcanic eruptions. She visited various islands looking for a place to live, but the sea constantly flooded the sites she chose for a home. She finally found refuge in the volcano of Kilauea.

Once settled in Kilauea, Pele traveled to a neighboring island and fell in love with a young chief named Lohiau. After returning home, Pele sent her young sister Hi'iaka to fetch the chief. She gave Hi'iaka **supernatural** powers, which the young woman used to overcome various obstacles during the journey.

When Hi'iaka arrived at the home of Lohiau, she found that the young chief had died of a broken heart caused by his longing for Pele. Hi'iaka caught his spirit and used her magical powers to restore him to life. Meanwhile, Pele became impatient, imagining that her sister had stolen Lohiau's love. The enraged Pele sent a stream of lava that killed Hopoe, the dearest friend of Hi'iaka.

When Hi'iaka finally brought the young chief to Kilauea, she learned of the death of Hopoe. Grief stricken, she embraced Lohiau, whom she had come to love. Pele saw this and sent more lava to kill Lohiau. Protected by her magical powers, Hi'iaka later restored Lohiau to life again and went to live with him on his home island.

† *See **Names and Places** at the end of this volume for further information.*

supernatural related to forces beyond the normal world; magical or miraculous

patron special guardian, protector, or supporter

Peleus

nymph minor goddess of nature, usually represented as young and beautiful

immortal able to live forever

Penelope

nymph minor goddess of nature, usually represented as young and beautiful

omen sign of future events

Many other legends deal with Pele's fiery temper and reveal how unpredictable and dangerous she could be. In some myths, she also appears as a water goddess who caused the seas to encircle the islands of Hawaii. Both Pele and Hi'iaka are considered **patrons** of magic and sorcery as well as of the hula, the ancient sacred dance of Hawaii. *See also* POLYNESIAN MYTHOLOGY.

Peleus, a figure from Greek mythology, is best known as the father of the Greek hero Achilles† and the husband of the sea **nymph** Thetis. As a youth, Peleus was banished from his homeland after he killed one of his brothers. Peleus suffered misfortune everywhere he went and fled from two kingdoms during his life.

Zeus† himself arranged for Peleus to marry Thetis. Zeus loved Thetis, but he decided to abandon his courtship when he learned that the fates had declared that Thetis's son would become more powerful than his father. After marrying Peleus, Thetis bore him a son named Achilles. She tried to make the infant **immortal** by holding him in fire to burn away his human weakness. Peleus, however, was horrified and stopped Thetis, leaving Achilles' heel vulnerable. Angered, Thetis abandoned her family and returned to the sea.

Peleus became king of Phthia, but he was overthrown by his enemies when Achilles left for the Trojan War†. Thetis took pity on Peleus and brought him back to her sea cave, where they lived together forever. *See also* ACHILLES; GREEK MYTHOLOGY; THETIS.

The wife of the hero Odysseus† in Greek mythology, Penelope was celebrated for her faithfulness, patience, and feminine virtue. For the 20 years that her husband was away during and after the Trojan War†, Penelope remained true to him and helped prevent his kingdom from falling into other hands.

Penelope's parents were Prince Icarius of Sparta and the **nymph** Periboea. Periboea hid her infant daughter as soon as she was born, knowing that Icarius had wanted a son. As soon as Icarius discovered the baby girl, he threw her into the sea to drown. However, a family of ducks rescued her. Seeing this as an **omen,** Icarius named the child Penelope (after the Greek word for "duck") and raised her as his favorite child.

When Penelope reached womanhood, Odysseus asked for her hand in marriage. Although reluctant to part with his daughter, Icarius agreed, and Penelope went with her new husband to his home on the island of Ithaca. Penelope and Odysseus were deeply in love, so it was with great sorrow that Odysseus later left her and their infant son, Telemachus, to fight in the Trojan War.

The Trojan War lasted ten years, and it took Odysseus another ten years to get home to Ithaca. During that time, Penelope received the attentions of many suitors. For a while, she put them off by saying that she would consider marriage only after she finished weaving a shroud for her father-in-law, Laertes, who was

grieving over Odysseus's absence. Each day Penelope would sit weaving the cloth, but at night she would secretly unravel her work. After three years, a servant revealed Penelope's secret, and she had to finish the shroud. When her suitors became insistent again, Penelope announced that she would marry the man who could shoot an arrow through the loops on a row of 12 ax heads.

Unknown to Penelope, Odysseus had arrived home disguised as a beggar. He wanted to review the situation in his kingdom before revealing his return. The disguised Odysseus won the archery contest and then killed all the suitors with help from his son Telemachus. At first Penelope would not believe that Odysseus was her husband, for the gods had hidden his identity from her. However, Odysseus revealed his true identity by telling Penelope a secret about their marriage that only they knew, and the loving couple were finally reunited. *See also* GREEK MYTHOLOGY; ODYSSEUS; ODYSSEY, THE.

Persephone

underworld land of the dead

In Greek mythology, Persephone was the beautiful daughter of Zeus, king of the gods, and of Demeter, the goddess of agriculture. Persephone became queen of the **underworld** when she married Hades. The Romans knew her as Proserpina.

As a young girl, Persephone traveled around the world with her mother, who ruled over the earth and everything that grew from it. Hades, the god of the underworld, wanted her for his wife. He spoke to his brother Zeus, who agreed to help him. One day Zeus caused a beautiful flower to grow in a place where Persephone was walking. The girl stooped to admire the flower. At that moment, Hades rode out of the underworld on a chariot, seized Persephone, and took her back to his kingdom.

Unaware of these events, Demeter searched everywhere for her missing daughter. For days she wandered the earth with a flaming torch in each hand and in her distress caused all crops to wither and die. Famine threatened. Zeus feared that humankind would perish, leaving no one to perform sacrifices to the gods. He begged Demeter to restore life to the earth, but she refused to do so unless Persephone was returned to her.

Zeus sent Mercury, messenger of the gods, to fetch Persephone from the underworld. As she was leaving, Hades gave her a sweet pomegranate, and she ate several of its seeds. Persephone did not realize that eating food from the underworld meant that she could not leave it. As a result, Zeus declared that Persephone

Hades, the god of the underworld, wanted the beautiful Persephone as his wife. This marble sculpture by Bernini from the 1620s shows Hades carrying Persephone off to his kingdom.

† *See Names and Places at the end of this volume for further information.*

would have to spend part of each year in the underworld with Hades and the remainder of the year on earth with her mother.

The story of Persephone was used to explain the cycle of the seasons. For most of the year, the earth is alive and covered with growing plants. However, during the barren months, when Persephone is with Hades, Demeter mourns her daughter's absence, and the earth lies bare and lifeless. *See also* DEMETER; HADES.

Perseus

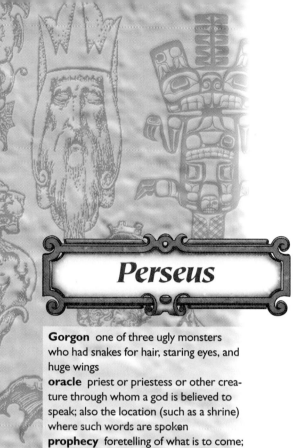

Gorgon one of three ugly monsters who had snakes for hair, staring eyes, and huge wings

oracle priest or priestess or other creature through whom a god is believed to speak; also the location (such as a shrine) where such words are spoken

prophecy foretelling of what is to come; also something that is predicted

nymph minor goddess of nature, usually represented as young and beautiful

In Greek mythology, Perseus was the heroic slayer of the **Gorgon** Medusa†. His mother was Danaë, daughter of King Acrisius of Argos. Before Perseus's birth, an **oracle** predicted that Danaë would bear a child who would one day kill his grandfather. Terrified by this **prophecy,** Acrisius imprisoned his daughter in a tower. However, Danaë received a visit in the tower from Zeus†, who had taken the form of a shower of gold, and she became pregnant.

After Danaë gave birth to Perseus, Acrisius had his daughter and her child locked in a box, which he threw into the sea. The box came ashore on the island of Seriphos and was found by Dictys, a fisherman. Dictys sheltered Danaë and Perseus in his home, and they remained with him for many years.

When Perseus had grown into a young man, King Polydectes of Seriphos fell in love with Danaë and tried to persuade her to marry him. Danaë refused, and Perseus protected his mother from the unwanted advances. Hoping to rid himself of Perseus, Polydectes set him a seemingly impossible task. Perseus was to obtain the head of Medusa†, a monster so hideous that anyone who even glanced at her face turned to stone.

Perseus received gifts from the gods to help him in his task: a pair of winged sandals, a sword, a helmet that made the wearer invisible, and a bronze shield from Athena† that was polished to shine like a mirror. Perseus then visted the Graeae, three old hags who were sisters of the Gorgons and who shared a single eye. Seizing their eye, he demanded to know where he could find the Gorgons. When they told him, Perseus threw the eye into a lake so that the Graeae could not warn their sisters.

With the winged sandals, Perseus flew to the home of the Gorgons. When he reached their cave, he advanced toward Medusa using Athena's shield as a mirror to avoid looking directly at the monster. Then he took the sword and cut off Medusa's head, which he placed in a bag. Drops of Medusa's blood that touched the ground changed into the winged horse Pegasus. Wearing the helmet that made him invisible, Perseus flew off on Pegasus.

On his way home, Perseus came upon the giant Atlas†, who held up the sky. Atlas tried to stop Perseus, but the hero took out the head of Medusa and turned the giant to stone. Next Perseus saw a beautiful woman chained to a rock. This was Andromeda, left as a sacrifice to a sea monster after her mother, Cassiopea, had boasted of her beauty and offended the sea **nymphs** known as the Nereids. Perseus killed the sea monster, rescued Andromeda, and asked her to marry him.

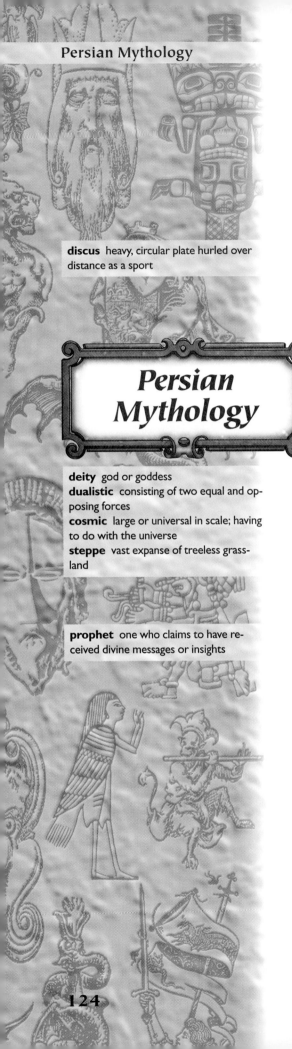

discus heavy, circular plate hurled over distance as a sport

deity god or goddess
dualistic consisting of two equal and opposing forces
cosmic large or universal in scale; having to do with the universe
steppe vast expanse of treeless grassland

prophet one who claims to have received divine messages or insights

Arriving back in Seriphos, Perseus found that his mother had taken refuge in the temple of Athena to avoid the advances of Polydectes. Furious, Perseus used Medusa's head to turn Polydectes and his soldiers to stone. Perseus returned the winged sandals, helmet, and shield to the gods and gave the head of Medusa to Athena, who placed it on her shield. He then took Andromeda to Argos, the kingdom of his grandfather Acrisius.

Hearing that Perseus had arrived, Acrisius fled to Thessaly, mindful of the prophecy made years before. Later, however, Perseus took part in an athletic contest there and threw a **discus** that accidentally killed Acrisius. The prophecy was fulfilled. *See also* ANDROMEDA; ATHENA; ATLAS; CASSIOPEA; DANAË; GORGONS; HEROES; MEDUSA; PEGASUS.

Persian Mythology

Persian mythology developed in what is now Iran after about 1500 B.C. About a thousand years later, a religion known as Zoroastrianism emerged in the region. It held on to many of the earlier beliefs but added new themes, **deities,** and myths. The result was a mythology based on a **dualistic** vision: a **cosmic** conflict between good and evil.

Background and Sources. The roots of Persian mythology lie in the **steppes** of southern Russia and Central Asia. Between 1500 and 1000 B.C., Indo-European peoples migrated south from the steppes into the regions now known as Turkey, Iran, and northern India. Those who settled in Iran became the Persians. Their mythology had much in common with that of the early Hindus and probably developed from a common Indo-European source. In time, the Persians also absorbed influences from Mesopotamia† on their western border.

The religious reformer and **prophet** Zoroaster (probably born around 628 B.C.) founded the faith that dominated Persia until the arrival of Islam in the A.D. 600s. Apart from somewhat unreliable accounts by ancient Greek historians, the earliest information about Persian mythology comes from Zoroastrianism's sacred book, the *Zend-Avesta* or *Avesta.* Much of the original *Zend-Avesta* was lost after Alexander the Great conquered Persia in 334 B.C. What survives is a set of writings gathered and arranged between A.D. 200 and 600. One section, the *Gathas,* consists of songs believed to have been composed by Zoroaster. Much mythological material can be found in another section containing *Yashts,* hymns addressed to angels and heroes.

Major Deities and Figures. The driving forces of Persian mythology were two powerful gods, sometimes presented as twin brothers. Ahura Mazda was the creator, a god of light, truth, and goodness. His enemy Ahriman, the spirit of darkness, lies, and evil, created only destructive things such as vermin, disease, and demons. The world was their battlefield. Although they were equally matched during this period of history, Ahura Mazda was fated to win

† *See **Names and Places** at the end of this volume for further information.*

the fight. For this reason, Ahura Mazda, the Wise Lord, was the supreme deity of Persian mythology. The Zoroastrians identified him with purifying fire and tended fires on towers as part of their worship.

The ancient Persian **pantheon** also included Mithras, a god associated with war, the sun, and law and order, who became the object of a widespread **cult** in the Roman empire. Anahita was a goddess of water and fertility. Verethraghna, a god of war and victory, appeared on earth in ten forms: as wind, a bull, a horse, a camel, a boar, a youth, a raven, a ram, a buck, and a man. Zoroaster reduced the role of these and other traditional deities and emphasized Ahura Mazda as supreme god. Religious scholars see this move as an early step toward **monotheism.** However, Ahura Mazda was said to have created seven archangels, called the Amesha Spentas, who represented truth, power, **immortality,** and other aspects of his being. These archangels may have taken over some features of the pre-Zoroastrian gods.

Heroes and kings also figured in Persian myth and legend. The hero Traetaona battled Azhi Dahaka, a three-headed demon controlled by Ahriman. When Traetaona stabbed the demon in the chest, snakes and lizards poured from the wound. To prevent the demon from poisoning the world, Traetaona locked him inside a mountain where he will remain until the world comes to an end. When that happens, Azhi Dahaka will break free—but then another hero, Keresaspa, will kill him.

The legendary king Bahram Gur appeared often in poems and tales as the inventor of poetry and a mighty hunter. The greatest hero was the warrior Rustum, whose adventures appear in the **epic** *Shah Namah* (Book of Kings), written by the poet Firdawsī around A.D. 1010.

Major Themes and Myths. The main theme of Persian mythology was the battle between good and evil. Ahura Mazda and Ahriman were not the only ones involved. Hosts of angels called the Yazatas and good spirits or *ashavans* fought on Ahura Mazda's side. Ahriman headed an army of evil spirits known as *dregvants* and of demons called *devas*. Humans took part in the conflict as well. Each person had to choose whether to follow the truth or the lie. Plants, animals, and other things could be good or evil, depending on whether Ahura Mazda or Ahriman created and controlled them.

Ahura Mazda made the world. Creation began when he cast a beam of his pure light into the empty void between him and Ahriman, who had attacked him. Ahura Mazda uttered a prayer that silenced Ahriman for 3,000 years, while Ahriman created the Amesha Spentas and the Yazatas. Ahura Mazda's final creation was Gayomart, the first man. Ahriman then awoke and began his evil work, sending a female demon to make Gayomart sicken and die.

Gayomart's body became the silver and gold in the earth, and in death he fertilized the ground so that a plant grew and became a man and a woman. These two people, Masha and Mashyoi, were

pantheon all the gods of a particular culture

cult group bound together by devotion to a particular person, belief, or god

monotheism belief in only one god

immortality ability to live forever

Star Wars

Perhaps influenced by stargazing Babylonian† astronomers, the ancient Iranians associated some of their deities with the stars. The star Sirius represented the rain god Tishtrya, whose main role was to battle Apausha, an evil star of drought. Tishtrya, in the form of a white stallion, and Apausha, a hideous black horse, fought for three days. Then with Ahura Mazda's help, Tishtrya defeated Apausha. Tishtrya and other star gods who protected agriculture also took charge of battling meteors, or shooting stars, which the Persians believed to be witches.

epic long poem about legendary or historical heroes, written in a grand style

This Persian drawing illustrates a scene from the epic *Shah Namah*. Written around A.D. 1010, the poem recounts the adventures of the hero Rustum.

the parents of the human race. Ahriman deceived them into thinking that he was their creator, and when they repeated this lie, evil and suffering entered the world. Zoroastrians believed that after 3,000 years, Zoroaster came into the world to break Ahriman's hold, leaving the two powers to fight into the future.

The legend of Rustum shows the part human heroes play in the great drama of good and evil. Rustum was so strong and brave that the king made him head of the army. Then the White Demon seized the king, and Rustum set out to rescue him. In the course of his travels, Rustum encountered a lion, a desert, a dragon, a demoness, and a demon army. He overcame all these obstacles with the help of his faithful horse Ruksh and a warrior named Aulad, whom he defeated in combat and who then became an ally. Rustum's adventure ended in a cave, the lair of the White Demon, where Rustum tore out the demon's heart.

Death in Persian mythology involved a journey into the afterlife. The soul of the dead person had to cross a bridge called Chinvat. Good souls found the bridge to be a wide and comfortable beam leading to heaven. For the wicked, it was a razor-sharp blade from which they fell headlong into hell.

Zoroastrianism was one of the first belief systems to include a vision of the end of the world. It would be signaled by the appearance of three saviors, sons of Zoroaster. Upon the arrival of Hushedar, the first savior, the sun would stand still for 10 days, and people would stop eating meat. When Hushedar-mar, the second savior, appeared, the sun would halt for 20 days, and people would stop drinking milk. Just as the world neared a state of purity, however, the evil demon Azhi Dahaka would break free from his mountain prison. Only after he had been killed would Soshyant, the third savior, arrive. People would stop eating plants and live only on water, and each soldier of good would fight and defeat a particular evil enemy.

Then the world would be enveloped in fire and molten metal for three days. Everyone who has ever lived would return to life to cross the fire, but only the wicked would suffer from the heat. This final judgment would purge sin and evil from the world, leaving an innocent human race in a cleansed world to worship Ahura Mazda.

Legacy. Persian religion and mythology had far-reaching influence. Historians of mythology think that certain beliefs in the Jewish,

† See **Names and Places** at the end of this volume for further information.

Christian, and Islamic faiths probably grew out of Persian traditions. The tendency of Zoroastrianism toward monotheism—turning multiple gods into aspects of one god—may also have helped shape those faiths.

Unlike some ancient belief systems, Persian mythology remains alive outside the covers of old books. It has survived continuously for thousands of years, and isolated groups of Iranians still worship Ahura Mazda. Other Zoroastrian communities exist in India, where the descendants of immigrants from Iran are known as Parsis or Parsees, a reference to their Persian origin. *See also* AHRIMAN; AHURA MAZDA; ANGELS; MITHRAS.

Phaedra

In Greek mythology, Phaedra was the daughter of King Minos and Queen Pasiphae of Crete and the younger sister of Ariadne. Phaedra married Theseus, king of Athens and slayer of the beast known as the Minotaur. Earlier, Ariadne had helped him kill the Minotaur and escape from Crete.

Theseus had a son named Hippolytus from a previous marriage to an Amazon queen, and after his marriage to Phaedra, they went to see him. Phaedra fell madly in love with Hippolytus, but he was disgusted by her feelings. Rejected, Phaedra killed herself and left a note saying that Hippolytus had raped her. When Theseus found the note, he asked the god Poseidon† to take revenge on Hippolytus. One day as Hippolytus was driving his chariot by the seashore, Poseidon sent a sea monster to frighten Hippolytus's horses. The horses bolted, tangling Hippolytus in the reins and killing him. The Greek playwright Euripides used the story of Phaedra and Hippolytus as the basis for his tragedy *Hippolytus*. *See also* ARIADNE; MINOS; THESEUS.

Phaethon

nymph minor goddess of nature, usually represented as young and beautiful

In Greek mythology, Phaethon was the son of the sun god Helios and the sea **nymph** Clymene. Phaethon's friends teased him because they did not believe that the sun was his father. Phaethon journeyed to Helios's palace to determine the truth. Helios replied that he was Phaethon's father and promised to grant his son a wish.

Phaethon asked to drive his father's chariot across the sky. Helios tried to discourage Phaethon, for no one except the sun could control the horses that pulled the chariot. However, Phaethon did not listen to the warning and insisted on driving the chariot. Helios could not take back his promise, so he let the youth take the reins. Soon after the chariot rose into the sky, Phaethon lost control of the horses, causing the sun to come too near the earth and burn it. To stop further destruction, Zeus† killed Phaethon with a thunderbolt, and the boy fell into the Eridanus River. Phaethon's sisters mourned for him so much that they turned into poplar trees on the banks of the river, and the tears they shed hardened into drops of amber.

Philemon

See *Baucis and Philemon*.

127

Philomela

In Greek mythology, Philomela was the daughter of Pandion, a legendary king of Athens. Her sister Procne married Tereus, king of Thrace, and went to live with him in Thrace. After five years, Procne wanted to see her sister. Tereus agreed to go to Athens and bring Philomela back for a visit. However, Tereus found Philomela so beautiful that he raped her. Then he cut out her tongue so she could not tell what had happened and hid her. He told Procne that her sister was dead.

Unable to speak, Philomela wove a tapestry depicting the story and arranged for an old woman to take it to Procne. When Procne saw the weaving, she asked the woman to lead her to Philomela. After rescuing her sister, Procne planned revenge on her husband. She killed their son Itys and served him to Tereus for supper. At the end of the meal, Philomela appeared and threw the boy's head on the table. Realizing what had happened, Tereus chased the women and tried to kill them. But before he could catch them, the gods transformed them all into birds. Tereus became a hawk (or a hoopoe), while Procne became a nightingale and Philomela a swallow. Roman writers reversed these roles, making Philomela a nightingale and Procne a swallow. The myth appears in Ovid's *Metamorphoses*†.

Phoenix

The phoenix is a legendary bird mentioned in Greek, Roman, and Egyptian mythology. According to ancient writers, the phoenix lived for 500 years, then died and was reborn. It had brilliant golden and scarlet feathers and grew to the size of an eagle.

Just before dying, the phoenix built a nest of fragrant herbs and spices, including cinnamon and myrrh. Then it set the nest on fire and died in the flames. However, a new phoenix rose from the ashes. When the young bird was strong enough, it placed the ashes of the dead phoenix in an egg made of myrrh. Then the young phoenix carried the egg to Heliopolis, the Egyptian city of the sun, and placed it on the altar of the sun god Ra (Re).

The phoenix was associated with **immortality** and eternal rebirth in Egypt, and the Romans used it on coins to symbolize Rome, the Eternal City. Early Christians saw the phoenix as a symbol of **resurrection.** The bird also appears as a sacred figure in both Chinese and Japanese mythology. ***See also*** BIRDS IN MYTHOLOGY.

immortality ability to live forever

resurrection coming to life again; rising from the dead

Pied Piper of Hamelin

The Pied Piper is the man who rid the town of Hamelin of rats. According to a **medieval** legend, the north German town of Hamelin was overrun with rats in 1284. Then one day, a mysterious man in a multicolored outfit appeared and offered to take care of the rats for a fee. After the people of Hamelin agreed to the deal, the man played his pipe and led the rats out of town.

Afterward, the people refused to pay the piper. So he came back a short time later and once again played his pipe. This time however, it was the children of Hamelin who followed him away. He led them to a cave in the mountains, where they disappeared.

medieval relating to the Middle Ages in Europe, a period from about A.D. 500 to 1500

†*See **Names and Places** at the end of this volume for further information.*

Another version of the story claims that the piper led the children to Transylvania, where they founded a colony. The story of the Pied Piper appears in a poem by the English writer Robert Browning.

Plants in Mythology

immortality ability to live forever

deity god or goddess

In many cases, human life ends with death and burial in the ground. Plants are just the opposite. They emerge from the earth and draw nourishment from it. For this reason, many mythological traditions associate plants with birth or rebirth and with the eternal cycle of life springing forth from death.

The magical plant or herb of **immortality** sought by Gilgamesh, the hero of ancient Mesopotamian mythology, provides one example of how myths use plants as symbols of life and of the healing power of nature. However, because some plants yield poisons and some die in winter, plants can also represent death and decay.

Various trees, shrubs, herbs, grains, flowers, and fruit appear in myths and legends as general symbols of rebirth, decay, and immortality. Some plants have acquired much more specific meaning in folklore.

Acanthus. The acanthus plant grows throughout much of the Mediterranean region. Its large leaves appear in many ancient sculptures, especially on top of columns in the Greek style called Corinthian. Legends says that after a young girl's death, her nurse placed her possessions in a basket near her tomb. An acanthus plant grew around the basket and enclosed it. One day the sculptor Callimachus noticed this arrangement and was inspired to design the column ornament.

Bamboo. The jointed, canelike bamboo plant plays a role in Asian folklore. Because bamboo is sturdy and always green, the Chinese regard it as a symbol of long life. In the creation story of the Andaman Islanders of the Indian Ocean, the first man is born inside a large stalk of bamboo. Philippine Islanders traditionally believed that bamboo crosses in their fields would bring good crops.

Beans. Beans have been an important food source for many cultures, except for the ancient Egyptians, who thought beans were too sacred to eat. Many Native Americans—from the Iroquois of the Northeast to the Hopi of the Southwest—hold festivals in honor of the bean. Europeans traditionally baked bean cakes for a feast on the Christian holiday of Epiphany, or Twelfth Night. Some ancient lore linked beans with the dead. The Greek philosopher Pythagoras thought that the souls of the dead resided within beans, while the Romans dreaded the lemures—the evil spirits of the dead—who brought misfortune on a home by pelting it with beans at night.

Cereal Grains. Grain-bearing cereal grasses, "the bread of life," are basic to the diets of most cultures. Rice is the staple grain throughout much of southern Asia. In many Asian cultures, people perform rituals to honor the rice spirit or a **deity** of rice, usually a

129

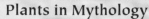

Plants in Mythology

pagan term used by early Christians to describe non-Christians and non-Christian beliefs

female. Some peoples, such as the Lamet of northern Laos, believe in a special energy or life force shared only by human beings and rice.

Although maize, a grain native to the Americas, is now called corn, many Europeans traditionally used the word *corn* to refer to such grains as barley, wheat, and oats. Europeans often spoke of female corn spirits, either maidens, mothers, or grandmothers. Grain waving in the wind, for example, was said to mark the path of the Corn Mother. Such sayings may have come from ancient beliefs that grains were sacred to harvest goddesses such as Greek Demeter and Roman Ceres.

In Central America, the Maya believed that human beings were made from maize. After attempts with other materials failed, the gods succeeded in creating people by using ground maize mixed with water.

Clover. The Druids† of the British Isles regarded clover as sacred, with both good and evil meanings. According to legend, however, St. Patrick later converted the **pagan** Irish to Christianity by using the three-part clover leaf as an example of the Trinity: God the Father, Son, and Holy Spirit in one. Clover came to represent fertility and prosperity in English folklore, and dreaming of clover foretold a happy marriage.

Coffee. Legends from various parts of the world tell how people learned of the stimulating properties of caffeine, contained in the beans of the coffee bush. An Ethiopian story says that a goatherd noticed that the beans from a particular bush made his goats unusually alert and frisky. People sampled the beans and determined that they might be useful for keeping people awake during evening religious ceremonies. Similar tales from Europe and South America also relate that people discovered the effects of caffeine in coffee by observing animals.

Ginseng. The ginseng root has long been prized in Asia for its medicinal properties. It was also thought to provide strength and sexual energy. A Korean legend says that a poor boy caring for his dying father prayed to the mountain spirit, who appeared to him in a dream and showed him where to find ginseng. A drink made from the root cured the father. Another legend tells of a man who found ginseng and tried to sell it at a high price. When his greed led to his arrest, he ate the root, which made him so strong that he overpowered his guards and escaped.

The acanthus plant, shown here in a mosaic from A.D. 200, was associated with death and immortality in Greek, Roman, and early Christian art.

130

† *See **Names and Places** at the end of this volume for further information.*

A Magical Wedding Gift

The Trio people of South America have a myth about Paraparawa, who lived before people were farmers. Paraparawa caught a big fish one day, but just as he was about to eat it, the fish became a beautiful woman. Paraparawa wanted to marry the woman, so she asked her father to bring a wedding feast. Out of the river he came, a huge alligator—some say a giant snake—with yams, yucca, sweet potatoes, and bananas. Following his bride's instructions, Paraparawa put the food in the ground. Each plant then became a hundred plants and provided plenty of food for all. Later Paraparawa planted the remains of the meal, which became another bountiful harvest. This is how people learned to farm.

nymph minor goddess of nature, usually represented as young and beautiful
oracle priest or priestess or other creature through whom a god is believed to speak; also the location (such as a shrine) where such words are spoken
patron special guardian, protector, or supporter
medieval relating to the Middle Ages in Europe, a period from about A.D. 500 to 1500

supernatural related to forces beyond the normal world; magical or miraculous

Ivy. The leaves and vine of the ivy, which remain green year round, often symbolize immortality. The plant was associated with Dionysus, the Greek god of wine (Roman Bacchus), who wore a crown of ivy and carried a staff encircled with the vine.

Laurel. The evergreen laurel tree or shrub occurs in many varieties, including cinnamon and sassafras. Greek mythology says that Daphne, a **nymph** who rejected the love of Apollo†, was turned into a laurel tree. The laurel was sacred to Apollo, whose priestesses were said to chew its leaves in order to become **oracles.** The Greeks also crowned some of their champions with laurel wreaths. According to English mythology, if two lovers take a laurel stick, break it in half, and keep the pieces, they will always remain faithful to each other.

Leek. The leek—a vegetable with a stalk of leaves layered like the skins of an onion—is the national emblem of Wales. According to legend, St. David, the **patron** saint of Wales, ordered a troop of Welsh soldiers to put leeks in their caps to identify each other during a battle. When the Welsh side won, the soldiers thanked the saint—and the leek—for the victory.

Mandrake. The mandrake plant has properties that bring on sleep or reduce pain. Many folklore traditions link the plant with sexual behavior. In the biblical book of Genesis, for example, Jacob's wife, Leah, obtains mandrake root to become pregnant. The Arabs called the plant devil's apples because they considered the arousal of sexual desire to be evil. **Medieval** Christians associated the mandrake with devil worship, and witches were believed to make images of their victims from mandrake root. According to one European tradition, a mandrake root cries out when pulled from the ground.

Manioc. Flour made from the manioc root is a traditional staple food of the Amazon peoples of South America. A story about Mani, an old, much-loved village leader, explains the origin of manioc. Before dying, Mani promised to come back to take care of his people, and he told them to dig in the ground a year after his death. What they found was the manioc root, Mani's body turned into food.

Mistletoe. The mistletoe plant, which grows in trees, appears in European legends as a symbol of fertility and eternal life, perhaps because it remains green all winter. Unlike most plants, mistletoe thrives without being rooted in soil. This may explain why many cultures have believed it to be heavenly or **supernatural.** Mistletoe has also been said to offer protection from sorcery and evil spells. The Druids believed that mistletoe had great healing properties, especially if it was gathered without the use of a knife and never allowed to touch the ground. Some Africans compare the mistletoe on a tree to the soul in the body, and they believe that

Bamboo appears in many Chinese stories as a symbol of long life. This silk painting shows seven sages in a bamboo grove.

mistletoe in a house brings good luck. In Norse† mythology, mistletoe was sacred to the beloved god Balder, but the evil god Loki used trickery to kill Balder with a stalk of mistletoe fashioned into a dart.

Myrtle. An evergreen shrub, myrtle is associated with birth and rebirth in European mythology. The ancient Greeks carried myrtle with them when they colonized new lands to symbolize the beginning of a new life. The Greeks also associated myrtle with Aphrodite, the goddess of love.

Parsley. The Greeks believed that the herb parsley grew from the blood of a hero named Achemorus who was killed by a serpent. At games held in his honor, they crowned the winners with parsley wreaths. Both the Greeks and the Romans regarded parsley as a symbol of death and rebirth. They often put parsley on tombs, and someone "in need of parsley" was on the verge of death.

Thistle. A Scottish legend tells how the thistle, a plant with purple blooms and prickly stems and leaves, became a national emblem. Around A.D. 950, Norse raiders invaded Scotland. As they crept toward a Scottish camp after dark, one of them stepped on a thistle. The resulting cry of pain awoke the Scots, who drove the invaders away and saved Scotland.

Tobacco. The tobacco plant originated in the Americas, and smoking dried tobacco leaves was part of many Native American **rituals.** Native Americans of different regions developed various

ritual ceremony that follows a set pattern

† *See **Names and Places** at the end of this volume for further information.*

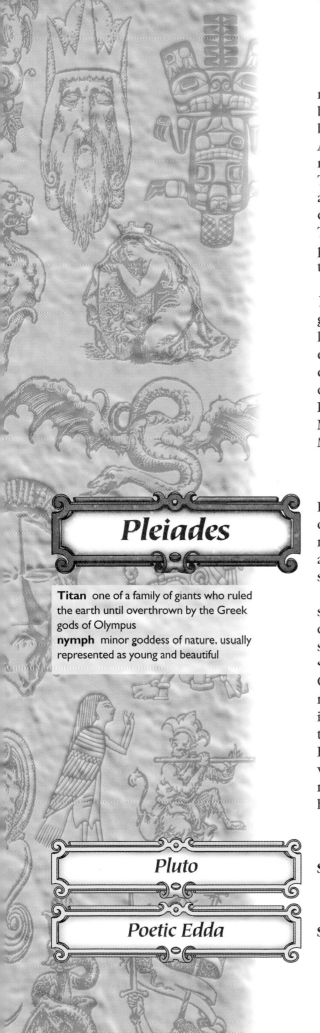

myths about tobacco. In the Southwest and Central America, tobacco is associated with rainfall because tobacco smoke resembles clouds that bring rain. A story from southeastern North America says that tobacco's origin was related to sex. A young man and woman who were traveling left the path to make love. They married soon afterward. Later the man passed the place again and found a sweet-smelling plant growing there. His people decided to dry it, smoke it, and call it "Where We Came Together." The couple's life together was happy and peaceful, so the flower produced by their love—tobacco—was smoked at meetings intended to bring peace.

Yam. In a myth from the African country of Kenya, the creator god Ruwa made humans immortal and gave them a paradise to live in but ordered them not to eat one plant growing there—the edible root known as the yam. One day Death told the people to cook the yam for him. When Ruwa learned what the people had done, he took away their immortality. *See also* ADAM AND EVE; BALDER; CORN; CREATION STORIES; EDEN, GARDEN OF; FLOWERS IN MYTHOLOGY; FRUIT IN MYTHOLOGY; GILGAMESH; INARI; TREES IN MYTHOLOGY; YGGDRASILL.

Pleiades

Titan one of a family of giants who ruled the earth until overthrown by the Greek gods of Olympus

nymph minor goddess of nature, usually represented as young and beautiful

In Greek mythology, the Pleiades were seven sisters who were the daughters of the **Titan** Atlas and the **nymph** Pleione. Their names were Maia, Electra, Taygete, Celaeno, Alcyone, Sterope, and Merope. The Pleiades are best known as a constellation in the sky consisting of seven stars.

According to one legend, Zeus† turned the Pleiades into a constellation after they had killed themselves out of sorrow over the death of their sisters, the Hyades. A better-known version of the story says that the giant hunter Orion fell in love with the seven sisters and pursued them constantly. To save the Pleiades from Orion's attentions, Zeus turned them into stars and set them in the night sky. However, this did not stop Orion. He, too, was changed into a constellation, the one that appears to chase the Pleiades through the heavens. One of the stars in the constellation of the Pleiades is not as bright as the others. Some say this is Merope, who was ashamed of her love for a mortal. Others say it is Electra, mourning for the destruction of Troy†, the city descended from her son Dardanus. *See also* ORION.

Pluto

See *Hades.*

Poetic Edda

See *Norse Mythology.*

deity god or goddess

Origin of Yams

The yam, or sweet potato, is one of the basic food crops of Polynesia. A number of myths explain the origin of this important food. One Maori myth tells how the god Rongo-maui went to heaven to see his brother Wahnui, the guardian of the yam. Rongo-maui stole the yam, hid it in his clothing, and returned to earth. Soon after, he made his wife, Pani, pregnant, and she later gave birth to a yam, the first on earth. Rongo-maui gave this food to humans.

pantheon all the gods of a particular culture
supernatural related to forces beyond the normal world; magical or miraculous

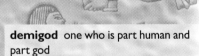

demigod one who is part human and part god
trickster mischievous figure appearing in various forms in the folktales and mythology of many different peoples
ritual ceremony that follows a set pattern
oracle priest or priestess or other creature through whom a god is believed to speak; also the location (such as a shrine) where such words are spoken
incantation chant, often part of a magical formula or spell
cult group bound together by devotion to a particular person, belief, or god

Polynesia is a vast region of the Pacific Ocean consisting of many hundreds of widely separated, culturally and politically diverse island groups. Ranging from Midway and Hawaii in the north to New Zealand in the south, the triangular area called Polynesia also includes Tahiti, Samoa, Tonga, Tuamotu, the Cook Islands, and the Pitcairn Islands. Although the mythology of Polynesia took different forms on various islands, many of the basic stories, themes, and **deities** were surprisingly similar throughout the region.

Foundations of Religion and Myth. Scholars believe that humans first migrated to Polynesia from Southeast Asia about 2,000 years ago. These people carried with them their mythological traditions about events, deities, and heroes. As time passed and people moved to different island groups, they adapted their mythology and religious beliefs to suit their new environments. In the process, they added new characters and events to the traditional myths and legends. Nevertheless, the basic elements of religion and myth remained relatively unchanged throughout the island groups, and a fairly distinct **pantheon** of gods and goddesses emerged.

Polynesian religion and mythology placed great emphasis on nature, particularly the ocean environment. The Polynesians became masters of navigation and other seafaring skills, and their religion and myths strongly reflected the importance of nature and the sea. Polynesians believed that all things in nature, including humans, contained a sacred and **supernatural** power called mana. Mana could be good or evil, and individuals, animals, and objects contained varying amounts of mana.

Because mana was sacred, Polynesians invented complicated rules to protect it. Ordinary people were not allowed, for example, to touch even the shadow of a great chief. Nor could they step inside sacred groves or temples. The punishment for breaking important rules, known as *tapus* (the source of the word *taboo*), was often death. Illness and misfortune were believed to come from breaking minor *tapus*.

The Polynesians' religion included many gods, local deities as well as the great gods of their pantheon. The people felt a close personal connection to their deities and to various heroes, **demigods,** and **tricksters** of their mythology. The most popular character was Maui, a hero-trickster well known throughout Polynesia.

Worship of the gods involved chants and prayers, elaborate **rituals,** and sacrifices (including human sacrifice) performed by various classes of priests, some of whom acted as **oracles.** Magic also flourished among the Polynesians, who used **incantations,** charms, and spells to summon the gods or ask for their guidance or assistance.

Priests usually organized and led religious festivals and celebrations. In some places, special **cult** organizations, consisting of storytellers, musicians, dancers, and other performers, took charge of staging ceremonial activities. Sacred ceremonies often included singing, dancing, storytelling, and dramatic performances. The Hawaiian hula dance originated as a sacred ceremonial dance.

Polynesian Deities

Deity	Role
Haumia	god of wild plants and vegetables
Kamapua'a	pig god
Kane	god of creation and growth
Ku	creator god
Lono	god of the heavens
Maui	trickster god and hero
Oro	war god
Papa, Po	supreme creator goddess, mother earth
Pele	fire goddess
Rangi, Ao	supreme creator god, father sky
Rongo	god of cultivated plants
Ta'aroa, Rua-i-tupra	supreme creator god
Tane	god of the forest
Tangaroa, Kanaloa, Tangaloa	god of the seas
Tawhiri	god of the wind and storms
Tu	god of war

Major Gods and Characters. The most important gods of the Polynesian pantheon were those associated with creation myths and legends. Best known were Rangi (Father Sky) and Papa (Mother Earth), the two supreme creator gods of the Maori people of New Zealand. According to Maori legend, Rangi and Papa served as the source from which all things came.

The counterparts of Rangi and Papa in Hawaiian mythology were Ao and Po. Ao represented the male force in the universe and was associated with the sky, the day, and light. Po, the feminine force, was linked with the earth, darkness, and night. According to Hawaiian myth, a creator god named Ku separated Ao from Po. Ku then worked with Lono, god of the heavens, and Kane, the chief god of generation and growth, to create the earth and all living things. After Kane made the first man and woman, he became angry at their bad behavior and decided that humans would be subject to death. He then left the earth and went to live in heaven.

In Tahitian mythology, the supreme creator deity was Ta'aroa, also called Rua-i-tupra (source of growth). Ta'aroa emerged from a **cosmic** egg and started the process of creation. To fill the emptiness around him, he used part of the egg to make the sky and the

135

other part to create the earth. Satisfied with his accomplishment, he filled the world with all the creatures and things that are now found in it. The Tahitians believed that Ta'aroa sent both blessings and curses, and they tried to appease him with human sacrifices.

The Maori gods Rangi and Papa had many offspring, including Tangaroa, the god of the seas. According to legend, Tangaroa fled to the sea to escape the wrath of his brother Tawhiri, the storm god. Tangaroa later quarreled with another brother, the forest god Tane, and forever after he enjoyed sinking canoes made from wood from Tane's forests. In Hawaiian mythology, Tangaroa was called Kanaloa and the Hawaiian counterpart of Tane was Kane. The Samoans and Tongans knew Tangaroa as Tangaloa.

Perhaps the best-known and most feared deity in Hawaii was the fire goddess Pele, a violent figure associated with volcanoes. Renowned for her beauty but also for her ability to destroy, Pele symbolized the power of natural forces. Many Hawaiian legends deal with her unpredictable temper and dangerous nature.

Another prominent deity in Hawaiian mythology was Kamapua'a, the pig god. Known both for his warlike nature and for his romantic exploits, this energetic god appeared in many tales. The

Captain James Cook visited the Hawaiian islands in 1778. When he came ashore, the people mistook him for one of their gods. This illustration shows the Hawaiians offering gifts to the English captain.

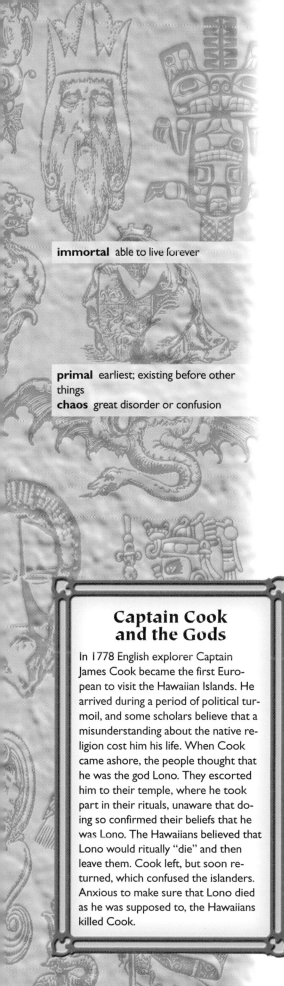

immortal able to live forever

primal earliest; existing before other things

chaos great disorder or confusion

Captain Cook and the Gods

In 1778 English explorer Captain James Cook became the first European to visit the Hawaiian Islands. He arrived during a period of political turmoil, and some scholars believe that a misunderstanding about the native religion cost him his life. When Cook came ashore, the people thought that he was the god Lono. They escorted him to their temple, where he took part in their rituals, unaware that doing so confirmed their beliefs that he was Lono. The Hawaiians believed that Lono would ritually "die" and then leave them. Cook left, but soon returned, which confused the islanders. Anxious to make sure that Lono died as he was supposed to, the Hawaiians killed Cook.

Hawaiians often sought Kamapua'a as an ally during war and used his adventures to explain various natural phenomena.

By far the most popular figure in Polynesian mythology was Maui, the trickster god and hero. Though small in stature, he displayed amazing strength and had various magical powers. The many tales about his adventures reveal a cunning and determined hero who performed many great and wondrous deeds, including creating the Pacific islands with a magical hook and providing humans with more hours of daylight by slowing the sun's passage across the sky. Maui also tried, but failed, to become **immortal.**

Major Themes and Myths. The best-known myths in Polynesia deal with creation and with the origin of gods, humans, and other living things. The adventures of characters such as Pele and Maui also figure prominently.

Some Polynesian myths describe creation as a process of growth or evolution from a **primal** state of **chaos,** nothingness, or darkness. The Hawaiian myths of Ao and Po, the male and female forces of the universe, reflect this idea. From a great watery chaos at the beginning of time, the creator god Ku separated Ao and Po, thus producing day and night and making the world possible.

Other Polynesian creation myths focus on a preexisting creator who lives alone and forms all things from nothingness. This idea is expressed in stories from Samoa and Tonga about Tangaloa. According to legend, while Tangaloa ruled over a vast expanse of ocean, his messenger, the bird Tuli, searched endlessly for somewhere to rest. Tangaloa eventually threw some rocks into the water, and these became the islands of Samoa and Tonga.

In the Maori creation myth, two primal beings—Te Po (Night) and Te Kore (Darkness)—existed in a realm of chaos at the beginning of time. From them sprang Rangi and Papa, the first gods of the universe. For many ages, Rangi and Papa were locked in an embrace, and their offspring, including numerous gods, were caught between them. The gods grew weary of their confinement and finally separated Rangi from Papa, thus providing room for themselves and for all things to grow and multiply.

The origin of humans and other living things is explained in various ways. According to myths about Tangaloa, after he created the islands of the Pacific, he used a vine to cover the bare land and provide shade. The vine spread, and parts of it decayed and became full of maggots. Tangaloa took the maggots and shaped them into humans. When he gave them a heart and soul, they came to life.

In Maori myth, several of the gods—especially Tane-mahuta, Tangaroa, and Rongo-ma-tane (the god of cultivated crops)—played an active role in creating lands, plants, and humans. According to some legends, all living creatures, including humans, emerged from Tangaroa's vast body.

In another myth, the god Tane went searching for a wife. He united with several different beings and produced mountains, rivers, and other living and nonliving things. Tane longed for a partner with a human shape, however, so he formed a woman out of

137

underworld land of the dead

The carving on this *hei tiki* jade pendant is a fertility symbol in the mythology of the Maori people of New Zealand. The figure represents the first man, Tiki, in the stories of other Polynesians.

Popol Vuh

sand and breathed life into her. This woman's name was Hine-hau-one (Earth-formed Maiden), and she had a daughter named Hine-titama (Dawn Maiden). Tane later took the girl—who did not know he was her father—as his wife, and they had many children. When Hine-titama discovered Tane's identity, she fled to the **underworld,** dragging her children after her. The relationship between Tane and his daughter resulted in the arrival of death for humans.

A Hawaiian myth tells how Kane longed for a companion in his own image. His mother, Papatuanuku, told him to make a likeness of himself from clay and to embrace it. When he did as she suggested, the clay figure came to life and became the first woman.

Numerous myths explain the origin of various plant foods and other things of value. According to some stories, humans had to steal food from the gods or trick them into giving up certain foods. In others, however, the gods felt sorry for humans and generously gave food to them. A number of myths also explain that foods were the offspring of a particular god or grew from part of the body of a god.

Some Polynesian myths tell about characters who possessed extraordinary or supernatural powers and acted as miracle workers, mischief makers, or tricksters. The Hawaiians called these figures *kapua* and loved to hear about their many adventures. The *kapua* were often raised by grandparents who used magic to help them in their adventures. They generally grew up to be monstrous creatures who could change shape and perform great feats of strength. Among the more popular tales were those in which the *kapua* slayed monsters, rescued maidens, defeated rivals, and competed with the gods.

Legacy. With the introduction of Christianity in Polynesia in the 1700s, traditional religious beliefs began to fade. Although the Polynesian gods no longer play a major role in religion in most parts of the region, the rich heritage of myths and legends remains part of the literature, folklore, and imagination of native cultures. *See also* CREATION STORIES; MAUI; MELANESIAN MYTHOLOGY; MENEHUNE; MICRONESIAN MYTHOLOGY; PELE; RANGI AND PAPA; TA'AROA; TIKI; TRICKSTERS.

The *Popol Vuh* is the most important source of information on the mythology of the ancient Maya. A sacred book of the Quiché Maya of Guatemala, it was written down in the mid-1500s. A Spanish priest discovered the *Popol Vuh* manuscript in the early 1700s. After copying the text, he translated it into Spanish.

The *Popol Vuh* is divided into five parts. The first contains an account of the creation of the world and of the failed attempts to produce proper human beings. The second and third parts tell of the adventures of the Hero Twins, Hunahpú and Xbalanqúe, and their forebears. The last two parts deal with the issue of creating humans from corn and then tell the story of the Quiché people, from the days before their history began to accounts of tribal wars and records of rulers up until 1550.

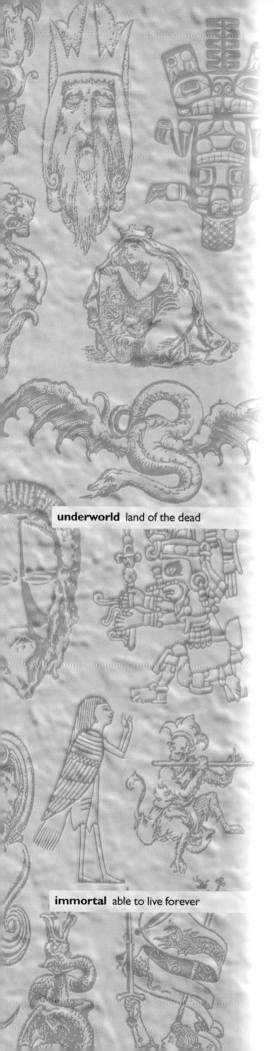

underworld land of the dead

immortal able to live forever

Creation of the World. At the beginning of time, the gods Hurucan and Gugumatz (also known as Quetzalcoatl) shaped the earth and its features and raised the sky above it. The gods then placed animals on the earth, hoping that they would sing the praises of the gods.

When the gods discovered that the animals could not speak, they tried again to make a creature that could praise its creator. Hurucan and Gugumatz called on the ancestral beings Xpiacoc and Xmucane to help, and together they created men of mud. However, these creatures talked endlessly and dwindled away. Next the gods fashioned humans out of wood. These beings populated the earth but soon forgot about their creators. The angry gods sent floods and various objects to destroy them.

The Hero Twins. In Part Two of the *Popol Vuh,* Hunahpú and Xbalanqúe appear and take on the self-important Vucub-Caquix, as well as his sons, Zipacna and Earthquake. Using blowpipes the twins knocked out Vucub-Caquix's jeweled teeth, which gave him his radiance. Vucub-Caquix accepted corn as a replacement for his teeth. But because he could not eat with his corn teeth and because they did not shine, he was defeated.

In Part Three of the *Popol Vuh,* the story goes back to an earlier time to Hun-Hunahpú and Vucub Hunahpú, the father and uncle of the Hero Twins. These two disturbed the lords of Xibalba, the **underworld,** with their constant ball playing. The lords commanded the brothers to come to the underworld for a contest. Tricked by the lords, the brothers lost the contest and, as a result, were sacrificed and buried in the ball court. However, the head of Hun-Hunahpú remained unburied and was placed in a tree.

A young goddess named Xquic heard of a strange fruit in a tree and went to see it. The fruit was actually the head of Hun-Hunahpú, which spat in her hand and made her pregnant. She later gave birth to the Hero Twins. Hun-Hunahpú already had another set of twins, Hun Batz and Hun Chuen, who resented their baby brothers. When the Hero Twins grew old enough, they outsmarted the older twins and turned them into monkeys.

The Hero Twins became great ballplayers, as their father and uncle had been, and one day the lords of Xibalba summoned them to the underworld for a contest. The twins saw this as an opportunity to avenge their father's death. Challenged to a series of trials, they passed every one they were given. They survived a night in the House of Cold, escaped death in the House of Jaguars, and passed unharmed through the House of Fire. They almost met defeat in the House of Bats, when a bat cut off Hunahpú's head. The lords of Xibalba took the head to the ball court as a trophy, but Xbalanqúe managed to return the head to his brother and restore him.

Knowing they were **immortal,** the Hero Twins now allowed the lords of Xibalba to defeat and "kill" them. Five days later, the twins reappeared, disguised as wandering performers, and entertained the lords with amazing feats. In one of these feats, Xbalanqúe sacrificed Hunahpú and then brought him back to life.

139

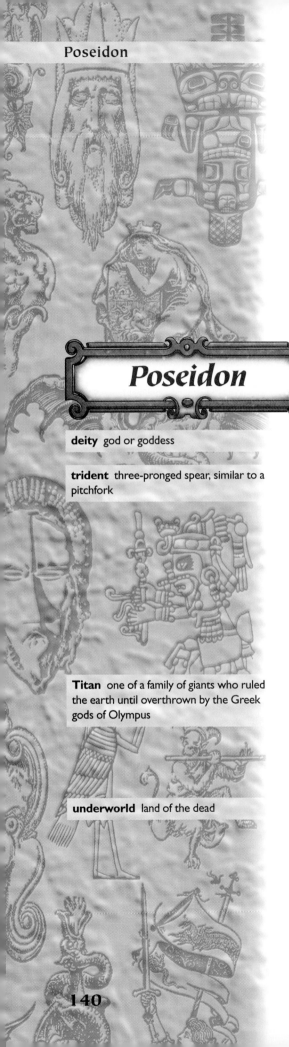

Astounded, the lords of Xibalba begged to be sacrificed themselves. The Hero Twins agreed to the request but did not restore the lords of Xibalba to life. The twins then dug up the bodies of their father and uncle and brought them back to life.

History. The final two parts of the *Popol Vuh* tell how the ancestral couple once again tried to make humans who would praise the gods. The four men they created from maize became the founders of the Quiché Maya. These people praised their creators and flourished. The generations that followed them are listed in the closing section of the *Popol Vuh*. ***See also*** HUNAHPÚ AND XBALANQÚE; MAYAN MYTHOLOGY; QUETZALCOATL; TWINS; XIBALBA.

Poseidon

deity god or goddess

trident three-pronged spear, similar to a pitchfork

Titan one of a family of giants who ruled the earth until overthrown by the Greek gods of Olympus

underworld land of the dead

One of the major **deities** in Greek mythology, Poseidon was the supreme ruler of the seas. The Romans called him Neptune. An awesome, unruly, and powerful god, Poseidon was associated with storms, earthquakes, and some other violent forces of nature. When angry, he could stir the sea to a fury. But he could also calm the raging waters with just a glance. One of his titles, Enosichthon (Earth-shaker), reflected his ability to cause earthquakes by striking the earth and mountains with his **trident.** Another name for Poseidon was Hippios (lord of horses), and the god presented horses as gifts to various individuals.

Poseidon rode the waves in a swift chariot drawn by golden sea horses. He used his mighty trident not only to provoke earthquakes and stir ocean waves but also to raise new land from beneath the sea or cause existing land to sink below the waters. Although often helpful to humans—protecting sailors at sea, guiding ships to safety, and filling nets with fish—Neptune could be a terrifying figure as well. Quick to anger, he directed his fury at anyone who acted against him or failed to show proper respect.

Poseidon's Siblings. The son of the **Titans** Cronus† and Rhea, Poseidon was swallowed at birth by his father. He was saved by his brother Zeus†, who tricked Cronus into taking a potion that caused him to vomit up Poseidon and the other siblings—Hades†, Demeter†, Hera†, and Hestia. Poseidon later joined Zeus and Hades in overthrowing Cronus, and the three brothers then divided the universe among themselves. Zeus received the sky, Hades ruled the **underworld,** and Poseidon became god of the seas.

Although Zeus was king of the gods, Poseidon often asserted his independence. Once he even plotted with the goddesses Hera and Athena† to overthrow Zeus. Together they managed to put Zeus in chains. However, the sea goddess Thetis saved Zeus by bringing a giant from Tartarus—a realm beneath the underworld—to release the king of the gods from his chains. As punishment for this rebellion, Zeus made Poseidon serve as a slave to King Laomedon of Troy for a year. During this time, Poseidon helped build great walls around the city. When the king refused to

Poseidon, the god of the seas, was one of the 12 Olympian gods in Greek mythology. Known for his terrible temper, Poseidon was associated with storms, earthquakes, and other violent forces of nature.

pay for this work, Poseidon took revenge by siding with the Greeks against Troy in the Trojan War†.

Love Life and Children. Poseidon had a turbulent love life and fathered many children, including a number of monsters and sea creatures. With his wife, the sea **nymph** Amphitrite, he had three offspring. One was the sea god Triton, a merman who resembled a human above the waist and a fish from the waist down.

Poseidon had children with other partners as well. After seducing his sister Demeter while disguised as a horse, he had two children: the divine horse Arion and a daughter, Despoina. A beautiful woman named Medusa† also bore Poseidon two children: the winged horse Pegasus and a son named Chrysaor. The goddess Athena, angered that Poseidon had made love to Medusa in one of her temples, turned the woman into a hideous monster, a **Gorgon.** Through his son Chrysaor, Poseidon became ancestor to some of the most fearsome monsters in Greek mythology, including Cerberus, the Hydra, the Nemean Lion, and the Sphinx.

Gaia, the earth, bore Poseidon two children: Antaeus, a giant, and Charybdis, a sea monster that almost destroyed Odysseus† during his journey home after the Trojan War. Another giant offspring of Poseidon—the one-eyed Cyclops Polyphemus—also threatened Odysseus on his voyage home. When Odysseus blinded the giant, he became a target of Poseidon's hatred.

When Poseidon tried to seduce the beautiful sea nymph Scylla, his wife, Amphitrite, became jealous and transformed her into a horrible sea monster with six dogs' heads. Like Charybdis, Scylla terrorized sailors, and she devoured several of Odysseus's companions.

Among Poseidon's other children were the evil Cercyon and Sciron, normal-sized offspring who threatened and killed travelers in Greece, and the giant Amycus, who forced people to fight with him and then killed them. Various ordinary mortals also claimed Poseidon as their father, including the famous Greek hero Theseus†.

Poseidon's Quarrels. Poseidon had numerous quarrels with other gods. One of his most famous disputes involved the goddess Athena. Both Poseidon and Athena claimed the city of Athens and the surrounding region of Attica as their own. A contest was held to see which god could give Athens the best gift. Athena created an olive tree; Poseidon produced a saltwater spring. When the Athenians judged Athena's gift to be superior, the angry Poseidon flooded the surrounding plain.

nymph minor goddess of nature, usually represented as young and beautiful
Gorgon one of three ugly monsters who had snakes for hair, staring eyes, and huge wings

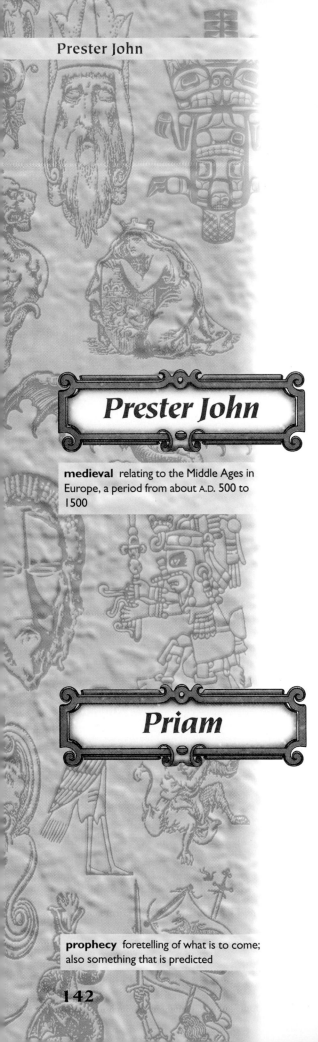

Poseidon also quarreled with the sun god Helios over control of the Greek city of Corinth. The giant Briareos settled the argument by giving the hill overlooking the city to Helios and the surrounding land to Poseidon. Satisfied with this decision, Poseidon caused no problems for the people of Corinth.

Another of Poseidon's famous quarrels was with Minos, the king of Crete. Minos asked Poseidon to send him a bull that he could sacrifice to the god. Poseidon sent such a magnificent bull that the king decided to keep it for himself instead of sacrificing it. Furious, Poseidon caused Minos's wife, Pasiphae, to fall in love with the bull and to give birth to the Minotaur, a monstrous beast that had the body of a man and the head of a bull. ***See also*** **ATHENA; CERBERUS; CYCLOPES; DEMETER; GAIA; HADES; HERA; HYDRA; MEDUSA; MINOS; MINOTAUR; MONSTERS; NEPTUNE; ODYSSEUS; PEGASUS; SCYLLA AND CHARYBDIS; SPHINX; THESEUS; ZEUS.**

Prester John

medieval relating to the Middle Ages in Europe, a period from about A.D. 500 to 1500

According to **medieval** legend, Prester John was a Christian king who ruled over an Asian land. The story of Prester John started around the time of the Crusades, the military campaigns undertaken by European Christians to retake the Holy Land from the Muslims.

A report written in 1145 called Prester John a mighty priest and king, who defeated the Persian Muslims and planned to help the Crusaders free Jerusalem. Twenty years later, a letter supposedly written by Prester John circulated in Europe. In it, he described his kingdom as a paradise on earth. He also promised to defeat the Muslims and recapture Christian holy places.

In 1177 Pope Alexander III sent a group to locate Prester John, but they were unsuccessful. Over the next few hundred years, many explorers and missionaries searched for him as they traveled throughout Asia. In the 1400s, a Portuguese traveler claimed to have found Prester John's kingdom in the present-day African country of Ethiopia.

Priam

In Greek mythology, Priam was the last king of Troy†, a ruler who witnessed the destruction of his city in the Trojan War†. His son Paris caused the war, while another son, Hector†, became the greatest Trojan hero during the long struggle against the Greeks.

Priam, the youngest son of King Laomedon of Troy, was originally named Podarces. While Podarces was an infant, the king promised his daughter Hesione to the great hero Hercules†. The king broke his promise, and Hercules killed him and all his sons except Podarces, who was sold as a slave. Hesione bought her brother at the slave market and changed his name to Priam.

When Priam was still a child, Hercules placed him on the throne of Troy. Priam grew up to be a capable and honest ruler who expanded Trojan rule and brought prosperity to the city. The king had several wives. His favorite, Hecuba, bore him many children, including Hector, Paris, and Cassandra, a young woman with the power of **prophecy** who foretold the destruction of Troy.

prophecy foretelling of what is to come; also something that is predicted

†*See **Names and Places** at the end of this volume for further information.*

Priam never forgot Hesione, the sister who had rescued him from slavery. She had been carried off to Greece by Hercules, who married her to his friend Telamon. Many years later, Priam sent his son Paris to Greece with a fleet of ships to bring Hesione back to Troy. Instead of returning with Hesione, however, Paris brought back Helen†, wife of King Menelaus of Sparta.

The **abduction** of Helen by Paris enraged the Greeks and led to the Trojan War. By the time the fighting began, Priam was much too old to take part in battle, so he let his sons manage the war. Sadly, as the war progressed, he saw his sons perish one by one.

Toward the end of the war, Priam went to the battlefield and asked the Greek hero Achilles† to return the body of his son Hector, killed in battle by Achilles. The Greeks greatly admired Priam for this show of courage. When Troy finally fell, Priam saw his son Polites killed in the royal palace by the warrior Neoptolemus. Aroused to fury, the aged king hurled a spear at the Greek, but his throw was too weak to cause any harm. Neoptolemus responded to Priam's act by dragging the king to the family altar and killing him. *See also* ACHILLES; CASSANDRA; HECTOR; HECUBA; HELEN OF TROY; ILIAD, THE; PARIS; TROJAN WAR.

abduction carrying away by force

Procrustes

In Greek mythology, Procrustes was a robber who lived near the city of Eleusis. He invited travelers to spend the night, offering them his hospitality.

However, as soon as the travelers were in his house, Procrustes would tie them to an iron bed. If they were shorter than the bed, he would stretch them on a rack until they were as long as the bed. If the guests were taller than the bed, Procrustes would cut off their legs until they fit. In either case, his victims died. Procrustes met his end at the hands of the Greek hero Theseus†, who killed him the same way that the robber took care of his victims. Today the term *Procrustean bed* means a standard or set of conditions, determined arbitrarily, to which everyone is forced to conform.

Prometheus

Titan one of a family of giants who ruled the earth until overthrown by the Greek gods of Olympus

nymph minor goddess of nature, usually represented as young and beautiful

Prometheus, one of the **Titans** in Greek mythology, was the god of fire. A master craftsman considered the wisest of his race, he was credited with the creation of humans and with giving them fire and various types of skills and knowledge. His name means "forethought."

Prometheus was the son of the Titan Iapetus and of either the sea **nymph** Clymene or the goddess Themis. Atlas† and Epimetheus ("afterthought") were his brothers; Hesione, daughter of the Titan Oceanus, was his wife.

When Zeus† and the other Olympian gods rebelled against the Titans, Prometheus sided with the gods and thus won their favor. He held Zeus's aching head so that Hephaestus (Vulcan)† could split it open and release the goddess Athena†. To show her gratitude, Athena taught Prometheus astronomy, mathematics, architecture, navigation, metalworking, writing, and other useful skills. He later passed this knowledge on to humans.

immortality ability to live forever

Champion of Humankind. Prometheus created humans by shaping lumps of clay into small figures resembling the gods. Athena admired these figures and breathed on them, giving them life. Zeus disliked the creatures, but he could not uncreate them. He did, however, confine them to the earth and denied them **immortality.** Prometheus felt sorry for humans, so he gave them fire and taught them various arts and skills.

Prometheus was given the task of determining how sacrifices were to be made to the gods. He cut up a bull and divided it into two portions. One contained the animal's flesh and skin, but they were concealed beneath the bull's stomach, the least appetizing part of the animal. The other consisted of the bones, wrapped in a rich layer of fat. Prometheus then asked Zeus to choose a portion for himself, leaving the other for humans. Fooled by the outward appearance of the portions, Zeus chose the one containing the bones and fat. Prometheus thus ensured that humans got the best meat.

Angered by this trick, Zeus punished humans by withholding fire from them so that they would have to live in cold and darkness and eat meat raw. Prometheus promptly went to Olympus†, stole a spark of fire from Hephaestus, and carried it back to humans. When Zeus discovered what Prometheus had done, he swore revenge. He ordered Hephaestus to create a woman from clay, and he had the winds breathe life into her. Athena and other goddesses clothed the woman, whose name was Pandora.

Zeus sent Pandora as a gift to Prometheus's brother Epimetheus, who married her despite warnings from Prometheus not to accept any gift from Zeus. Pandora brought with her a box containing evil, disease, poverty, war, and other troubles. When Pandora opened the box, she released these sorrows into the world, and Zeus thus gained his revenge on humankind.

In Greek mythology, Prometheus was a wise craftsman who taught humans many useful skills, including navigation, writing, and architecture. Here, Prometheus gives fire to man.

†*See **Names and Places** at the end of this volume for further information.*

Prometheus's Punishment. To punish Prometheus, Zeus chained the god to a rock on a mountain peak. Every day an eagle tore at Prometheus's body and ate his liver, and every night the liver grew back. Because Prometheus was **immortal,** he could not die. But he suffered endlessly.

Prometheus remained chained and in agony for thousands of years. The other gods begged Zeus to show mercy, but he refused. Finally, Zeus offered Prometheus freedom if he would reveal a secret that only he knew. Prometheus told Zeus that the sea nymph Thetis would bear a son who would become greater than his father. This was important information. Both Zeus and his brother Poseidon† desired Thetis, but they arranged for her to marry a mortal so that her son would not pose a challenge to their power.

Zeus sent Hercules to shoot the eagle that tormented Prometheus and to break the chains that bound him. After his years of suffering, Prometheus was free. To reward Hercules for his help, Prometheus advised him how to obtain the golden Apples of Hesperides, one of the 12 labors the famous hero had to accomplish.

Legacy. The story of Prometheus's suffering and ultimate release from his torment has inspired artists and writers for centuries. Among the most important early works dealing with the myth were a series of plays written by the Greek playwright Aeschylus. Only one of these works, *Prometheus Bound,* survives. The Roman poet Ovid incorporated parts of the story in his work the *Metamorphoses.* Prometheus has also been the subject of more modern works of art, music, and literature by such individuals as the composer Beethoven and the poets Byron, Shelley, and Longfellow. ***See also*** Atlas; Greek Mythology; Hercules; Pandora; Titans; Vulcan; Zeus.

Prose Edda

See *Norse Mythology.*

Proserpina

See *Persephone.*

Proteus

Proteus was an ancient Greek god also known as the old man of the sea. He served as a shepherd for the sea god Neptune†, watching over his flocks of seals. In return, Neptune gave Proteus the gift of **prophecy.**

Proteus possessed knowledge of all things—past, present, and future—but was reluctant to reveal his knowledge. He would answer questions only if caught. The only way to catch him was to sneak up on him at noontime when he took his daily nap. However, Proteus also had the ability to change shape at will. Once he was seized, it was necessary to hold him tightly until he returned to his natural form. Then he would answer any question put to

immortal able to live forever

prophecy foretelling of what is to come; also something that is predicted

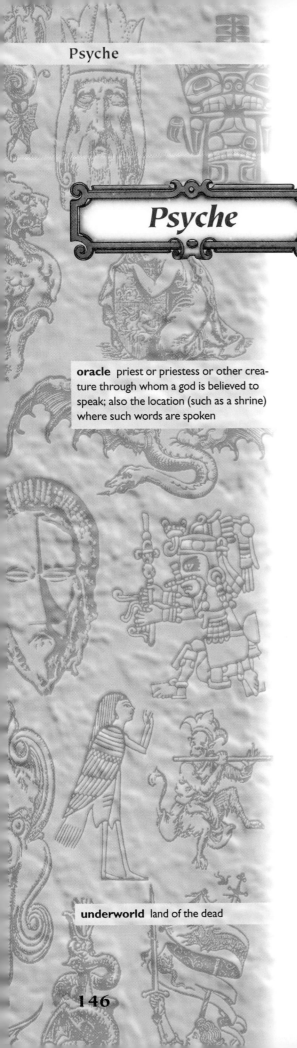

Psyche

oracle priest or priestess or other creature through whom a god is believed to speak; also the location (such as a shrine) where such words are spoken

underworld land of the dead

him. The legend of Proteus gave rise to the term *protean,* which means able to assume different forms. ***See also*** Greek Mythology; Neptune.

In Greek and Roman mythology, Psyche was a princess of such stunning beauty that people came from near and far to admire her. In turning their adoration toward Psyche, however, they neglected to worship the goddess Aphrodite†. Jealous that so much praise was flowing to a mortal girl, Aphrodite decided to punish Psyche.

The goddess summoned her son Eros (also known as Cupid), the god of love, and told him to make Psyche fall in love with some ugly, mean, and unworthy creature. Eros prepared to obey his mother's wishes, but when he laid eyes on the beautiful Psyche, he fell in love with her.

Eros asked Apollo† to send an **oracle** to Psyche's father, telling him to prepare his daughter for marriage. He was to send her to a lonely mountain, where an ugly monster would meet her and take her for his wife. Full of sorrow for his daughter but afraid of making the gods angry, Psyche's father obeyed.

While Psyche stood on the mountain, Zephyrus, the god of the west wind, sent a breeze to pick her up and carry her to a beautiful palace in a valley. When Psyche entered the palace, a friendly voice guided her around, and invisible attendants waited upon her and fulfilled her every need.

That night and on the nights that followed, Eros came to Psyche in the darkness of her bedroom and made love to her. Psyche could not see Eros in the darkness, but he told her that he was her husband. He also warned Psyche not to ask his identity and never to look at him. Psyche grew to love her unseen husband, but she felt very lonely.

When she asked if her sisters might visit, Eros reluctantly agreed. Her sisters admired her palace and life of luxury, but when they discovered that Psyche had never seen her husband, they told her that he must be a monster and might kill her. They convinced her to take a knife and lamp to bed with her.

When Eros fell asleep that night, Psyche lit the lamp and prepared to stab her husband. But instead of a monster, she saw the handsome god of love. Startled, she let a drop of hot oil from the lamp fall on Eros. He awoke, realized that Psyche knew his identity, and flew away. Psyche fainted. When she awoke, the palace had vanished, and she found herself alone in a strange country.

Psyche wandered the countryside searching for Eros. Finally she asked Aphrodite for help, and the goddess gave her a set of seemingly impossible tasks. With the help of other gods, however, Psyche managed to sort a roomful of grain in one night and gather golden fleeces from a flock of sheep. For the final task, Aphrodite told Psyche to go the **underworld** and bring back a sealed box from Persephone†. Psyche retrieved the box and on her way back, overcome by curiosity, peeked inside it. The box released a deep sleep, which overpowered her.

*†See **Names and Places** at the end of this volume for further information.*

Cupid, the god of love, fell in love with a beautiful Greek princess named Psyche. He took her to Mount Olympus, where Zeus made Psyche immortal and allowed Cupid to marry her.

By this time Eros, could not bear to be without Psyche. He flew to where she lay sleeping, woke her, and took her to Olympus†, where Zeus† commanded that the punishment of Psyche cease and gave permission for the lovers to marry. Zeus then gave Psyche a cup of ambrosia, the food of the gods, which made her **immortal**. *See also* **APHRODITE; EROS; GREEK MYTHOLOGY.**

Ptah

In Egyptian mythology, Ptah was the chief **deity** of the ancient city of Memphis. He was worshiped as the creator of all things and the **patron** of various crafts, such as sculpting and metalworking. At Memphis, Ptah belonged to a group of three deities

147

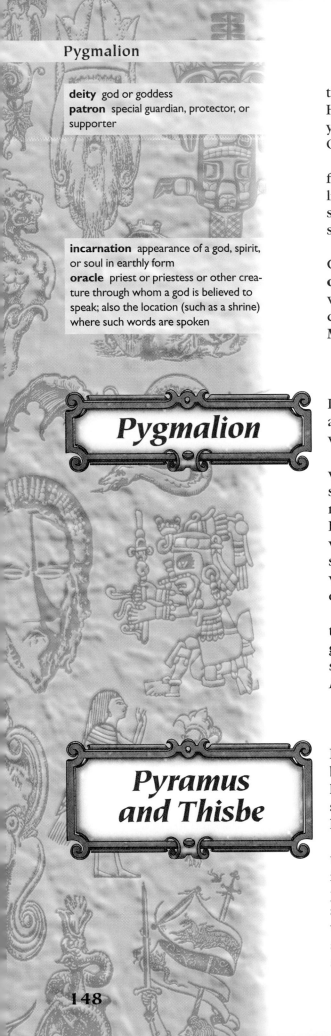

incarnation appearance of a god, spirit, or soul in earthly form
oracle priest or priestess or other creature through whom a god is believed to speak; also the location (such as a shrine) where such words are spoken

that included the goddess Sekhmet and the young god Nefertum. However, legends about Ptah spread throughout Egypt and beyond, and he was sometimes combined with the gods Seker and Osiris to form a new god.

Egyptian creation stories say that Ptah made the other gods by first imagining them in his heart and then using his voice to breathe life into them. He went on to produce other creatures from metal, stone, and wood. He also brought forth towns and religious shrines, and he established ceremonies for worship.

In Memphis, Ptah's temple housed a sacred bull known as Apis. Considered an **incarnation** of the god, the bull served as Ptah's **oracle.** In works of art and temple decorations, Ptah is shown wearing a skullcap, close-fitting garments, and a short beard and carrying a staff that symbolizes his authority. *See also* EGYPTIAN MYTHOLOGY; OSIRIS.

Pygmalion

In Greek mythology, Pygmalion was a king of the island of Cyprus and a sculptor. He spent many years carving an ivory statue of a woman more beautiful than any living female.

Pygmalion became fascinated by his sculpture and fell in love with it. He pretended it was an actual woman. He brought it presents and treated it as if it were alive. However, the statue could not respond to his attentions, and Pygmalion became miserable. Finally, he prayed to Aphrodite, the goddess of love, to bring him a woman like his statue. Aphrodite did even better. She brought the statue to life. Pygmalion married this woman, often called Galatea, who gave birth to a daughter (some versions of the story say the child was a boy).

The writer George Bernard Shaw took the name *Pygmalion* as the title of his play about an English professor who turns a poor girl from the streets into a fashionable society woman. Shaw's story was the basis of the later Broadway musical and movie *My Fair Lady.*

Pyramus and Thisbe

Pyramus and Thisbe are young lovers in a Babylonian† story told by the Roman poet Ovid in the *Metamorphoses.* The lovers, who lived next door to each other, were forbidden by their parents to see or speak to each other. But the two communicated through a hole in the wall between their houses.

Deciding to elope, Pyramus and Thisbe agreed to meet at night under a mulberry tree outside the city. Thisbe arrived first, wearing a veil over her face. When she heard a lion roar, she fled, dropping her veil. The lion, whose jaws were bloody, found the scarf and tore it up. When Pyramus arrived, he saw the stained, tattered veil and assumed that Thisbe was dead. He drew his sword and stabbed himself. Thisbe then returned to find Pyramus dying, and she used his sword to kill herself as well.

†See **Names and Places** at the end of this volume for further information.

It is said that, before this incident, the fruit of the mulberry tree was white. However, the blood from Pyramus and Thisbe turned its fruit deep red, and it has been that color ever since. ***See also*** **METAMORPHOSES, THE; TREES IN MYTHOLOGY.**

Quetzalcoatl

Mesoamerica cultural region consisting of southern Mexico and northern regions of Central America
deity god or goddess
culture hero mythical figure who gives people the tools of civilization, such as language and fire

pantheon all the gods of a particular culture

For thousands of years, Quetzalcoatl was one of the most important figures in the traditional mythologies of **Mesoamerica.** As **deity, culture hero,** or legendary ruler, Quetzalcoatl appeared in some of the region's most powerful and enduring stories. He represented life, motion, laughter, health, sexuality, and the arts and crafts of civilization, such as farming, cooking, and music.

The name *Quetzalcoatl* means "Feathered Serpent." It brings together the magnificent green-plumed quetzal bird, symbolizing the heavens and the wind, and the snake, symbolizing the earth and fertility. Quetzalcoatl's name can also be translated as "precious twin," and in some myths, he had a twin brother named Xolotl, who had a human body and the head of a dog or of an ocelot, a spotted wildcat.

Historical Background. Quetzalcoatl occupied a central place in the **pantheon** of the Aztec people of central Mexico, but he dates back to a time long before the Aztecs. Images of the Feathered Serpent appear on a temple building in Teotihuacán, a Mexican archaeological site from the A.D. 200s. These images are found with images of rain and water, suggesting close ties between Quetzalcoatl and the god of rain and vegetation.

Quetzalcoatl, the Aztec god also known as the Feathered Serpent, appears on structures in the ancient city of Teotihuacán in Mexico.

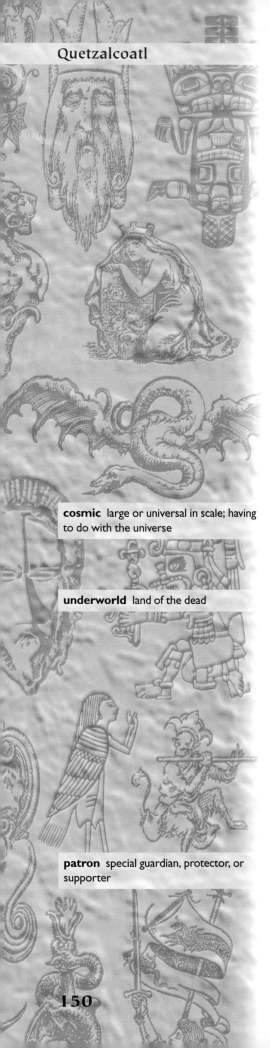

cosmic large or universal in scale; having to do with the universe

underworld land of the dead

patron special guardian, protector, or supporter

To the Toltecs, who flourished in the region from the 800s to the 1100s, Quetzalcoatl was the deity of the morning and evening stars and the wind. When the Aztecs rose to power in the 1400s, they brought Quetzalcoatl into their pantheon and made him a culture hero, a bringer not just of life but also of civilization. These old myths merged with legends about a priest-king named Quetzalcoatl, possibly a real historical figure. Later as groups from central Mexico migrated into southern Mexico and the Yucatán peninsula, blending with the local Maya population, the Feathered Serpent took his place in the Mayan pantheon under the name Kukulcan.

The God. Quetzalcoatl was portrayed in two ways. As the Feathered Serpent, he was a snake with wings or covered with feathers. He could also appear in human form as a warrior wearing a tall, cone-shaped crown or cap made of ocelot skin and a pendant fashioned of jade or a conch shell. The pendant, known as the "wind jewel," symbolized one of Quetzalcoatl's other roles, that of Ehecatl, god of wind and movement. Buildings dedicated to this god were circular or cylindrical in shape to minimize their resistance to the wind.

According to some accounts, Quetzalcoatl was the son of the sun and of the earth goddess Coatlicue. He and three brother gods created the sun, the heavens, and the earth. In the Aztec creation myth, Quetzalcoatl's **cosmic** conflicts with the god Tezcatlipoca brought about the creation and destruction of a series of four suns and earths, leading to the fifth sun and today's earth.

At first there were no people under the fifth sun. The inhabitants of the earlier worlds had died, and their bones littered Mictlan, the **underworld.** Quetzalcoatl and his twin, Xolotl, journeyed to Mictlan to find the bones, arousing the fury of the Death Lord. As he fled from the underworld, Quetzalcoatl dropped the bones, and they broke into pieces. He gathered up the pieces and took them to the earth goddess Cihuacoatl (Snake Woman), who ground them into flour. Quetzalcoatl moistened the flour with his own blood, which gave it life. Then he and Xolotl shaped the mixture into human forms and taught the new creatures how to reproduce themselves.

The Hero. Besides creating humans, Quetzalcoatl also protected and helped them. Some myths say that he introduced the cultivation of maize, or corn, the staple food of Mexico. He did this by disguising himself as a black ant and stealing the precious grain from the red ants. He also taught people astronomy, calendar making, and various crafts and was the **patron** of merchants. Carlos Fuentes, one of modern Mexico's leading writers, compares Quetzalcoatl with the mythic figures Prometheus†, Odysseus†, and Moses. All three had to leave their cultures but obtained gifts or wisdom that renewed those cultures. Stories about a Toltec king named Topiltzin Quetzalcoatl, famed as an enlightened and good ruler, may have contributed to the image of Quetzalcoatl as a culture hero.

†*See* **Names and Places** *at the end of this volume for further information.*

Quetzalcoatl's departure from his people was the work of his old enemy, Tezcatlipoca, who wanted people to make bloodier sacrifices than the flowers, jade, and butterflies they offered to Quetzalcoatl. Tezcatlipoca tricked Quetzalcoatl by getting him drunk and then holding up a mirror that showed Tezcatlipoca's cruel face. Believing that he was looking at his own imperfect image, Quetzalcoatl decided to leave the world and threw himself onto a funeral **pyre.** As his body burned, birds flew forth from the flames, and his heart went up into the heavens to become Venus, the morning and evening star. Another version of the myth says that Quetzalcoatl sailed east into the sea on a raft of serpents. Many Aztecs believed that he would come back to his people one day after a period of 52 years. In the early 1500s, the Spanish conqueror Hernán Cortés took advantage of this belief by encouraging the people of Mexico to view him as the return of the hero-god Quetzalcoatl. *See also* AZTEC MYTHOLOGY; COATLICUE; HUITZILOPOCHTLI; MAYAN MYTHOLOGY; TEZCATLIPOCA.

pyre pile of wood on which a dead body is burned in a funeral ceremony

Names and Places

Achilles foremost warrior in Greek mythology; hero in the war between the Greeks and the Trojans

Aeneas Trojan hero who founded Rome; son of Aphrodite (Venus) and the Trojan Anchises

Aeneid epic by the Roman poet Virgil about the legendary hero Aeneas and the founding of Rome

Agamemnon Greek king and commander of Greek forces in the Trojan War; later killed by his wife, Clytemnestra

Ajax Greek hero of the Trojan War

Amazons female warriors in Greek mythology

Aphrodite Greek goddess of love and beauty (identified with the Roman goddess Venus)

Apollo Greek god of the sun, the arts, medicine, and herdsmen; son of Zeus and Leto and twin brother of Artemis

Ares Greek god of war; son of Zeus and Hera (identified with the Roman god Mars)

Artemis in Greek mythology, virgin goddess of the hunt; daughter of Zeus and Leto and twin sister of Apollo (identified with the Roman goddess Diana)

Arthurian legends stories about the life and court of King Arthur of Britain

Asia Minor ancient term for modern-day Turkey, the part of Asia closest to Greece

Assyria kingdom of the ancient Near East located between the Tigris and Euphrates Rivers

Athena in Greek mythology, goddess of wisdom and war; the daughter of Zeus (Roman goddess Minerva)

Atlas Titan in Greek mythology who held the world on his shoulders

Baal god of the ancient Near East associated with fertility and rain

Babylonia ancient kingdom of Mesopotamia; **Babylon** city in Babylonia; **Babylonians** (noun) people of Babylonia; **Babylonian** (adj) referring to kingdom or people

Brahma Hindu creator god

Canaan name given to Palestine and Syria in ancient times; **Canaanites** people of Canaan

Celtic referring to the **Celts,** early inhabitants of Britain whose culture survived in Ireland, Scotland, Wales, Cornwall, and Brittany

Ceres Roman goddess of vegetation and fertility; mother of Proserpina (Greek goddess Demeter)

Cronus Greek deity, king of the Titans; son of Uranus and Gaia

Cyclopes one-eyed giants in Greek mythology

Delphi town on the slopes of Mount Parnassus in Greece that was the site of Apollo's temple and the Delphic oracle

Demeter Greek goddess of vegetation; sister of Zeus and mother of Persephone (Roman goddess Ceres)

Devi Hindu goddess; wife of the god Shiva

Diana Roman goddess of hunting and childbirth (Greek goddess Artemis)

Dionysus Greek god of wine and fertility; son of Zeus by Theban princess Semele (Roman god Bacchus)

Druids priests and political leaders of an ancient Celtic religious order

Euripides (ca. 480–406 B.C.) Greek playwright who wrote many tragedies

Franks early Germanic people who invaded and eventually ruled Gaul (present-day France) between the A.D. 200s and the mid-800s

Golden Fleece hide of a magic ram that hung in a sacred grove guarded by a serpent

Hades Greek god of the underworld; brother of Zeus and husband of Persephone (Roman god Pluto)

Hector in Greek mythology, a Trojan prince and hero in the Trojan War

Helen of Troy in Greek mythology, a beautiful woman and the wife of the king of Sparta; her kidnapping by a Trojan prince led to the Trojan War

Hephaestus Greek god of fire and crafts; son of Zeus and Hera and husband of Aphrodite (Roman god Vulcan)

Hera Greek goddess, wife and sister of Zeus; queen of heaven (Roman goddess Juno)

Hercules (Heracles) Greek hero who had 12 labors to perform; Roman god of strength

Hermes in Greek mythology, the messenger of the gods; escorted the dead to the underworld (Roman god Mercury)

Hesiod (ca. 700 B.C.) Greek poet who wrote the *Theogony*

Homer (ca. 700s B.C.) Greek poet thought to be the author of the great epics the *Iliad* and the *Odyssey*

Iliad Greek epic poem about the Trojan War composed by Homer

Indo-Iranian having to do with the peoples and cultures of northern India, Pakistan, Afghanistan, and Iran

Isis Egyptian goddess of rebirth and resurrection; mother of Horus

Jason Greek hero and leader of the Argonauts who went on a quest for the Golden Fleece

Jupiter Roman god of the sky and ruler of the other gods (Greek god Zeus)

Mars Roman god of war (Greek god Ares)

Medusa in Greek mythology, a monster whose hair was made of snakes and whose face turned humans to stone

Mercury Roman messenger god (Greek god Hermes)

Mesopotamia area between the Tigris and Euphrates Rivers, most of present-day Iraq

Metamorphoses narrative poem by the Roman author Ovid

Mongol referring to an empire in southeastern Asia that existed from about 1200 to the 1700s

Neptune in Roman mythology, god of the sea (the Greeks called him Poseidon)

Norse referring to the people and culture of Scandinavia: Norway, Sweden, Denmark, and Iceland

Odin in Norse mythology, one-eyed deity and ruler of the gods

Odysseus Greek hero who journeyed for ten years to return home after the Trojan War

Odyssey epic by the Greek poet Homer that tells the story of the journey of the hero Odysseus

Oedipus in Greek mythology, king of Thebes

Olympus in Greek mythology, home of the gods

Orpheus Greek hero known for his musical skills; son of Apollo and Calliope

Osiris in Egyptian mythology, the chief god of death

Ovid (ca. 43 B.C.–A.D. 17) Roman poet who wrote the *Metamorphoses*

Palestine ancient land located on the site of modern Israel and part of Jordan

Pegasus in Greek mythology, a winged horse

Perseus Greek hero, son of Danaë and Zeus, who cut off the head of Medusa

Persia ancient land in southwestern Asia, including much of present-day Iran and Afghanistan

Philistines ancient people who lived along the coast of Canaan (present-day Palestine and Syria)

Phoenicia ancient maritime country located in an area that is now part of Lebanon

Phrygia ancient country located in present-day Turkey

Pindar (ca. 522–438 B.C.) Greek poet

Plutarch (ca. A.D. 46–120) Greek author who wrote biographies of important Greeks and Romans

Poseidon Greek god, ruler of the sea, and brother of Zeus (Roman god Neptune)

Prometheus in Greek mythology, Titan said to have created the human race

Pueblos Native American groups of the southwestern United States, including the Hopi, Keresan, Tewa, Tiwa, and Zuni

Quetzalcoatl Feathered Serpent god of Central America; Aztec god of learning and creation

Ra (Re) in Egyptian mythology, the sun god

Saturn Roman god of the harvest

Semitic relating to people of the ancient Near East, including Jews, Arabs, Babylonians, Assyrians, and Phoenicians

Set in Egyptian mythology, god of the sun and sky; brother of Osiris

Sophocles (ca. 496–406 B.C.) Greek playwright who wrote many tragedies

Sparta ancient Greek city-state

Sumer part of ancient Babylonia in southern Mesopotamia; **Sumerians** people of Sumer

Thebes ancient Egyptian city on the Nile River

Theogony epic written by the Greek poet Hesiod explaining the creation of the world and the birth of the gods

Theseus Greek hero who killed the Minotaur of Crete with Ariadne, the daughter of King Minos of Crete

Thor in Norse mythology, the thunder god

Titan one of a family of giants who ruled the earth until overthrown by the Greek gods of Olympus

Trojan War legendary war between the Greeks and the people of Troy that was set off by the kidnapping of Helen, wife of the king of Sparta; inspiration for Homer's epics the *Iliad* and the *Odyssey*

Troy ancient city that was the site of the Trojan War; present-day Turkey near the Dardanelles

Valhalla in Norse mythology, the home of the dead heroes

Valkyrie in Norse mythology, one of the handmaidens to the god Odin

Virgil (ca. 70–19 B.C.) Roman poet who wrote the *Aeneid* explaining the founding of Rome

Vishnu Hindu god, preserver and restorer

Vulcan Roman god of fire (Greek god Hephaestus)

Zeus in Greek mythology, king of the gods and husband of Hera (Roman god Jupiter)

Index

Italicized page numbers refer to illustrations or charts.

Acanthus plant, 129, *130*
Achilles
  Myrmidons and, 73
  Odysseus and, 102
  Paris and death of, 118
  Peleus, father of, 121
  Priam and, 143
Acoma people of the American
    Southwest, myths of, 35–36
Acrisius, 123, 124
Adam and Eve, 28, 34
Adaro, 45–46
Aeacus, 73
Aeëtes, King, 12, 41–42
Aegeus, 42
Aegisthus, 110
Aeneas, 25
Aeolus, 104
Aeschylus, Orestes portrayed by,
    111
Aesir, 91, 99
Aeson, King, 11, 42
African mythology
  Katonda and, 19
  Kibuka in, 19
  Lebe in, 26
  Leza in, 27
  moon in, 69, 70
  Mujaji in, 71
  Mulungu in, 71
  Mwindo in, 72–73
  Nummo in, 95–96
  Nyame in, 97
  Ogun in, 108
  Olorun in, 109–10
Afterlife
  in Melanesian mythology, 47
  in Micronesian mythology, 58
  Osiris, judge in, 114
  in Persian mythology, 126
Agamemnon, 1, 48, 110
Agelaus, 117, 118
Agemo, 110
Agnar, 100
Ahab, 14
Ah Puch (Yum Cimil), 38, 39
Ahriman, 124, 125, 126
Ahura Mazda, 62, 124–25
Akan people of Ghana, myths of,
    97
Alexander III, Pope, 142
Alfheim, 93
Allfather. *See* Odin
Aluluei, 56, 58
Ama-no-uzume, 10
Amaterasu, 5, 7, 9–10, 11, 88
Amazon people, myths of, 131
Ambrosius, 48, 50
Ambundu people of Angola,
    myths of, 66
Ameinias, 76
American frontier, myths of,
    16–17, 119–20
Amesha Spentas, 125

Amma, 95
Amphitrite, 141
Amycus, 141
Anahita, 125
Ancestor worship, Melanesian,
    43–44
Andromeda, 123
Angels, 28, 125
Angrboda, 29
Animals in mythology
  Loch Ness Monster, 28
  manticore, 33
  in Melanesian mythology,
    45–46
  in Mexican mythology, 54
  in Micronesian mythology, 58
  Myrmidons from ants, 73–74
  in Native American mythology,
    81–82
  Nemean Lion, 84
Antaeus, 141
Anticlea, 101
Antigone, parents of, 15, 107
Antiphas, 24
Anu, Ishtar and, 1
Anubis, Osiris and, 114
Ao and Po. *See* Rangi and Papa
Aoede, 72
Apausha, 125
Aphrodite, 132
  judgment of Paris and, *118,*
    118
  punishment of Psyche by, 146
  Pygmalion and, 148
Apis, 148
Apollo, 114–15, 131
  Midas and, 59
  Muses and, 71
  Orestes and, 110, 111
  Orpheus, son of, 112–13
Apsu, 34
Apsyrtus, 13, 42
Ararat, Mount, 89
Areoi, 112
Areopagus, 111
Ares, Mars identified with, 35
Argonauts, *12,* 12–13, 41–42, 112
Ariadne, 60, 127
Arion, 141
Arjuna, 22, 31
Artemis, 1, 98
Arthur, King
  Lady of the Lake and, 22
  Lancelot and, 22–24
  Merlin and, 48, *49,* 50
  Morgan Le Fay and, 70–71
Arthurian legends
  Lancelot in, 22–24, *23*
  Merlin in, 48–50, *49*
  Morgan Le Fay in, 70–71
Asgard, 93
Ashanti people of Ghana, myths
    of, 97
Asterius, 60

Atargatis, 30
Athena, 88–89, 105
  judgment of Paris and, *118,*
    118
  Poseidon and, 140, 141
  Prometheus and, 143
Atlas, 123, 143
Atreus, 48
Augustus, 115
Aulad, 126
Australian mythology, 67
Avalon, 22, 71
Ayom people of Papua New
    Guinea, myths of, 46
Azhi Dahaka, 125, 126
Aztec mythology, 37, 39, 52, 69
  Mixcoatl in, 62–63
  Quetzalcoatl in, *149,* 149–51

Baal, 14, 27
Babylonian mythology, Marduk
    in, *34,* 34
Bacabs, 41
Balarama, 21
Balder, 91, 92, 93, 95
  Loki and, *29,* 29
  mistletoe and, 132
  Odin, father of, 99
Balor, 30
Bamboo, 129, *132*
Ban, King, 22
Bantu people of Tanzania, myths
    of, 67
Bariaus, 46
Basilisk, 54
Beans, 129
Bears in Native American mythol-
    ogy, 81–82
Bellerophon, 120
Bellona, 35
Beowulf, 67
Berserks, Odin worshiped by,
    100–101
Bhagavad Gita, 22, 31, 32
Bhagavatam, 20
Bhima of Vidarbha, 75
Bhutas, 66
Bible, Old Testament of
  Jezebel in, 14
  Job, Book of, *14,* 14–15
  Jonah, Book of, 17
  Leviathan in, 27
  Noah in, 89
Big Rong, 58
Birds in mythology, 82, 128
Blackfoot Indians, myths of,
    79–80, 108–9
Black Legend, 53
Bloodletting, 41
Bragi, 92
Brahma, Nagas and, 74
Briareos, 142
Brunhilde, in *Nibelungenlied,*
    85–86

Buddhism and mythology, 9, 74,
    117
Bue, 57
Buganda people of East Africa,
    myths of, 19
Bunyan, Paul, 15

Cacus, 67
Calendars, 38, *40*
California region, myths of, 78
Callidice, 102
Callimachus, 129
Calliope, 72, 112
Calypso, 103, 105
Camaxtli, 62
Camenae. *See* Muses
Cardea, 6
Cargo cults, 44
Cassandra, 142
Cassiopea, Perseus and, 123
Celtic mythology
  King Lear in, 25
  leprechauns in, 26
  Lug in, 30–31
  Merlin in, 48–50, *49*
  Oisin in, 108
Centaurs, 67
Cephissus, 76
Cerberus, 112
Cercyon, 141
Cereal grains, 129–30
Chac, 38, 39, 51
Chaga, 67
Chanson de Roland, 115
Chapman, John. *See* Johnny
    Appleseed
Charlemagne, *115,* 115
Charon, 112
Charybdis, 141
Chilam Balam, 38
Child of Water, 80, 83
Chimaera, 66–67
Chinese mythology, 66, 97,
    116–17
Chinigchinich, 80
Chiron, 11
Chivalry, 87
Chrétien de Troyes, Lancelot in
    romances of, 23
Christianity, 52, 54–55. *See also*
    Saints
Chrysaor, 43, 141
Cian, 30
Cihuacoatl (Snake Woman), 150
Circe, 102, 104, 105
Cizin (Kisin), 38, 39
Clio, 72
Clover, 130
Clymene, 127, 143
Clytemnestra, 1, 102, 110–11
Coatlicue, 150
Cocalus, 60, 61
Coffee, 130
Columba, St., 28

Conquistadors, 53
Cook, James, *136*, 137
Cordelia, 25
Corn, 18, 130, 150
Corn Mother, 130
Cortés, Hernán, 53, 150
Creation stories
    in Japanese mythology, 8–9
    Marduk and, 34
    Masewi and Oyoyewi and,
        35–36
    in Mayan mythology, 39–41
    in Melanesian mythology,
        44–45, 46
    in Micronesian mythology,
        56–58
    in Native American mythology,
        78, 82–83
    in Norse mythology, 93
    Nu Wa in, 97
    Odin in, 99
    Old Man in, 108–9
    Pandora in, 116
    Pan Gu in, 116–17
    in Polynesian mythology,
        137–38
    in *Popol Vuh,* 139
    Prometheus and, 144–45
    Ptah in, 148
    Quetzalcoatl in, 150
Creon, 13, 42
Cronus, 140–42, *141*
Crusades, 142
Ctesias, 33
Cuchulain, 30–31
Culture heroes
    Manco Capac, 32–33
    Masewi and Oyoyewi, 35–36
    Maui, 36
    in Micronesian mythology, 57
    in Native American mythology,
        80, 81
    Quetzalcoatl, 150
    tricksters as, 81
Cyclopes, 68, 104

Daedalus, 60–61
Dagon, 50
Damayanti. *See* Nala and
    Damayanti
Danaë, 43, 123
Daphne, 114–15, 131
David, St., 131
Day of the Dead, *54*, 55
Death, 69, 83, 109, 126
Dechtire, 30
Delphi, Oedipus and, 106–7
Demeter, 122–23, 140, 141
Demodocus, 72
Despoina, 141
Devaki, 21
Devils and demons, 33
    in Japanese mythology, 8
    Krishna and, 21
    Lilith, 28
Dhritarashtra, 31, 32
Dictys, 123
Diego, Juan, 53

Diocletian, 62
Dionysus, 59, 131
Divination, 39, 44, 99, *100*
Dogon people of Mali, myths of,
    26, 95–96
Dracula (Stoker), 64
Dragons, 67
    Loch Ness Monster, 28
    Mwindo and, 73
    Pan Gu accompanied by, 117
Draupadi, 31, 32
Druids, plants and, 130, 131
Dryads, 98
Dudugera, 45
Dwarfs and elves, 26, 85, 91, 95
Dzoavits, 67

Ea, Ishtar and, 1
Earth Diver myth, Native Ameri-
    can, 82–83
Earth Woman, 83
Easter Bunny, 64–65
Echo, Narcissus and, 76
Efik Ibibio people of Nigeria,
    myths of, 70
Egyptian mythology
    Isis in, 2–4, *3*
    Nut in, *96*, 96–97
    Osiris in, *113*, 113–14
    Ptah in, 147–48
Ehecatl, 150
Eight Deer, 62–63
Elaine of Astolat, 23
Elder Edda. See Poetic Edda
Electra, 110–11, 133
Elijah, 14
Emergence myths, 82
Endymion, 70
Enkidu, 2
Enlil, Ishtar and, 1
Enosichthon. *See* Poseidon
Enuma Elish, Marduk in, 34
Epic of Gilgamesh, Ishtar in,
    1–2
Epimetheus, 116, 143
Ereshkigal, 2
Eris, 118
Eros, Psyche and, 146–47, *147*
Eskimo mythology. *See* Inuit
    mythology
Eteocles, 15
Ethlinn, 30
Etzel, King, *86*, 87
Euripides, Orestes portrayed by,
    111
Europa, 60–61
Eurydice, 98, 112
Eurystheus, 84
Euterpe, 72
Evil Twin, 83
Excalibur, 22, 50, 71

Fafnir, *90*
Father Sky, 79
Fenrir, 29, 66, *67*, 92, 95
Fianna, 108
Finn, 108
Firdawsī, 125

Fire, *144,* 144
Floods, 33–34, 89
Flying Head, 67, 68
Formorians, 30
Frankenstein, 63–64
Freud, Sigmund, 107
Freyja, 29, 91, 92
Freyr, 91, 92
Frigg, 91, 92
Furies, 111

Gaia, Poseidon and, 141
Galahad, 23–24
Galatea, 148
Games, Mayan, *37,* 37–38
Garcilaso de la Vega, Inca, 32–33
Garuda, 74
Gayomart, 125
Geb, 2, *96,* 96–97, 113–14
Geirrod, 100
Geoffrey of Monmouth, 25, 49
Germanic mythology, *Nibelung-
    enlied* and, 85–87, *86*
Gguluddene. *See* Katonda
Giants
    Loki and, 29
    Mimir, 59–60
    in Norse mythology, 91, 94
    Pan Gu, 116–17
Gilgamesh, 1–2, 129
Ginseng, 130
Glauce, 42
Gluskap, 68, 80
Golden Fleece, 11, *12,* 12–13,
    41–42
Goneril, 25
Gong Gong, 97
Good Twin, 83
Gorgons, 42–43, 123
Graeae, 123
Great Ennead of Heliopolis, 2
Great Spirit, 79
Greek mythology, 50–51, 66–67,
    68, 69, 70, 97–99, *98*
    Iphigenia in, 1
    Jason in, 11–13, *12*
    Jocasta in, 15
    Laocoön in, *24,* 24
    Lethe in, 26–27
    Medea in, 41–42
    Medusa in, 42–43
    Menelaus in, 48
    Midas in, 60–61
    Minos in, 60–61
    Minotaur in, *61,* 61
    Mithraism in, 62
    Muses in, 71–72, *72*
    Myrmidons in, 73–74
    Narcissus in, 76
    Nemean Lion in, 84
    Nike in, 88–89
    Odysseus in, 101–2
    Odyssey in, 102–5, *103*
    Oedipus in, *106,* 106–7
    Orestes in, 110–11
    Orion in, 111
    Orpheus in, 112–13
    Pan in, 115–16

Pandora in, 116
Paris in, 117–18, *118*
Pegasus in, 120
Peleus in, 121
Penelope in, 121–22
Persephone in, *122,* 122–23
Perseus in, 123–24
Phaedra in, 127
Phaethon in, 127
Philomela in, 128
Pleiades in, 133
Poseidon in, 140–42, *141*
Priam in, 142–43
Procrustes in, 143
Prometheus in, 143–45, *144*
Proteus in, 145–46
Psyche in, 146–47, *147*
Pygmalion in, 148
Grendel, 67
Grimnir, 100
Gudrun, in *Nibelungenlied,* 85–87
Gugumatz. *See* Quetzalcoatl
Guinevere, 22, 23–24, 70
Gunnar, in *Nibelungenlied,* 85,
    87

Hachiman, *6, 7,* 8
Hades, *122,* 122, 123, 140
Hagen, 86–87
Hamadryads, 98
Haumia, 135
Hawaiian mythology, 120–21,
    135, 136–37, 138
Hecate, 69
Hector, 118, 142
Hecuba, 117, 142
Heimdall, 92
Hel, 29, 92
Helen of Troy, 48, 101, 118, 143
Helenus, 102
Helios, 105, 127, 142
Hera
    Jason and, 11
    judgment of Paris and, *118,* 118
    Poseidon, brother of, 140
    Roman Juno, 35
Hercules, 68, 84, 142, 145
Hermione, 111
Hermod, *94*
Heroes, 63–64
    Manco Capac, 32–33
    Masewi and Oyoyewi, 35–36
    Maui, 36
    in Micronesian mythology, 57
    Mwindo, 72–73
    in Native American mythology,
        80, 81
    in *Nibelungenlied,* 85–87
    Pecos Bill, 119–20
    in Persian mythology, 125
    Quetzalcoatl, 150
Hero Twins. *See* Hunahpú and
    Xbalanqúe
Hesiod, 72, 88–89
Hesione, 142, 143
Hidalgo y Costilla, Miguel, 53
Hi'iaka, 120, 121
Hildebrand, 87

Index

Hina, 36, 69
Hina-tu-a-uta, 112
Hinduism and mythology, 66, 69
    Juggernaut in, 17
    Krishna in, 20–22, 21
    Mahabharata in, 31–32
    Manu in, 33–34
    Nagas in, 74
    Nala and Damayanti in, 75,
        75–76
Hine-hau-one, 138
Hine-titama, 138
Hippios. *See* Poseidon
Hippolytus, Phaedra and, 127
Hoa-tabu-i-te-ra'i, 112
Höd, 29
Hoenir, 59
Homer, 102–5, 103, 107
Hopi Indians, myths of, 18–19,
    20, 79, 80, 82–83
Hopoe, 120
Horus, 3–4, 96, 114
Hunab Ku, 4
Hunahpú and Xbalanqúe, 38, 39,
    40–41, 139–40
Hun-Hunahpú (Ah Mun), 38, 39,
    40, 139
Hunin, 79
Hurucan, 39, 139
Hushedar, 126
Hushedar-mar, 126
Hyades, 133

Iapetus, 143
Iatiku, 35, 36
Idun, 92, 94
Igaluk, in Native American
    mythology, 78
Iliad, 72, 73–74, 101, 102
Inanna. *See* Ishtar
Inari, 7, 8
Inca mythology, 32–33, 69
Indra, in *Mahabharata*, 32
Inuit mythology, 67, 69, 78
Iphigenia, 1, 110
Irish myth, St. Patrick in, 119
Iroquois people, myths of, 79, 82,
    83
Ishtar, 1–2, 2
Isis, 2–4, 3, 96, 113–14
Ismene, 15, 107
Itys, 128
Itzamná, 4, 38, 39
Ivan the Terrible, 4–5
Ivy, 131
Ixchel, 4, 38, 39
Iyangura, 73
Izanagi and Izanami, 5, 7, 8–9
Izumo Cycle, 8, 10–11

Janus, 6
Japanese mythology, 6, 6–11, 9,
    51, 67
    Izanagi and Izanami in, 5, 7,
        8–9
    Kojiki and, 19–20
    Nihongi in, 88
Jason, 11–13, 12, 41–42

Jehoram, 14
Jehu, 14
Jerome, St., 13–14
Jewish mythology, 14, 14–15, 17,
    28, 89
Jezebel, 14
Jimmu Tenno, 10
Jizô, 8
Job, 14, 14–15
Jocasta, 15, 106
John Henry, 15–16
Johnny Appleseed, 16–17
Jonah, 17
Jormungand, 29, 93, 95
Jotunheim, 93
Judgment of Paris, 118, 118
Juggernaut, 17
Julian Hospitaller, St., 17–18
Juno, 35. *See also* Hera
Jupiter. *See* Zeus

Kachinas, 18, 18–19, 20, 35, 80
Kadru, 74
Kagingo. *See* Katonda
Kagura dances, 11
Kagutsuchi, 5, 7, 9
Kali, 76
Kamapua'a, 135, 136–37
Kambel, 45
Kamsa, King, 21
Kanaloa. *See* Tangaroa
Kane, 135, 136, 138
Kannon, 8
Kappa, 8
Kapua, 138
Kasyapa, 74
Katonda, 19
Kauravas, 22, 31–32
Keraki of Papua New Guinea,
    myths of, 46
Keresaspa, 125
Kibuka, 19
Kilauea, 120
Kimbiji kia Malenda, 66
Kingu, 34
Kinich Ahau, 4, 38, 39
Kinioka kia Tumba, 66
Kiwai of Papua New Guinea,
    myths of, 45, 46, 47
Kojiki, 6, 8, 19–20
Kokopelli, 20
Kokopell' Mana, 20
Krishna, 17, 20–22, 21, 32
Ku, 135
Kukulcan. *See* Quetzalcoatl
Kuwaan Kokopelli, 20
Kvasir, 100

Lady of the Lake, 22, 23, 50,
    70–71
Laertes, King, 101, 105
Laestrygonians, 104
Laius, King, 15, 106
Lakota people, myths of, 79
Lamia, 67
Lancelot, 22–24, 23, 70
Laocoön, 24, 24
Laomedon, King, 140

Lares and Penates, 25
Laurel, 131
Leah, 131
Lear, King, 25, 25
Leda, 26
Lei Jen Zu, 66
Leimoniads, 98
Leiriope, 76
Lemures, 129
Leprechauns, 26, 31
Lethe, 26–27
Leviathan, 27
Leza, 27
Lilith, 28
Little Rong, 58
Loa, 57
Loch Ness Monster, 28
Lohiau, 120
Loki, 28–29, 29, 91, 92, 94, 132
Lono, 135, 137
Lucius Tarquinius Collatinus, 30
Lucretia, 30
Lug, 26, 30–31
Luna, 69, 70

Maenads, 112–13
Magic, 44, 46, 99, 100, 134
Mahabharata, 31–32, 32
    Krishna in, 20, 22
    Nala and Damayanti in, 75,
        75–76
Maize. *See* Corn
Malinche, 53
Mama Ocllo, 33
Mana (supernatural power), 44,
    134
Manannan Mac Lir, 108
Manco Capac, 32–33
Mandrake, 131
Mani, 131
Manioc, 131
Manticore, 33
Manu, 33–34
Maori mythology, 69, 135, 136,
    137
Marawa, 45
Marduk, 27, 34, 34, 74
Mars, 35
Marsalai, 46
Marsyas, Midas and, 59
Masewi and Oyoyewi, 35–36
Masha and Mashyoi, 125–26
Maui, 36, 134, 135, 137
Mayan mythology, 36–41, 37, 40,
    69
    Itzamná in, 4
    Mexican mythology and, 52
    Popol Vuh in, 138–40
    Quetzalcoatl in, 150
Medea, 12–13, 41–42
Medusa, 42–43, 120, 123–24, 141
Medus (Medeius), 42
Melanesian mythology, 43–47,
    45, 47
Melete, 72
Meliae, 98
Melpomene, 72
Melqart, 65

Menehune, 47
Menelaus, 48, 118
Mercury, 122
Merlin, 22, 48–50, 49, 71
Mermaids, 50–51
Merope, 106–7, 111, 133
Metamorphoses, 51, 114–15,
    145, 148–49
Metra, 69
Mexican mythology, 51–55, 52,
    54. *See also* Native Ameri-
    can mythology
Micronesian mythology, 55–59,
    56, 58
Mictecacuiatl, 69
Midas, 59
Midgard, 93
Mimir, 59–60, 92, 99
Mimisbrunnr, 59
Minerva. *See* Athena
Minos, 60–61, 127, 142
Minotaur, 60, 61, 61, 67, 142
Mistletoe, 29, 29, 131–32
Mithras, 62, 125
Mixcoatl, 62–63
Mneme, 72
Mnemosyne, 27, 71
Modern mythology, 63–65, 64
    Loch Ness Monster in, 28
Moloch, 65–66
Monsters, 33, 64, 66–68, 67
    Loch Ness Monster, 28
    in Melanesian mythology, 46
    Minotaur, 61, 61
Monster Slayer, 80, 83
Moon, 68–70, 69
Mordred, 24
Morgan Le Fay, 70–71
Moses, 66
Mother Corn, 79
Mother Earth, 79
Motikitik, 57
Muchalinda, 74
Mugodo, 71
Muisa, 73
Mujaji, 71
Mukasa, 19
Mulungu, 71
Munin (Memory), 100
Muses, 71–72, 72, 113, 120
Music, 44, 112–13, 115
Mwindo, 72–73
Myrmidons, 73–74
Myrtle, 132

Na Atibu, 57
Nabu, 74
Nagas, 74, 76
Naiadhiyacarita, 75, 75–76
Naiads, 98
Nala and Damayanti, 75, 75–76
Namorodo, 67
Namuginga. *See* Katonda
Naniumlap, 57
Nanna, Ishtar and, 1
Napi. *See* Old Man (Napi)
Narcissus, 76
Nareau (Spider Lord), 56–57

Narfi, 29
Native American mythology,
      76-83, 77, 78, 79, 81. See
      also Mexican mythology
   kachinas in, 18, 18-19
   Masewi and Oyoyewi in,
      35-36
   monsters in, 67, 68
   moon in, 70
   Old Man in, 79-80, 108-9
   tobacco in, 132-33
Navajo Indians, myths of, 80, 82,
      83
Nawang Wulan, 70
Near Eastern mythology. See
      Egyptian mythology;
      Persian mythology;
      Semitic mythology
Nefertum, 148
Nei Teukez, 57
Nei Tituaabine, 57
Nemean Lion, 84
Nennius, 48
Neoptolemus, 102, 143
Nephthys, 2, 96
Neptune, 84, 140, 145. See also
      Poseidon
Nereids, 50, 98, 98
Nereus, 98
Niamh, 108
Nibelungenlied, 85-87, 86, 92
Nicholas, St., 87-88
Nidavellir, 93
Nidhogg, 93
Niflheim (Hel), 93
Nihongi, 6-7, 19-20, 88
Nihonshoki. See Nihongi
Nike, 88-89
Nimrod, 89
Nimuë. See Lady of the Lake
Ningyo, 51
Ninigi no Mikoto, 10
Ninshubur, 2
Njord, 91
Noah, 34, 89
Norns, 93
Norse mythology, 69, 90, 90-95,
      94, 132
   Loki in, 28-29, 29
   Mimir in, 59-60
   in Nibelungenlied, 85-87, 86
   Odin in, 99-101, 100
Nuada, King, 30
Nuga, 46
Numa Pompilius, 35
Nummo, 95-96
Nut, 2, 96, 96-97, 113
Nu Wa, 97
Nyame, 97
Nyamwezi people of Tanzania,
      myths of, 71
Nyamwindo, 72
Nyanga people of central Africa,
      myths of, 72-73
Nymphs, 97-99, 98

Oannes, 50
Oba-Orun. See Olorun

Obatala, 109-10
Oceanids, 98
Odin, 91, 92, 93, 99-101, 100
   Loki as companion of, 28, 29
   Mimir and, 59-60
Odysseus, 68, 101-2, 105
   in Odyssey, 102, 103-5
   Penelope, wife of, 121-22
   Poseidon's hatred of, 141
Odyssey, 72, 101, 102-3, 103
Oedipus, 15, 106, 106-7
Oenone, 98-99, 117, 118
Oenopion, 111
Ogun, 108
Ohrmazd. See Ahura Mazda
Oisin, 108
Ôjin, 8
Ôkuninushi, 8, 10-11
Old Man (Napi), 79-80, 108-9
Old Woman Who Never Dies, 69
Olifat, 57, 58
Olmec civilization, 37
Olodumare. See Olorun
Olofin-Orun. See Olorun
Olokun, 109, 110
Olorun, 108, 109-10
Oluluei, 57
Omori-kane, 10
Oni, 8
Ô no Yasumaro, 19
Orestes, 1, 110-11
Orestiads, 98
Orion, 111, 133
Oro, 112
Orpheus, 42, 112-13
Orunmila, 108, 109, 110
Osiris, 113, 113-14
   Isis, sister of, 2, 3
   Nut, mother of, 96
   Ptah and, 148
Ossian. See Oisin
Ovid, 51, 114-15

Paladins, 115, 115
Palraiyuk, 67
Pälülop, 58
Pan, 59, 115-16
Pandavas, 22, 31-32
Pandion, 128
Pandora, 116
Pandu, 31
Pan Gu, 116-17
Pani, 134
Papa. See Rangi and Papa
Papatuanuku, 138
Paraparawa, 131
Paris, 117-18, 118
   Menelaus and, 48
   Oenone, wife of, 98-99
   Priam, father of, 142-43
Parsley, 132
Pasiphae, 60, 61, 127, 142
Patrick, St., 119, 130
Patu-pai-arehe, 47
Pawnee people, myths of, 79
Pecos Bill, 119-20
Pegasus, 43, 120, 123, 141
Pele, 120, 120-21, 135, 136

Peleus, 121
Pelias, 11, 13, 42
Pelleas, Lady of the Lake and, 22
Penates. See Lares and Penates
Penelope, 101, 102, 105, 121-22
Periboea, 121
Persephone, 122, 122-23, 146
Perseus, 43, 120, 123-24
Persian mythology, 62, 124-27,
      126
Phaeacians, 103, 105
Phaedra, 127
Phaethon, 127
Philoctetes, 102
Philomela, 128
Phoenix, 117, 128
Picus, 35
Pied Piper of Hamelin, 128-29
Pierides, 72
Plains people, myths of, 78, 82
Plants in mythology, 129-33,
      130, 132
Pleiades, 111, 133
Pluto. See Hades
Podarces. See Priam
Poetic Edda, 90
Polites, 143
Polybus, 15, 106-7
Polydectes, 43, 123, 124
Polyhymnia, 72
Polynesian mythology, 51, 69,
      134-38, 136, 138
   Maui in, 36
   Menehune in, 47
   Oro in, 112
   Pele in, 120, 120-21
Polynices, 15
Polyphemus, 104, 141
Popol Vuh, 38, 39, 138-40
Poseidon, 140-42, 141
   Minos and, 60
   Neptune identified with, 84
   Pegasus, son of, 120
Prester John, 142
Priam, 117-18, 142-43
Procne, 128
Procrustes, 143
Prometheus, 116, 143-45, 144
Prose Edda, 90. See also Norse
      mythology
Proserpina. See Persephone
Proteus, 145-46
Psyche, 146-47, 147
Ptah, 147-48
Pueblo Indians, myths of, 18-19,
      20, 80, 82
Putana, 21
Pygmalion, 148
Pylades, 110
Pyramus and Thisbe, 148-49
Pyrrha, 116
Pythagoras, 129

Qat, 45
Quetzalcoatl, 40, 149, 149-51
   in Mayan mythology, 38, 39
   Mixcoatl, father of, 63
   in Popol Vuh, 139

Quiché Maya of Guatemala,
      myths of, 138-40

Ra (Re), 3, 96-97
Ragnarok, 29, 95, 99
Rangi and Papa, 135, 136, 137
Ratatosk, 93
Regan, 25
Rhea, 140-42, 141
Rhpisunt, 81
Rice, 129-30
Riiki, 57
Rituparna of Ayodhya, 76
Roland, as paladin, 115
Roman mythology, 50-51, 67
   Janus in, 6
   Laocoön in, 24, 24
   Lares and Penates in, 25
   Lethe in, 26-27
   Lucretia in, 30
   Mars in, 35
   Midas in, 59
   Mithraism in, 62
   Neptune in, 84
   Nike in, 88-89
   Ovid in, 114-15
   Psyche in, 146-47, 147
Rome, 35
Romulus and Remus, 35
Rongo, 135
Rongo-ma-tane, 137
Rongo-maui, 134
Round Table, Merlin and, 50
Rua-i-tupra. See Ta'aroa
Ruban, 45
Rukmini, 22
Ruksh, 126
Russian mythology, Ivan the
      Terrible in, 4-5
Rustum, 125, 126, 126
Ruwa, 133

Sabines, 6
Sacrifice, 41, 65-66
Sadb, 108
Sagas, 90-91
Sahagun, Bernadino de, 52
Saints
   Jerome, 13-14
   Nicholas, 87-88
   Patrick, 119
Saktasura, 21
Salacia, 84
Salii, 35
Santa Claus, 64, 87-88
Satan, Job and, 14, 14
Saxo Grammaticus, 90-91
Sciron, 141
Scylla and Charybdis, in Odyssey,
      104-5
Sedna, 78
Seker, 148
Sekhmet, 148
Selene, 70
Semitic mythology, 69
   Ishtar in, 1-2, 2
   Job and, 14, 14-15
   Leviathan in, 27

Index

Lilith in, 28
Moloch in, 65–66
Nabu in, 74
Nimrod in, 89
Noah in, 89
Seneca, 107
Serpents and snakes
Laocoön crushed by, 24, 24
Leviathan, 27
Loch Ness Monster, 28
in Melanesian mythology, 46
Nagas in form of, 74
Set, 2, 3–4, 96, 113–14
Sextus Tarquinius, 30
Shakespeare, William, 25
Shamash, Ishtar and, 1
Shamrock, 119
Shelley, Mary Wollstonecraft, 63–64
Shemwindo, 72–73
Shesha, 74
Shipap, 35
Shoshone people, myths of, 83
Shriharsha, 75, 75–76
Shu, 96
Shuster, Joseph, 63
Siegel, Jerry, 63
Sigurd, 85–87, 90, 92
Silenius, 59
Sirens, 51, 103, 104
Sirius, 125
Sisyphus, 101
Sleipnir, 29, 100
Solomon, King, 66
Sophocles, 107
Soshyant, 126
Spanish conquistadors, 53
Sphinx, 15, 106, 106
Spider Woman, 80, 82–83
Stoker, Bram, 64
Strophius, 110
Sturluson, Snorri, 90
Sudika-mbambi, 66
Sun, Old Man identified with, 109
Superman, 63
Susano-ô, 5, 7, 9–10
Svartalfaheim, 93
Syrinx, 115

Ta'aroa, 112, 135–36
Tacitus, 91
Tagaro, 45
Tahitian mythology, gods in, 112, 135–36
Tammuz (Dumuzi), 2
Tane, 135, 136, 137–38
Tane-mahuta, 137
Tangaloa. See Tangaroa
Tangaroa, 36, 135, 136, 137
Taoism, Japanese mythology and, 7
Tarzan, 63
Tawa, 82–83

Tawhiri, 135, 136
Tefnut, 96
Te Kore, 137
Telamon, 143
Telegonus, 102, 105
Telemachus, 101, 103, 105, 121, 122
Tengu, 8, 9, 67
Teotihuacán, 149
Tepeyac, 53
Te Po, 137
Tereus, 128
Terpsichore, 72
Tezcatlipoca, 62, 150
Thalia, 72
Thamyris, 72
Themis, 143
Theseus
Medea and, 42
Minos and, 60
Minotaur and, 61, 61
Phaedra, wife of, 127
Poseidon, father of, 141
Procrustes and, 143
Thetis, 121, 145
Thilefial, 57
Thisbe. See Pyramus and Thisbe
Thistle, 132
Thor, 91, 92, 95
Loki as companion of, 28
Odin, father of, 99
St. Nicholas and, 88
Thoth, 4, 96, 114
Thymbraeus, 24
Tiamat, 27, 34
Tiki, 138
Tirawa, 79
Tiresias, 76, 104, 105
Tir Na Nog, 108
Tishtrya, 125
Titans, 116, 143–45, 144
Tiwaz, 91
Tobacco, 132–33
To-Kabinana and To-Karvuvu, 45, 46
Toltecs, myths of, 37, 150
Tonántzin, 53
Toneri, Prince, 88
Tooth Fairy, 65
Totem poles, 81
Totoima, 68
Traetaona, 125
Trees in mythology
mulberry tree, 148–49
plants and, 129–33, 130, 132
Tricksters, 81
Loki, 28–29, 29
Maui, 36
in Melanesian mythology, 45–46
in Micronesian mythology, 57, 58
in Native American mythology, 78, 80–81

Old Man, 108–9
in Polynesian mythology, 134, 138
Trident, 84, 140
Trinavarta, 21
Trio people of South America, myths of, 131
Tritons, 50, 141
Trojan War, 24, 48, 73–74, 142–43
Odysseus in, 101–2
Odyssey, story of journey after, 102–5, 103
Paris in, 117–18, 118
Penelope during, 121–22
Tsuki-yomi, 5, 7, 9
Tuatha Dé Danaan, 30–31
Tuli, 137
Tumbrenjak, 46
Tutankhamen, 96
Twins
Hunahpú and Xbalanqúe in Popul Vuh, 139–40
Masewi and Oyoyewi, 35–36
in Mayan mythology, 40–41
in Melanesian mythology, 45, 46–47
in Native American mythology, 80, 83
Nummo, 95–96
Tyndareus, Odysseus and, 101
Tyr, in Norse mythology, 92, 95

UFOs (unidentified flying objects), 64, 65
Ulysses. See Odysseus
Underworld
Ishtar in, 2
Isis in, 4
Izanagi and Izanami in, 5
in Japanese mythology, 9
Lethe, river in, 26–27
in Norse mythology, 93
in Odyssey, 104, 105
Osiris, god of, 113, 113–14
Psyche in, 146
Unicorn, Pan Gu accompanied by, 117
Urania, 72
Urban legends, 63
Uther Pendragon, 49, 50

Vahuka, 76
Vairaumati, 112
Valhalla, 93, 99, 100
Vali, 29
Valkyries, 92, 100
Vampires, 64, 67
Vanaheim, 93
Vanir, 59, 91
Vasudeva, 21
Vatea, 51
Ve, 99
Verethraghna, 125

Vesta, 25, 140
Vikings, 100–101
Vili, 99
Villa, Francisco "Pancho," 53, 54
Virgin of Guadalupe, 53
Vishnu, Krishna as eighth incarnation of, 20–22
Vision Serpents, 41
Viviane. See Lady of the Lake
Volsunga Saga, 92
Voluspa, 90, 93
Vortigern, 48, 50
Vucub-Caquix, 139
Vucub Hunahpú, 139
Vulgate, 13
Vyasa, 31

Wagner, Richard, 85, 95
Wahnui, 134
Wakan Tanka, 79
Walumbe, 19
Werewolves, 64, 67
Woman Who Fell from the Sky, 82

Xibalba, 41, 139–40
Xmucane, 39, 139
Xolotl, 149, 150
Xpiacoc, 39, 139
Xquic, 139

Yadavas, 22
Yahweh, 14, 14–15, 17, 27
Yam, 133, 134
Yazatas, 125
Yggdrasill, 93, 95
Mimir and, 59
Odin and, 99, 101
Yin and Yang, Pan Gu and, 116
Ymir, 91, 92, 93, 99
Yomi-tsu Kuni, 9
Yoruba people, myths of, 108, 109–10
Yoshitsune, 9
Young Spider, 57
Yudhishthira, 31

Zapata, Emiliano, 53
Zend-Avesta (Avesta), 124
Zephyrus, 146
Zeus
Minos, son of, 60–61
nymphs, daughters of, 97–99, 98
Pandora and, 116
Paris and, 118
Persephone, daughter of, 122–23
Poseidon, brother of, 140
Prometheus and, 143, 144
Zhu Rong, 97
Zipacna, 139
Zoroaster and Zoroastrianism, 62, 124–27. See also Persian mythology